Building an Effective Information Security Policy Architecture

Building an Effective Information Security Policy Architecture

SANDY BACIK

CRC Press
Taylor & Francis Group
Boca Raton London New York

CRC Press is an imprint of the
Taylor & Francis Group, an **informa** business
AN AUERBACH BOOK

CRC Press
Taylor & Francis Group
6000 Broken Sound Parkway NW, Suite 300
Boca Raton, FL 33487-2742

First issued in paperback 2019

ISBN-13: 978-1-4200-5905-2 (hbk)
ISBN-13: 978-0-367-38730-3 (pbk)

Library of Congress Cataloging-in-Publication Data

Bacik, Sandy.
    Building an effective information security policy architecture / author, Sandy Bacik.
        p. cm.
    Includes bibliographical references and index.
    ISBN 978-1-4200-5905-2 (alk. paper)
    1. Computer security. 2. Computer networks--Security measures. I. Title.

QA76.9.A25B335 2008
005.8--dc22

2008011392

Visit the Taylor & Francis Web site at
http://www.taylorandfrancis.com

and the CRC Press Web site at
http://www.crcpress.com

Dedication and Thanks

This book is dedicated to my family, especially my mother, who was a teacher early in her career. It is also dedicated to friends who have assisted me over the years in the Information Security field.

Presenting at various security industry events has enabled me to share my knowledge of policy architecture and evaluation. Thank you to all who have participated in my sessions.

Sandy Bacik

Contents

Preface

Many times, security professionals need a reference for reviewing, developing, and implementing a security policy architecture. This text will walk the reader through the process for an effective policy architecture for a small, medium, or large enterprise. Whether the reader is a novice or an experienced security professional, this text will give examples and hints on how to review an existing security policy architecture and develop it from scratch. The reader also will receive tips on how to gain enterprise support and communicate the security policy architecture to the enterprise, whether the enterprise is a global company or a private firm. At times, security professionals need to validate their own security policy development direction against others in the industry. This book will assist any security professional who has the responsibility of developing and maintaining a security policy architecture.

The Author

Sandy Bacik, CISSP, ISSMP, CISM, CHS-III

Ms. Bacik has more than 12 years of direct development, implementation, and management information security experience in the areas of Audit Management, Disaster Recovery/Business Continuity, Incident Investigation, Physical Security, Regulatory Compliance, and Standard Operating Policies/Procedures, and an additional 10 years in various Information Technology positions.

Throughout her career, Ms. Bacik has managed, architected, and implemented comprehensive information assurance programs and managed internal, external, and contracted/outsourced information technology audits to ensure various regulatory compliance for state and local government entities and Fortune 200 companies. Ms. Bacik has developed methodologies for risk assessments, information technology audits, vulnerability assessments, security policy and practice writing, incident response, and disaster recovery. She has implemented cross-functional Business Continuity Programs and developed an enterprise-wide security-conscious culture through information assurance programs. Ms. Bacik has performed and managed engagements for the following assessment types and frameworks to ensure corporate compliance: Committee of Sponsoring Organizations of the Treadway Commission (COSO), Control Objectives for Information and related Technology (CobIT), Gramm–Leach Bliley Act (GLBA), Health Insurance Portability and Accountability Act (HIPAA), International Standards Organization (ISO) 17799, IT Infrastructure Library (ITIL), Sarbanes–Oxley Act (SOX), Cardholder Information Security Program (CISP), Restriction of Hazardous Substances (RoHS), and Waste Electrical & Electronic Equipment (WEEE).

Ms. Bacik has been heavily involved with local, national, and international security industry events. She is a Certified Information Systems Security Professional (CISSP), Information System Security Management Professional (ISSMP), Certified Information Security Manager (CISM), and Certified in Homeland Security (CHS)—Level III. Ms. Bacik is a regular presenter at MIS Training Institute security and audit conferences and has volunteered with the Washington State

Criminal Justice Training Commission in developing and instructing public and private sector personnel in electronic investigations. She is involved with various groups that promote cooperative relationships between public and private sector security professionals for high-tech investigation and training. Ms. Bacik was a member of Agora; a founding member of the Puget Sound Chapter of ISSA; former Vice President, webmaster, and instructor for Computer Technology Investigators Northwest (CTIN); and was a former Chair of Highline Community College's CIS Advisory Committee. Ms. Bacik is a certified instructor for The Internet and Your Child, a comprehensive education and safety program for adults.

Chapter 1

Introduction

You walk into a server room or office and you see a note literally taped to the front of a network device stating:

> UNAUTHORIZED ACCESS TO THIS NETWORK DEVICE IS PROHIBITED. You must have explicit permission to access or configure this device. All activities performed on this device may be logged, and violations of this policy may result in disciplinary action and may be reported to law enforcement. There is no right to privacy on this device.

Is this a good display of a warning notice in a server room? How about in an office area? Does it emphasize the endorsement of security? Yes, it displays the endorsement for the physical security and walking up to the network device console. No, it does not display a necessary endorsement of security for anyone remotely accessing the network device. As an information security team displays notices, they need to ensure that the message is going to the correct location in the enterprise for the right access. Information security teams have the continual challenges of increased need for regulatory compliance, increased acquisition and merger activities, increasing (and decreasing) staff numbers, increased information risk, increased privacy requirements, and expanding business requirements. The information security teams need to develop and maintain a set of documents that demonstrate due diligence in protecting the enterprise assets, an information security policy architecture. Using business requirements, the information security team needs to identify (and document) safeguards and controls to protect enterprise assets from constantly changing risks and threats.

For the purposes of the book, an information security policy architecture is a set of documents (policy, guideline, standard, procedure, and memo) that make up how the enterprise protects its assets. The defining of a policy architecture to an enterprise is one of the most important items that an information security team can do to assist in protecting the enterprise's assets. A well-written, comprehensive policy architecture is one of the most effective management tools and is probably the most neglected one. An information security policy architecture provides the glue for defining appropriate behavior for asset use, standardization of tools for work and monitoring, and communication of appropriate messages. There are plenty of excuses to avoid producing an efficient and effective policy architecture: too little time and too much work, uncertainty about the policy architecture's content, or an unwillingness to put too much in writing. Underlying all these reasons is the failure to recognize just how vital a policy architecture is to protecting enterprise assets, reducing enterprise asset risk, providing for regulatory compliance, and protecting the privacy of staff and enterprise data.

Nicolò Machiavelli once said that it must be remembered that there is nothing more difficult to plan, more doubtful of success, nor more dangerous to manage than the creation of a new system. What Machiavelli was trying to say was that change is essential in an enterprise if that enterprise is to grow and remain competitive. Those who have ever had to develop, implement, or update an information security policy architecture know this firsthand. Although the danger is not physically life-threatening, it is definitely dangerous to our sanity. This book will take you through the process of creating a new information security policy architecture and evaluating an existing information security policy architecture. Changes can be positive for an organization and an information security policy architecture may create anxiety and resistance. Creating the architecture using the enterprise culture and business requirements will lessen that anxiety and resistance because staff will understand how it will fit into making the enterprise better.

Many decades ago, employees were loyal to a single company for a whole career; today, a company is lucky if it can keep staff for five years. Back then, companies ran on a handshake and the concept of giving your word for a deal or a contract, so there was no need to write anything down. Ronald Reagan said, "Trust but verify." Today, we need to trust that our employees will perform their job effectively and efficiently, but many times loyalty, integrity, and trust can be an issue when completing jobs effectively and efficiently. If you can state that

- You know who you are dealing with from the beginning to the end of a transaction;
- You know what is going to happen with that asset or information from beginning to end of the transaction;
- You know that you are protected from any wrongdoings with that asset or information from the beginning to the end of the transaction;

- You know that the asset or information will not be shared outside of the parties within the transaction;
- You know that the asset or information transacted is only between yourself and the other party.

Then you can state that you trust that entity. Because the value of trust may have decreased over the decades, it is a requirement that an enterprise has an information security policy architecture to protect all of its assets. In setting up an information security policy architecture that works with the business, the architecture verifies the trust of information access. In addition to the employee trust factor, you need to look at the risk, the compliance, the privacy, and the information security in order to protect the enterprise, to gain market share, and to be able to back what the enterprise believes in should anything go wrong. This trust factor also extends to vendors and the hardware and software that the vendors produce. Buggy hardware and software may seem to be a current way of life. It is that lack of trust that puts fear into users for losing their jobs, puts fear into executives for losing intellectual property, and puts fear into the enterprise for implementing and updating existing hardware and software and the loss of access and control. The information security policy architecture can bring back a balance of trust into the enterprise.

1.1 History of Policy Documents

Employees at many enterprises ask if policies actually make a difference within the organization. Policies and policy architectures do have a long history within enterprises. Although much effort has been spent in creating and maintaining the policy architecture, it is often ignored. Many times, a group is thrown together, and they go out and download what they can find as policy that might fit their enterprise. They do a cut and paste, do a change-all, to match the enterprise title and attempt to get a sign-off. When they do get the sign-off, they have the problem of enforcing the policy. So, from that standpoint, that policy may not make a difference. What difference do you want to make with the policy? A policy is "a plan or course of action" as of a government, political party, or business intended to influence, determine decisions, actions, and other matters (as per the *American Heritage Dictionary of the English Language*).

A few decades ago, when information security policies first came out, they appeared in a Human Resource manual. Enterprise Human Resource manuals were two- to three-inch-thick hardcopy documents. In today's environment, policies change so fast that they cannot be in a binder. They have to be readily available for staff, so paper is ineffective. And you do not really want to call it a manual, because a manual implies that that is what it is; there are no exceptions, you must follow this. However, the manual continues to grow.

This book will take that old policy architecture and update it with today's business life styles. Throughout this book, policies are that guiding behavior and the enterprise guidelines, standards, procedures, processes, and work instructions support those policies. The main reason for policies is to ensure a change in attitudes practiced by the staff. A policy architecture should be acknowledged by staff for awareness and understanding relevance to the enterprise.

The first step to making a security policy architecture work is to realize that there is more to do than just ensuring staff can find the policy documents. Staff must be able to interpret and act on the information they find. So what do you do? This book will break down the concepts of how to write policies in plain and simple language so that, if you are a multinational company, you will be able to translate them into the language of all of your employees. An enterprise must ensure that the policies are designed to communicate to the staff in a way that they understand.

1.2   Why Do We Really Need Policies?

Fraud and reporting scandals have been extremely prevalent over the past few years. Sometimes, management thinks that throwing technology at an issue will solve the problem. Yes, it may be helpful, but it is not necessarily effective. Enterprises need ways to protect themselves and their assets. An enterprise information security program that includes an information security policy architecture will assist enterprises in protecting assets. Many enterprises do not know the location of many enterprise assets. Home and remote offices purchase equipment that becomes an enterprise asset when purchased through the enterprise procurement system. Do the expense system and procurement system then add those assets to the master enterprise list and assign an owner and purpose to those assets? If the enterprise has a specific formula used to calculate the profit on the sale of a widget and a staff member e-mails a copy of a master spreadsheet with that formula to a competitor, does that formula now become public knowledge because it was not protected? The details within a policy architecture, the standards, guidelines, and procedures, document how that information should be protected and used. A policy architecture (and technology) can save or cripple an enterprise if it is involved with civil or legal litigation.

Privacy is a hot topic for global enterprises. What is the meaning of personally identifiable information in the United States versus China versus France? Can I have one set of documents that covers privacy for my enterprise? An executive in the company accidently sends out a file containing employee names, titles, location, and salary to the entire enterprise. The Information Technology (IT) department reviews the mail logs and contacts all employees who forwarded that e-mail to an address outside the enterprise. A non-U.S.-based employee claims a privacy violation, because he did not know that his e-mail transactions were monitored. Is this a legitimate claim or not? Depending on the country's privacy laws, the enterprise ownership, and the enterprise policy, it could be a legitimate claim.

An employee laptop contains nonstandard tools to monitor the network, and then the employee starts running scans against the network to gain additional privileges for his or her account. Is this a "business use" of the asset? Maybe, if it was part of an information security professional's job description. Was there any damage done? Should the employee be terminated? What happens if this situation is being done by a contractor who is stationed at an enterprise location?

So what are some of the other trends that businesses have to look at? The worms, the keystroke loggers, and unprotected desktops and laptops continue to be top concerns for security professionals. People walking away with intellectual property—partners, contractors, or consultants assisting you. Who owns that intellectual property when they are done with an assignment are additional concerns. Whose equipment do contractors and partners work on?

An information security policy architecture is required within an enterprise. Staff view policies as an impediment to their productivity and a measure to control behavior ("Big Brother is watching"). Policies affect everyone within the enterprise, and changes at times, produce fear, uncertainty, and doubt (FUD). The FUD factor manipulates how staff view security and can elevate tension among departments. An information security team needs to reduce the political and fear aspects by planning and talking to the user community and using their business requirements to explain the need for implementation.

The questions posed here and many others can help to mitigate risk through the definition of an information security policy architecture. An information security policy architecture documents the responsibilities of everyone who accesses enterprise assets. Documenting expectations helps staff understand what is required of them and the consequences of violation. A policy architecture with a common glossary and acronym reference will demonstrate a common set of items across the enterprise. In having a common glossary and acronym reference, document interpretation becomes limited in translation into other languages. A policy architecture will allow an enterprise to

- Have a strong commitment to ethics and asset protection;
- Form a benchmark to progress measurement;
- Evaluate how an organization is doing with its information security program;
- Evaluate how service level agreements are being met through security monitoring;
- Ensure consistency in what the enterprise wants to protect;
- Serve as a guide for information security, risk, privacy, compliance;
- Define acceptable use of enterprise assets.

The first step in making an information security policy architecture work is to realize that there is more to do than just ensuring staff can find the policy documents. Staff must be able to interpret and act upon the information they find. In today's society, we are seeing the convergence of information security, audit, risk, and compliance (see Figure 1), and your information security policy architecture also needs to take into account the convergence of those topics.

Figure 1   Convergence.

An information security policy architecture can be successful if the information security team (or policy architecture team) understands what the enterprise's mission, goals, and objectives are. The team needs to build or improve your existing policies and procedures to match the strategic direction of the enterprise. The team will need:

- The names of business unit leaders and general organizational charts;
- Existing corporate strategic plans, including IT's and information security's strategic plans;
- A copy of the existing information security policy architecture documents;
- Listing of key business projects for the current fiscal year and points of project contact;
- Listing of staff and management who would be a good reference point for ideas on how to proceed with the information security policy architecture.

Rarely is a policy or procedure document drafted and implemented immediately. Typically, documents go through revisions. The processes described in the book will reduce the lead time of review and implementation of a documented information security policy architecture. When an information security policy architecture is developed in a comprehensive way, the architecture will

- Work with the business unit to understand the business functions and will promote teamwork and improve human relations;
- Understand the business processes will promote clarity, consistency, and continuity of performance, and with this understanding comes better and more comprehensive management decisions;
- Establish approved, measurable standards of performance for compliance and monitoring for a competent practice;
- Provide a tool for staff orientation on an annual basis and the training of new staff;
- Document proper delegation and define limits of authority and levels of responsibility;
- Serve as source documentation for regulatory and accrediting agency reviews.

1.3   What Follows

The names of the information security teams and the titles for members of that team, as well as the title of the person who has enough status to implement and enforce the policies, are different within each enterprise. As titles, teams, and positions are used in this book, equate the title, team, and position to the particular person in your current enterprise. For example, the chief information security officer or chief security officer mentioned through this book may be your senior security architecture or engineer. Do not get hung up on the titles, but use the concept to apply to your current enterprise.

By reading this book, you have acknowledged that there is probably a need to build or improve existing information security policies and procedures to match the strategic direction of the enterprise. Items needed to move forward are as follows:

- Knowing business requirements, details, tips, samples, and guides to assist in accomplishing specific objectives such as understanding and knowing the audience and the culture for which the information security policy architecture is being developed and implemented;
- Knowing how to gain support and implement the policy and procedures right the first time, understanding how IT fits into the organization's strategic plan for support;
- Identifying alliances for support;
- Being able to be detailed, yet not extremely controlling and dictating;
- Knowing to check the ego at the door when speaking with a nontechnical person and writing documents to the level of everyone in the organization.

Developing and implementing an information security policy architecture may seem overwhelming, especially when starting from scratch. A logical plan makes it much simpler but not necessarily easier depending on the enterprise organizational structure. The following documents the basic outline of the process and how the book will work through the process:

- Explore the definition of a policy architecture, what should be included in a policy architecture. We will go through creating and drafting some policies and what a policy architecture is and making it fit into the organization.
- Before getting into writing a policy architecture, determine what is already present, what needs to be improved, and where do we go from here. Many times, companies do not know if they will throw everything out and start from scratch or try and see what they can muddle through and fix. Walking through developing a list of topics and base definition for the policy architecture is one of the first steps.
- Make enterprise operational goals from top management the first line of documents created. Creating that manual of style will ensure similar formatting

and design of the document. The drafting of the documents is the most tedious part of the architecture.

■ Review and circulate the drafts to ensure compliance with institutional philosophy and regulatory requirements, and compatibility with other department policies for feedback.
■ Finalize policies, have them approved by appropriate executive management, and publish them in various forms. Executive management needs to make it clear that staff will be held accountable for reading and complying with the policy architecture content.
■ Put it all together with how to get support and the actual writing.
■ Setup review processes to ensure architecture changes and, when new problems arise, the enterprise need to make prompt and accurate amendments.

The author of this book learns by reading samples. This book is formatted with explanations supported with samples of how to implement the processes.

Please remember in reviewing and using the samples that you must think about how this fits into your enterprise's culture and existing architecture. Do not try to force a fit because you will be doomed to failure. Learn your enterprise environment first and find out what the business requirements are and what executive management's position is on information security. As a reader, you should be able to answer the following questions as you go through this book:

■ What do you want your policy architecture to accomplish?
■ Is a policy architecture absolute?
■ Are we doing things to industry standards?
■ Are we delivering value to the organization?
■ Where does the organization want to go with this policy architecture and, more important, where is the enterprise now?
■ Does this policy architecture have a clearly defined scope? Is it clear to which systems and which staff members this policy architecture applies?
■ Is it clear who is responsible for enforcement, for monitoring? Is that document actually enforceable? Can it be applied in a concrete manner so that such compliance can be measurable? Is the policy adaptable?
■ Does the policy architecture comply with law and with duties to third parties?

Whether you are starting from scratch or have taken on an existing structure, take your time in developing and update the information security policy architecture. Figure 2 shows the continuous process needed to develop and maintain an effective security policy architecture.

All of the figures and tables within this book are based on the author's years of experience within information technology, information assurance, corporate governance, risk, audit, and compliance.

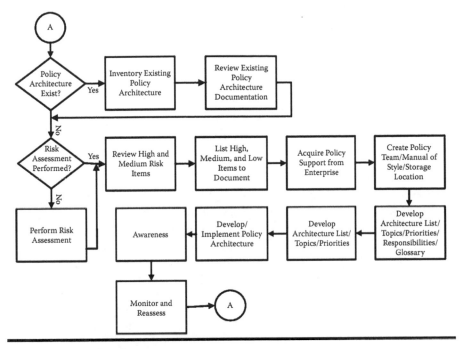

Figure 2   Mapping the process.

Chapter 2

The Enterprise

No matter the size of an enterprise, whether it is a public or private enterprise or whether it is a single or multicountry enterprise, there is a need for an information security professional in the organization. The information security professional's responsibilities can be far and wide, depending on the size of the organization. Can an enterprise afford a team of information security professionals? How many should be dispersed through the enterprise? These questions need to be answered through an enterprise risk assessment before an information security team can be built and assigned to an enterprise organization. There is no right or wrong placement within the enterprise, as long as the mission and tasks can be completed by the information security team.

2.1 Policy Architecture Design Process

The initial information security policy architecture design process can be set up as a standard project, using the enterprise project plan methodology. The project sponsor needs to be an executive team member. The person coordinating and giving direction to the project should be the highest person within the security chain of the enterprise, such as the corporate information security officer, the director of information security, or the lead business information security officer. The following is an outline for a basic information security policy architecture design project:

1. Selecting an information security policy architecture development/review team. The size of the team will vary depending on the organization size. A suggestion for the policy development team would be as follows:

   a. Senior administrator (servers, network devices);
   b. Management team member who will be assisting with enforcement;
   c. Counsel team member;
   d. Internal audit team member;
   e. User community member (this person could be the policy interpreter before implementing into the enterprise);
   f. Writer—a technical writer, if possible.
2. Reviewing the information security team's reporting structure to ensure appropriate staffing for monitoring and appropriate level of authority for enforcement.
3. Deciding on the scope, mission, and objectives of the policy architecture.
4. Selecting a sample staff and support population for review and input before implementation.
5. Acquiring sign-off from the executive management team, depending on the level of document being implemented.
6. Implementing the information security policy architecture and setting up user awareness sessions.
7. Documenting the review and maintenance process of the information security policy architecture.

The development and implementation time for an information security policy architecture will depend on the scope of the information security policy architecture, the size of the organization, and the priority of this initiative for the executive management team.

2.2 Setting the Reporting Structure

Each enterprise has the responsibility to protect its assets and to have control over those assets. An enterprise's assets can be tangible (cash, buildings, equipment, records, information), intangible (goodwill or reputation), and strategic (a relationship between two or more entities). An enterprise's operations rely on accurate and timely access to information and some of that information needs to remain confidential. An enterprise security team will assist in accomplishing that goal. It helps that the United States has the Computer Security Act of 1987, which requires businesses to put an effort into security. Most countries around the world have similar laws or regulations. Three things are required by the Computer Security Act of 1987:

■ Sensitive data (and systems) must be identified;
■ Plans for security and access control must be created;
■ User training must be in place.

This can be one of the justifications for a formalized information security program that requires documentation: an information security policy architecture. If any enterprise wants to protect its assets, then these are the basic business requirements for that protection.

An enterprise would hope that there would be a standard message about information protection that is simple, to the point, and understandable to all. An enterprise should have a "tone at the top." The enterprise's executive team should have a stance on how they stand on the protection of and access to enterprise assets. A common statement is, "Assets should be protected to the level of importance to the enterprise" or "Assets should be secured to the level of importance to the enterprise." *Protected* versus *secured*—is there a difference? *Protected* would mean using the security triad (confidentiality, integrity, and availability) to ensure the protection of assets and imply that it is the responsibility of everyone via administrative, technical, and physical methods. *Secured* would mean that assets are protected through technical and physical methods, leaving out the administrative method of policies and procedures. The tone at the top will assist the information security organization in implementing the information security program. Do business units throw around the terms *security administration, secure the access,* or *we have security*? This could imply that enterprise is once again interested in just the technical and physical methods to securing the assets. If business units use terms that relate to limiting or lowering risk, then the information security program has a better chance of survival. Limiting or lowing risk in an enterprise would mean looking at the security triad and using administrative, technical, and physical means to protect the assets. When a statement comes back to the information security group, unsolicited, that a business unit has requested the team's assistance in reducing the risk to a set of assets, it is a great accomplishment for a new information security team.

What happens when business units and the executive team think that security is synonymous with compliance or that you were hired with a security title and your only responsibility is compliance? Although it is more difficult, an information security program can be developed based on the primary responsibility of compliance. Determining with what you need to be compliant can lead to requirements for a security program. Many of today's regulatory requirements have a security or risk component. On the down side, the security regulatory components are vague and leave much to the individual enterprise. Regulators then come in and base their audits on their standards.

If the enterprise is large enough and the position is justified enough, the highest level risk, security, privacy person would report to the Chief Executive Officer (CEO) who would report to the Board of Directors (BOD). Figures 3 and 4 represent a great organization security structure when security, privacy, risk, and compliance are the primary goals and objectives for the enterprise. More than likely, a security organization is within the organization structure shown in Figures 5 and 6.

The higher up in the organization the security function is, the more responsibility, the more accountability, and the larger the operating budget. Higher up in the organization structure does not necessarily mean respect, trust, or reliability.

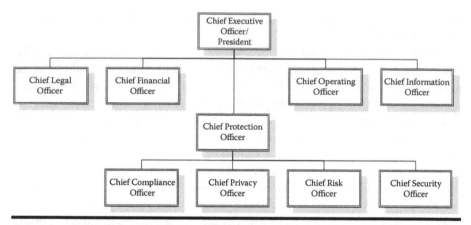

Figure 3   Ultimate organization structure (1).

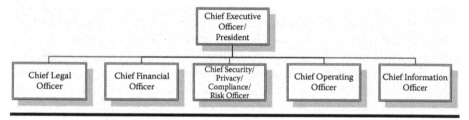

Figure 4   Ultimate organization structure (2).

Those aspects of an information security organization must be gained individually. *The communication style, reputation, knowledge, resources, and contacts within the information security organization create the respect, trust, and reliability with the rest of the enterprise.* It does not matter where the information security, privacy, risk, and compliance function reports, as long as the group understands the enterprise and understands the business requirements of the enterprise.

When the information security organization (or security organization) structure is determined, then the executive team needs to determine what the scope of responsibility is for the group. The group will include the responsibilities of the following

■ Asset protection (physical or logical)
■ Compliance
■ Risk
■ Privacy

Most information security teams that maintain the information security policy architecture have basic responsibilities of logical asset protection, compliance, risk,

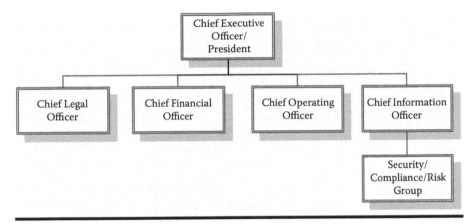

Figure 5 Standard organization structure (1).

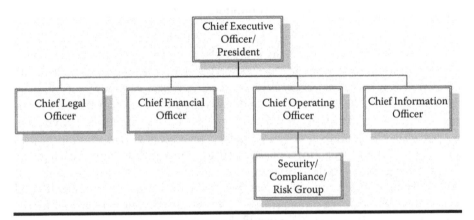

Figure 6 Standard organization structure (2).

and privacy. These are business requirements for the enterprise, no matter in what country the enterprise resides.

2.3 Determining the Mission

Before any enterprise develops an information security policy architecture, the team needs to develop its mission, goals, and objectives to work toward and to be evaluated on. Most information security teams are assigned the mission to protect the assets of the enterprise. This can mean many things to many people. Security professionals know and understand that information security is a continuous process (see Figure 7).

Figure 7 Information security—a continuous process.

An information security policy architecture is at the heart of a successful information security program and at the heart of business requirements. Security professionals also know that when it comes to risk and protecting assets, people are the largest risk to an enterprise. With a proper business continuity and disaster recovery program, the data, software, and hardware present lower risks to the enterprise. Although we can put technical and physical controls around asset protection, the person at the controls needs to be guided by a set of documentation to provide a desired outcome, an information security policy architecture. Although we are protecting the enterprise assets, we have to consider confidentiality, integrity, and availability of data compliance and privacy while being stored, accessed, and transmitted. What are the consequences if there are no controls in place to limit the risk to the enterprise assets? What would the enterprise lose?

We need to create a mission statement for the information security team to be able to start the building of the information security policy architecture. Using the theories of protection, compliance, risk, and privacy, a sample mission statement for the team can be as follows:

> The Information Security Program (ISP) and its policies and processes establish accountabilities and provide reliable protection to limit the risk of attacks, improper activity of employees, and accidental damage by authorized personnel. This extends to providing reliable information security and security awareness education to within the My Company ("MYC"). The ISP will be thoughtful stewards in helping MYC protect all of its information assets through access control.
>
> The ISP will accommodate all regulatory and privacy requirements and best business practices with response to information security and is

designed to assure a high degree of protection for the technology environment. This program establishes a baseline of policies, standards, and procedures that apply to all MYC-wide and Information Technology (IT) systems and services, both operational and administrative.

This program is intended to be distributed throughout MYC and therefore contains no information which could be classified as sensitive or business proprietary, or that would pose a threat to the security of the MYC information resources. Where necessary, organizations and titles are referenced rather than individual names.

The Chief Information Security Officer (CISO) is responsible for the development, management, and maintenance of this program.

These statements provide the information security group with the overall mission to develop an information security policy architecture. But what is the scope for fulfilling that mission? Something simple would be as follows:

This program applies to all current and future MYC information resources for all organizations, regardless of business line association or information technology resource subsystem. MYC information resources due to their inter-connectivity, inter-reliability and inter-operability, include but are not limited to all computer hardware and software, printers, FAX machines, network routers, hubs, gateways, switches, controls, telecommunication system, and cabling and all operating systems, applications, databases, information, and data stores. Additionally, this plan applies to all connections, modes or methods of connection, access, or utilization of any and all MYC information resources.

Facilities Protection has primary responsibility for physical security, and the ISP will help support and enhance the physical security requirements and needs of Facilities Protection.

This plan applies to all persons who in any way connect to or make use of MYC information resources for any reason, including but not limited to MYC full- and part-time employees, MYC contract employees, business partners, vendors, and others.

There is a general mission and scope, but what is the information security's group philosophy on asset protection? The group's philosophy could be something similar to the following.

Information security is the management of information technology risk in pursuit of business objectives. Within our day-to-day function, we may perform the following:

- Handle sensitive client information that you are expected to keep in confidence;
- Handle information which you have legislative obligations to protect.

A significant part of your business processes relies on Information Systems.

Prolonged failure of the business process can cause significant disruption and may affect long-standing relationships with clients and partners. An even more significant risk would be the unauthorized disclosure of information given in confidence. Information security will allow you to better understand the risks to your business and put in place strategies to mitigate the risks you feel are unacceptable. Therefore, an ISP needs to be a critical part of any business architecture.

Security is an important component of business as the lack of a properly implemented and up-to-date security policy can result in the loss of valuable information assets. The ISP will implement a program governed by the following ideas:

- In an organization in which one of the assets is confidential information, the results of the improper use of that information can be disastrous;
- Access to MYC computing environment is given on a need-to-know basis;
- Having access to data on the MYC network does not qualify one as being authorized to access that information;
- The proactive identification of important assets, security threats, and how the threats could be realized will allow MYC to minimize the risks of those threats;
- It is better to minimize the damage that could be inflicted by realizing a threat than to catch the perpetrator of the security breach; and
- Committing an act out of ignorance does not relieve responsibility for the action nor its outcome.

2.4   Strategic Plans

Normally, after a risk assessment is performed, an enterprise will come up with key issues that need to be addressed based on a standard enterprise architecture similar to Figure 8.

Key issues that an enterprise can face are as follows:

- When MYC uses a partner for supporting product development, MYC is liberal with giving the partner information about its infrastructure and granting access.
- Current operating system and application patch management is currently not supported on a regular basis.

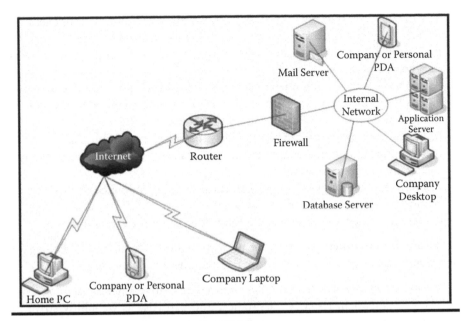

Figure 8 Basic enterprise network architecture.

- Log monitoring and alerts are a passive and post activity. Intrusion detection technology is not implemented to ensure that egress and ingress points are actively monitored and acted upon.
- Standard device configurations are not consistently used and implemented across the enterprise.
- Business continuity and disaster recovery ensure that the business would be able to continue operations in the case of an emergency. Business continuity and disaster recovery have not been formally implemented and tested within the enterprise network environment.
- Internally executed or outsourced network vulnerability assessments provide insight to weak points within the network architecture at regular intervals. Regular scans within the enterprise network are not currently implemented.

When a member of the executive team sees an assessment containing these statements, emotions can go out the windows and a statement may be made: "Lock down EVERYTHING." Security professionals know this cannot be done, and information security requirements need to be based on business requirements. And the basic business requirement is to protect enterprise assets.

The basic strategy of an information security team building a policy architecture is to understand the business and its requirements. Although senior management realizes that major changes in information technology will be necessary to meet the needs of the business, there is also a concern for the bottom line. Information security strategic priorities include the following:

1. Assessing and protecting key information assets and critical infrastructure, including interdependent physical and cyberinformation systems.
2. Limiting the risk to enterprise assets through the use of administrative, technology, and physical means.
3. Ensuring privacy of information related to employees, partners, and customers.
4. Ensuring the enterprise is compliant with all required regulations and other regulations that may affect clients and partners.
5. Fusing and sharing information security among all business units.
6. Planning for and providing continuity of business operations before, during, and after large-scale disasters.
7. Protecting and supporting continuous functioning of interoperable communication systems surrounding information assets.
8. Executing proactive deterrence, preemption, and prevention initiatives.

Using these priorities, we can come up with strategic themes for developing an information security policy architecture that include the following:

1. *Partnership and Leadership.* Promote a collaborative environment for sharing information, resources, assistance, and expertise as we jointly strive to enhance our Information Assurance environment.
2. *Communication.* Provide interoperable systems that provide critical information in a timely fashion to those who need it and in a form that is easy to use and understand.
3. *Preventing Attacks.* Initiate a wide spectrum of prevention efforts including intelligence and warning capabilities to ensure situational awareness and hardening of critical infrastructure.
4. *Reducing Vulnerabilities.* Protect our enterprise by improving the protection of the individual pieces and interconnecting systems that make up our critical information infrastructure.
5. *Compliance and Privacy.* Have environmental compliance with corporate policies and regulations to ensure the privacy of information used, stored, and transmitted.

2.5 Summary

Where and to whom an information security team reports within an enterprise may not have any real meaning, as long as the team has the trust and the reputation with the business units. Looking at the enterprise and determining a mission with goals and objectives gives the information security team a strategic direction to protect the enterprise assets. The mission, goals, objectives, and strategic direction form the basic set of information for building an information security policy architecture. For samples of information security program documents, see Appendix A and Appendix B.

Chapter 3

What Is a Policy Architecture?

In general, policy is a plan or course of action that a business uses to influence and determine decisions, actions, and other matters, and an architecture is the art and science of designing and building something. A security policy architecture is a set of documents built and designed to demonstrate the business's course of action to protect the enterprise and its assets. It is an interlocking set of documents that provides guidance for business requirements. An information security policy architecture is the foundation of building blocks for the information security program (see Figure 9).

This simple statement takes on huge meaning and value, and of course, takes a tremendous amount of time to development, implement, and maintain for an enterprise. The concept of an information security policy architecture needs to be talked about in the concept of a set of documents, not a manual to do business by. By using the concept of document sets, the enterprise does not have to memorize everything that is in print. The enterprise can then use the document sets to supplement their business requirements when divesting or acquiring new entities, evaluating software for implementation, or enforcing consequences when someone abuses privileges within the organization. The information security policy architecture is the enterprise's approach toward information security, the framework, and the guiding principles of the information security strategy, and it will explain to future generations why the enterprise did what it did. The information security policy architecture shows your due diligence in protecting the enterprise's assets. And you must remember that an information security policy architecture is not an absolute. It grows and changes with the enterprise and its business requirements.

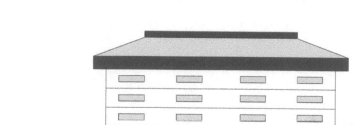

Strong Business Foundation is Built on a
Strong Policy Architecture

Figure 9   Building foundation.

The information security policy architecture, information security program, and information security strategic plan must fit and complement the enterprise's business model and requirements. Do not write an information security policy architecture for the sake of writing it and having something documented.

Network and software engineers develop and maintain architectures as part of their daily responsibilities. Security professionals start with the enterprise's business goals and objectives, create an information security concept, and develop an information security policy architecture that supports the business needs and requirements. We must remember that the information security policy architecture is written to support the business and not to be written and implemented just for the sake of security. As stated earlier, a policy architecture will allow an enterprise to

- Have a strong commitment to ethics and asset protection
- Form a benchmark to progress measurement
- Evaluate how an organization is doing with its information security program;
- Evaluate how service level agreements are being met through security monitoring
- Ensure consistency in what the enterprise wants to protect
- Serve as a guide for information security, risk, privacy, compliance
- Define the acceptable use of enterprise assets

A policy architecture is not a checklist to show you are in compliance or that the enterprise has reduced asset risk. A policy architecture enhances the enterprise's ability to protect assets; it serves as a guide for information security, risk, privacy, and compliance, and most of all defines acceptable use. A policy architecture is coordinating the lines of the business; looking at the risk; balancing it with information security, regulatory; and audit requirements; and using technology to implement it. The whole policy architecture may not be enforced through automation and technology. With an information security program, your policy architecture can document your strategies. It shows a mature escalation process for incidents as you move forward.

So what is a policy architecture? It is a continuous process. Although your initial implementation or your annual review can be done as a project, your policy architecture is an ongoing a process; it is at the heart of charting your business course and of assessing your risk of baselining. If you don't have an underlying architecture, how are you going to move forward? It assists with your compliance. It gives you guidelines, standards, and processes to monitor and respond to things within your organization. And it also is a basis for user awareness training. An information security policy architecture will allow you to spell out that there is no implied privacy in the use of corporate assets. A risk management program can be incorporated into your policy architecture. A statement for the information security program could be that the program was developed in conjunction with industry best practices and guidelines for information security, reducing the risk to enterprise assets, and safeguarding confidential customer information or internal intellectual property information. As you look at potential threats, how are those threats mitigated? Just like risks. Strategies need to be developed based on the information security policy architecture. Your policy architecture includes the identification of information and information systems to be protected including electronic systems and physical components used to access, store, transmit, protect, and eventually dispose of information. Information and information systems can be both paper-based and electronic-based. You need to look at governance, which is achieved through management structure, assignment of responsibilities, and authority to enforce and to establish policies and procedures with the allocation and resources for monitoring and accountability. You need to continually review that. For the most part, your policy architecture is designed to protect critical information systems, system owners, and system users through physical and virtual controls.

Before you continue in your policy architecture development, you should sit down and document the answers to the following questions:

- What do we want our policy architecture to accomplish?
- Are we doing the right things and the right way?
- Are we getting things done?
- Will this policy architecture deliver value to the organization?

You need to look at where do we want to go with this policy architecture and, more important, where we are now.

Without being able to answer these questions, how can you move forward to examine things?

Another area that must be considered is the culture of the organization with its relationship to policies. Many smaller enterprises like one large document rather than several smaller documents. Other enterprises prefer several smaller documents, which are modularized and easier to maintain and review. Within the enterprise culture, especially global enterprises, a determination needs to be made on whether all documents apply to all locations and environments. The culture plays into FUD because all countries and locations interpret documentation differently. From an international culture standpoint, the policy architecture must

- Be implementable and enforceable
- Be concise and easy to understand (and translate)
- State why the document is needed
- State what is covered by the document
- Define responsibilities
- Define contacts for questions (and exceptions)
- Define how violations will be handled
- Balance the protection required with the need for productivity

3.1 Basic Document Definitions

For the purposes of developing the concept of an information security policy architecture, Table 1 defines terms for an information security policy architecture. It defines the types of documents that will be described in this book to complete an enterprise policy architecture.

So how does this fit together? See Figure 10, which illustrates how each document type molded into another. What you need to look at is the policy at the high

Table 1   Types of Document Definitions

Policy	A high-level statement for goals, behaviors, and consequences. Do not forget about the consequences because if you have one that violates the policy without a consequence, how do you know or why would you even want to know whether someone violated it. Policies are technology neutral. They are somewhat abstract because they need to be supported with guidelines, standards, and processes.
Guideline	An outline for a statement of conduct. This is a guide for how someone or something should perform, such as acceptable use of the Internet.
Standard	A set of rules and procedures that are required.
Procedure, process, or work instruction	Whatever the term within your organization, these are documented step-by-step instructions to get to a goal. Examples of a procedure would be setting up an account for a new hire, removing access on termination, access control issues, and access control assignments.

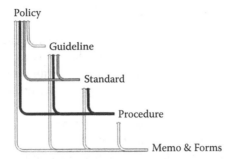

Figure 10   Layering the policy architecture.

level. If you write a guideline, it has to feed into a policy. A practice must reference a guideline or a standard. A procedure must reference a standard, guideline, and/or policy. You can have forms and memos that support any one of these other four levels. If you keep this in mind, you will have an information security policy architecture that is not difficult to maintain.

3.2   Effective Policy Architecture

Before any development is begun on a security policy architecture, the information security team needs to remember that information security is an enterprise problem. In creating an effective policy architecture, you need to remember a few things. First and foremost, the documents need to be written in plain and simple language. Should the enterprise go global, then translating these documents into other languages may be done more easily. Using plain and simple language, the documents can be communicated to the staff with understanding and no misinterpretation. As you format the documents ensure the formatting is suitable for online use. And lastly and more importantly, ensure that the content is related to the business and business requirements. As an effective policy architecture is developed, the following items need to be considered:

- Explain why the issue is important, why a decision needs to be made
- Provide essential facts and supporting evidence
- Provide clear courses of action
- If this will be effective over time

Apply a SMART principle while developing the information security policy architecture (**S**pecific, **M**easurable, **A**greeable, **R**ealistic, and **T**ime-bound) to ensure it continues to meet the enterprise business requirements.

3.3   Scope of the Architecture

All enterprise and departmental policies need to have a defined scope: how much does the policy encompass. For the most part, when an enterprise policy is written, it includes anyone and anything it connects to, communicates with, or is accessed by. Like a project without a defined scope, the policy architecture can become ineffective and inefficient.

Entities and people who work for/with (get paid) or volunteer for/with the enterprise are staff members. Within the scope of all documentation, the types of staff members to whom the document applies need to be defined. This portion of the scope lets people know if they are obligated as a staff member to follow or enforce the document. The definitions given in Table 2 are the different types of staff being used for the samples within this book. Your enterprise needs a master set of definitions for the types of staff that your policy architecture will encompass.

After the scope of staff is defined for the enterprise, the definition of an asset needs to be included in the scope. Many staff members think that if they cannot see an item, if something is not concrete, then it is not an asset. An asset definition needs to be given in terms of type, ownership, and location because an asset has different meanings to different departments within an enterprise. Accounting cares about a fixed asset, PPE (property, plant, and equipment), or tangible assets, that are purchased for continued and long-term use in earning profit in a business or long-term investments, for example. To the IT department an asset can be equipment as well as data stored in electronic form. There are also intangible assets that lack physical substance and are usually very hard to assign value. These include patents, copyrights, franchises, goodwill, trademarks, trade names, and so on. A simple definition of an asset for a policy architecture could be as follows:

> An asset is any item of value or use that is owned or created by the entity. The following is a basic, but not inclusive, list of MYC assets: hardware, software, data, people, documentation, supplies, intellectual property, and client and community information. Assets are owned by MYC. Personnel do not have privacy in the use of enterprise assets. Items brought onto MYC property will be considered an extension of MYC assets, unless specifically identified as the property of other parties, and subject to auditing, monitoring, and logging by MYC.

You have created basic definitions of staff members and assets, now what about the location of these items. Within the scope of the document, the location of staff and assets needs to be defined to ensure the proper locations are included. We know that location is a physical item where assets and staff members are housed. This can include a specific area, geographic region, country, or body of water. A simple definition of location for a document is as follows

Table 2   Definition of Staff Types

Client	A party for which professional services are rendered.
Consultant	Someone who gives expert.or professional advice. A consultant's time is normally set up through a purchase order agreement or through a contract.
Contractor (PO)	A person or business who performs services for another person under an express or implied agreement and who is not subject to the other's control or right to control the manner and means of performing the services; not an employee. This person's services are done through a purchase order for payment.
Contractor (Regular)	A person or business who performs services for another person under an express or implied agreement and who is not subject to the other's control or right to control, the manner and means of performing the services; not an employee. This person's services are through a standard vendor and he or she is considered staff augmentation.
Co-Op	One who is enrolled or attends classes at a school, college, or university.
Customer	A party who buys goods or services.
Employee	A person who is hired by MYC at a wage or fixed payment in exchange for personal services and who does not provide the services as part of an independent business.
Partner	A company that is associated with MYC in performing activities from a non-MYC facility using a non-MYC infrastructure. Offshore partner: Located at a distance from the shore; located or based in a foreign country. Onshore/Nearshore: Located within or contiguous with the United States.
Staff	Any person or entity that falls into the categories of Client, Consultant, Contractor (PO), Contractor (Regular), Co-Op, Customer, Employee, Partner, Student, Vendor, or Volunteer.
Student	One who is enrolled or attends classes at a school, college, or university.
Vendor	A seller. One who disposes of an item in consideration of money.
Volunteer	A person who performs or offers to perform a service voluntarily without pay.

In the protection of assets, the scope of this document covers all locations where enterprise assets are housed and accessed by any staff member.

If you define the staff, the assets and the location, you have a complete scope of what the document will cover through its details. Placing these definitions within a master glossary enables all documents to use a common terminology set which reduces the misinterpretation of terms and also can shorten the maintenance cycle during review periods.

3.4 Top-Level Topics

The concepts presented for document writing within the information security policy architecture are topics that should be included. If the creative writing skills of the team are good, then some of these topics can be combined into a single document.

At an enterprise level, an information security policy architecture should start with the following topics, not necessarily in individual documents:

- Employment practices (and discipline)
- Standards of conduct (ethics)
- Conflict of interest (asset ownership)
- Compliance (in general)
- Corporate communications (internal/external)
- Corporate authority and responsibility
- Privacy
- Risk
- Information security
- Asset ownership and classification (contracts, procurement, IP)
- Physical and environmental security
- Business continuity and disaster recovery

These topics set the executive tone for the behavior and culture of protecting enterprise assets. Included in these topics can be the undertones of the following topics, not necessarily in individual documents:

- Network security
- Access control
- Authentication
- Encryption/key management
- Segregation of duties
- Auditing/logging/monitoring/review

- Software security
- Security awareness
- Incident response
- Device configurations
- Procurement and contracts
- System development lifecycle
- Document retention

Depending on the enterprise's business requirements, the topic priorities will be different and even the topics themselves may be difference. Know and understand the enterprise business requirements before embarking on an information security policy architecture task.

Chapter 4

Getting Ready to Start

4.1 Reviewing What Is in Place

Every business is handled differently because people in command of each business have their own styles. For every staff member within the enterprise there is a different way to handle the review of the information security policy architecture. The process below will walk through the review in a logical manner looking at the CIAA (confidentiality, integrity, availability, accountability) principle using the administrative, technical, and physical controls. Because every enterprise is not the same, it is extremely hard to list what needs to be included as someone reviews the existing policy architecture. No matter what methodology is being used, you must first identify the enterprise assets and any data protection or regulatory requirements. Identifying enterprise assets can be difficult, especially if there is not a documented formal asset (tangible and intangible) inventory or a documented asset definition. The array of data protection laws and global regulatory bodies seems to grow on a daily basis. For example, as of this writing:

- Twenty-seven countries are involved with the European Union (EU) data protection directives;
- Five countries outside the EU have equivalent data protection directives;
- Twenty-one countries in the Asia–Pacific Economic Cooperative have developed a voluntary privacy framework;
- Thirty-four states within the United States have adopted security breach notification laws;
- Fifty-one countries have their own specific data protection laws.

Has anyone documented this within the enterprise?

Next, you have to identify threats (any circumstance or event with the potential to cause harm to the enterprise's information or information system); common threats can be natural, human, or environmental in nature. And you have to incorporate business requirements so local, remote, and off-shore staff can access the assets needed to perform their function. This is not a mandatory requirement for a privacy, compliance, or risk assessment to be performed to determine the key areas of business requirements. It is getting to know the enterprise and the culture of acceptance for an information security policy architecture. Some general questions that an enterprise needs to answer when reviewing its existing information security policy architecture include the following:

1. Is there an executive directive/statement to ensure there is an information security architecture that includes risk, governance, ethics, compliance, privacy, and protection of enterprise assets? Are enterprise roles, responsibilities, and accountabilities defined? Are the executive team and the board of directors on the same page?
2. Are there data/information requirements stating that it must be available, accessed by need to know or have, and in the most accurate format?
3. Are staff required to acknowledge policies on new hire and termination, and at regular intervals? Are the staff types of enterprise network access defined? Is an enterprise asset defined?
4. What types of services and applications are permitted on the enterprise network, who is permitted to perform the installs and removals, and who is permitted to perform the monitoring? How are connections (hardwired, wireless, remote) defined to the enterprise network?
5. How are access roles, accountabilities, and responsibilities defined for network, applications, and devices? How are monitoring, logging, and reporting defined for goals and objectives?
6. Who is permitted onsite and permitted to plug what type of device into the enterprise network? What is the standard authorization and authentication mechanism for the enterprise?
7. How are staff going to request access to a network, application, device, or service, who will grant access, and who will be required to monitor logs and access? How do staff access the building, business areas, and communication rooms? Is electrostatic training required for anyone who enters a data center? Is the building segmented by badge control?
8. How are incidents/exceptions reported, to whom are they reported, how are incidents/exceptions reviewed? (These are not necessarily security breaches.)
9. How are the enterprise network devices configured? How are they monitored and put back into compliance? What is the exception process to the standard? Are all ingresses and egresses documented within the enterprise?
10. If something happens in the enterprise environment, how is it reported and how are systems and information recovered?

11. Is there an asset and information classification matrix and are the risks defined for the asset classification? Is there a statement about the protection of the enterprise assets?
12. Within the information security team and operational duties is there a document listing the segregation of duties and responsibilities, so no one person has the responsibility of complete end-to-end transaction processing?
13. If the enterprise should happen to lose is information security team, are there enough details and documents to permit a third party or another business unit to take over the duties and continue the business until the team is replaced?
14. Is the location of all documents documented and known to all staff members? Is there a document management system? Is there a review process and an owner assigned to each document?

If these questions do not match the enterprise, then putting it into a matrix format and responding to gaps may work. See Table 3 and Appendix D for a sample gap matrix for reviewing the existing enterprise information security policy architecture. Should the table format be used, the information security team will need to add additional requirements based on business needs. If the answers are in the affirmative, then the enterprise more than likely has a good information security policy architecture foundation. If staff are aware of information risks, compliance, governance, and privacy, then the user awareness program is more than likely strong. And if the information security team is invited to project meetings, software evaluation sessions, and requirements gathering sessions, then the information security team has performed its function in aligning with the business requirements and units of the enterprise. This book can be used as a validation of what is implemented within the enterprise. For the enterprise lacking full term implements, this book will walk through the process of creating the information security policy architecture to ensure the enterprise has a strong foundation for complying with business requirements.

Now, if you are starting from scratch, these questions and the table also can be used to get you started in developing the outline of what is needed.

4.2 Basic Assessment

All businesses have four different layers of architectures:

■ Business: The mission and goals of the enterprise;
■ Information: What is required to accomplish the enterprise mission and goals;
■ Application: What is being used to access that information for the business;
■ Technical: Who will be accessing the business information and how.

Table 3 Policy Gap Matrix

	Standard	Topic Documented	Possible Location to Add Topic
Administrative Safeguards	Authorization Policy		
	Information System Security Activity Review		
	Assigned Security Responsibility		
	Workforce Security		
	Workforce Clearance Procedure		
	Termination Procedures		
	Access Control Management		
	Access Establishment and Modification		
	Security Awareness and Training		
	Security Reminders		
	Protection from Malicious Software		
	Log-in Monitoring		
	Password Management		
	Security Incident Procedures		
	Contingency Plan		
	Data Backup Plan		
	Disaster Recovery Plan		
	Emergency Mode Operation Plan		
	Applications and Data Criticality Analysis		
	Business Associate Contracts and Other Arrangements		
	Written Contract or Other Arrangement		

Table 3 (continued)   Policy Gap Matrix

	Standard	*Topic Documented*	*Possible Location to Add Topic*
Physical Controls	Facility Access Controls		
	Contingency Operations		
	Facility Security Plan		
	Access Control and Validation Procedures		
	Maintenance Records		
	Workstation Use		
	Workstation Security		
	Data Disposal		
	Media Re-use		
	Accountability		
	Data Backup and Storage		
Technical Controls	Access Control		
	Unique User Identification		
	Emergency Access Procedure		
	Automatic Logoff		
	Encryption and Decryption		
	Audit Controls		
	Integrity		
	Mechanism to Authenticate Electronically Protected Information		
	Person or Entity Authentication		
	Transmission Security		
	Integrity Controls		
	Encryption		

Understanding the importance of business information allows the information security team to assist in the documentation of potential loss and the exposure risk of that business information. By understanding the business information and information use, the information team can start performing gap assessments within an enterprise to determine priorities and documents or statements that need to be developed first. The assessment needs to combine risk, compliance, privacy, business requirements, and asset protection.

- Risk Assessment: What is our exposure and what do we need to do?
- Compliance Assessments: How well are we achieving ongoing compliance as our business model changes?
- Privacy Assessments: How well are we limiting the exposure of information?
- Security Assessments: How well are our security mechanisms protecting information?

When developing the information security policy architecture, all of these components must be included. This could be termed a readiness assessment evaluating if you have implemented adequate controls throughout the enterprise to protect and use information in a manner that does not pose a risk to the enterprise? Should any one of the components be missing, the information security policy architecture will be out of balance and nonconformance of protecting enterprise assets will exist. Developing an assessment plan defines the objects to be assessed as well as the tasks and responsibilities of the assessments, the planning schedule, and the resources required for the realization. This assessment plan will determine the state in which the assets are currently protected, by whom, and by what means. The assessment will give you a baseline for what assets are missing protection within the enterprise and assist in performing a quality assessment of what is currently in place. This baseline will allow the information security team to documenting the following:

- How hardened are the electronic assets?
- How are the information and assets classified for their level of importance?
- What is being monitored, how, and by whom?
- What is being audited, how, and by whom?
- Who is doing the enforcing for violations and for incidents?
- Does anything need to be encrypted and what methods are being used?

There are many books and white papers on how to perform the various assessments. This introduction is not to take their place, but it will give you an idea of what needs to be thought about as you develop your information security policy architecture. Please see Appendix E for a sample risk assessment.

4.3   Policy Writing Skills

A good policy writer has performed business and industry research to ensure the business requirements and enterprise mission and objectives are integrated into the writer's statements. Everyone, well almost everyone, hates to do documentation. Many times, it is a technical person who is tasked with writing the information security policy architecture documentation. And there are many resources out there for the technical person to copy and manipulate, and a document can be written in their technical language. Information security and technical professionals many times use their own acronyms without explanation and document complex and confusing topics, then the staff comfort levels in understanding and following these documents drops. However, the needs and skill level of a novice staff member may not be addresses. Many information security and technical personnel lack writing and technical writing skills, meaning the documentation may not be readable, concise, and effective to read. This book is not going to concentrate on how to achieve technical writing skills, but it will give some guidance on how to write a better document for the enterprise.

As a writer, you need to concentrate on the 5Ws and 1H (who, what, when, where, why, and how) when building the information security policy architecture. When performing incident response, you must get back to the basics when reviewing and presenting information. The same is true for writing documentation. This also provides a consistent framework for the information security policy architecture and improves the comfort levels of the enterprise when implementing and maintaining the policy architecture. And, finally, it reduces how a staff member interprets the document. Less interpretation and less confusion join for better trust and alignment with the business requirements.

Following basic grammar rules means a staff member will be comfortable in reading the document. Basic business writing uses nouns and verbs. Consider:

> MYC uses technological resources, which are MYC assets, to protect investments that are high in enterprise monetary value.

What does that mean? It would be simpler to state:

> All MYC assets are protected to the level of importance using technology resources.

Wow, now that is easy to understand. Short, sweet, and to the point. It tells you what is being protected, who is protecting the assets, and how much they are protected. The rest of the document or subdocuments will then go more in depth on the where, when, and how the assets are protected.

Write in active and not passive voice. In passive voice the subject is the recipient of the action, and use verbs such as "to be" and "to have." Using the basic grammar rules, it should be easy to state the document in active voice—who does what; for example:

> A foundation for enterprise asset protection is established by the information security policy architecture.

Or rewriting it to state:

> The information security policy architecture establishes a foundation for enterprise asset protection.

The second statement is more clear and concise, leaving little to interpretation.

Know the business requirements, culture, and user environment before starting to write. As with any presentation, a presenter tries to know who will be in the audience and presents the topics in a way the audience will understand. The same is true for document writing. Writing short, simple sentences will lessen the confusion of the reader. Writing at an eighth to tenth grade level may seem like "dumbing down" the writing, when in fact it will increase the comprehension and make the document easier to understand; for example:

> Using the RSA authentication with the IPSEC VPN tunnel will reduce the need for MD5 hash encryption when performing trans-border data transfer.

Yeah, right, when all a staff member needs to hear is

> MYC uses two-factor authentication for remote access to protect the internal information resources.

As a normal staff member, I do not need to know the technology the enterprise is using, but I do need to know why. For a technical procedure between two information technology departments, the first sentence is perfect.

Shorter is better. The higher level documents are what the author calls "bathroom reading," short and to the point. No chance in not finishing the document and losing the reader before the point is demonstrated. The "shorter is better" ideal does not necessary work for guidelines, standards, or work instructions, because more detail is required in these documents. As people enter a bookstore, do they choose the largest book on the shelf not minding the title or content or do they look at the content and title and determine if the length is worth reading? The "shorter is better" concept will assist an enterprise in determining if the information security policy architecture document needs to be one large document or multiple interrelated documents.

4.4 A Framework or Set of Standards?

There can be no standard set of recommendations for a specific framework or set of standards to implement into each organization. Each enterprise has a different set of business requirements that include massive sets of regulations. Take the various frameworks that are out there (e.g., ISO17799, SAS70, PCI DSS, Basel II, international privacy) and pick the best mesh that fits with your business requirements. As an enterprise, the information security team needs to know all the information controls required to meet the objectives. One disadvantage of creating a custom framework is that the information security team will need to validate and justify the framework to the regulators more and have to perform regular research on the base frameworks the enterprise used to construct their custom framework. While this requires more work up front, in the end, it may reduce the amount of work for pulling (auditing) data for the regulators. If you create a master matrix for compliance and privacy, expanding for global regulations, the enterprise can map gaps of risk and compliance based on the above performed assessments. See Table 4 for a sample.

Once the initial matrix is completed, the enterprise area column can be broken down into more detail and the distinction can be made between enterprise, department, and information technology responsibilities. This can also be mapped to the gaps in the assessments performed to get the priorities that need to be focused on within the information security policy architecture. Then as with all risk, regulations, frameworks, and assessments, the enterprise will need to plan, implement, monitor, and assess (see Figure 11) against the various capability maturity models that are out there.

The framework and style selection is based on the enterprise culture and business requirements. As long as the homework is done for the justification for the enterprise and the regulators understand this, the customized framework will work for the enterprise. Within the framework there are standards. Standards come in all shapes and sizes from simple to complex. If the enterprise does not know how to use the selected standards or know what the standards are, it will be a waste of time, effort, and money. As the enterprise selects the framework and standards, the enterprise must determine the level of security that needs to be applied to each level of information based on the business requirements. As you work through selecting a framework and set of standards, the enterprise needs to remember the following items:

■ Strategic/business alignment
■ Efficiency and effectiveness (value) of delivery
■ Risk mitigation
■ Resource management to monitor and maintain the performance

Table 4   Initial Framework

Enterprise Area	ISO 17799	SAS70 Type II	GLBA	PCI DSS	EU Privacy	CobIT	Common Criteria	Generally Accepted Privacy Principles	Generally Accepted Security Principles
Access Control	X	X	X	X	X	X	X	X	X
Application Development	X	X			X	X	X		X
Asset Management	X	X		X	X				X
Business Operations	X	X		X	X	X	X	X	
Communications	X	X	X	X	X	X	X	X	X
Compliance	X	X	X	X	X	X			
Corporate Governance	X				X	X			
Customers	X	X	X	X	X	X		X	X
Incident Management	X	X	X	X	X	X		X	X
IT Operations	X	X	X	X	X	X	X	X	X
Outsourcing	X	X		X	X	X	X	X	X
Physical/Environmental	X	X					X		X
Policies & Procedures	X	X		X	X	X	X	X	X
Privacy	X	X	X	X	X			X	
Security	X	X		X	X	X	X		X

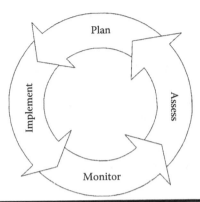

Figure 11   Work cycle.

4.5   Manuals of Style

Each enterprise probably has a communications group or a group that controls press releases or documents to the organization. This group has a standard format documenting what is contained in each document and how the document is constructed. They have a style guide that outlines standards for design and writing for a specific publication or enterprise. Depending on the type of document, the style can focus on graphic design, covering such topics as typography and white space. A Web site style guide can be different from a hard copy style guide because its focus is on a publication's visual and technical aspects rather than prose style, best usage, grammar, punctuation, spelling, and fairness. The style guide does not address the author's voice, yet it gives the author a standard format to follow for documents. The old reliable *Chicago Manual of Style* book, the *Associated Press Stylebook*, and the *MLA (Modern Language Association) Handbook* are a few well-known manuals of style. A documented style manual is a style guide that aims for consistency in formatting and making documents easier to read. Before documents are written within an enterprise, the enterprise needs to have a formal manual of style to provide consistency to the enterprise for the information security policy architecture, as well as any other publication for and by the enterprise.

As you begin to understand and learn additional business requirements to build the information security policy architecture and start the development process, you need to also remember and consider a few items about the writing style:

- The author needs to write from a neutral point of view.
- As the information security policy architecture is being written you need to ensure the policies are enforceable through monitoring and auditing.

■ Remember that if you copy from another's policy architecture, the policy architecture content must fit into your enterprise's culture and business requirements.
■ Write in a way that matches the enterprise's communication style, a way that everyone in the organization will understand.
■ Do not hesitate to rewrite what is currently written, as long as it fits into the enterprise's business requirements. By contrast, do not overstate or ramble within the information security policy architecture documents.
■ Make sure the information security policy architecture documents are written to information staff of who is endorsing and enforcing the documents.
■ Be clear and do not use unnecessary acronyms.

If an enterprise style manual exists, then follow that manual of style for the information security policy architecture. Using an established format will assist in the implementation and acceptance of the information security policy architecture. The manual of style should include the following defined areas:

■ Font and pitch
    Signature sheet
    For document approval
    For regular staff acknowledgement
■ Header/footer information
    Title
    Owner
    Effective date
    Last review date
    Document number
    Revision number
■ Revision history including
    Date
    Revision number
    Author
    Description of what was updated
■ Purpose/Scope
    Supporting details
    Definitions, if there is no master glossary
    Acronyms, if there is no master acronym reference
    References to other documents
    Responsibilities/functions/duties
■ Reviewing and approval groups
    The review group members
    The approval process members

- Template
    Instructions on how to use the document format
    Required and option sections of the document
    The location of documents that provide conformance evidence, such as
        meeting minutes, audit reports, databases, software.

If the enterprise considers the information security policy architecture as intellectual property belonging to the enterprise, and it should, each architecture document should have somewhere in the document a statement similar to the following:

> This document and the information disclosed is proprietary and is not to be reproduced, used, or disclosed to anyone without the written permission of MYC. A hard copy of this document is for reference only and the latest approved version is located in the enterprise document management system.

Before using this statement within your documents, please verify with your Human Resource department and Counsel.

See Appendix C for a sample set of document format sections for policies, guidelines, standards, and procedures.

A naming and numbering convention for the documents should be within a style guide. If there is an automated program to keep track of the numbers and owners (document management), the review cycle will be easier in the future. The numbering system can be every number, every other number, every fifth or tenth number, depending on the enterprise style. The document naming convention can be generic, based on a prefix and the number generator matched with a title, which is one of the simpler methods of naming. A sample document prefix convention could be something similar to Table 5.

4.6   Do I Need to Create a Committee?

Does the enterprise need an information security committee (ISC)? It depends on the enterprise culture and the information security team's mission statement. When anything new is being implemented, staff will go through the avoidance and resistance phases, then they will refocus and adjust their habits for compliance with the requirements. See Figure 12 for a sample of the cycle of issues that will be encountered and actions that can be taken when implementing an information security policy architecture.

An ISC is a group of staff and executives through which the information security program can be guided. This committee will consist of executive team members who will assist the enterprise's information security program in following

Table 5 Document Prefixes

PL	Policy
ST	Standards
GD	Guidelines
WI	Work instruction
LT	Memo or letter
FM	Form
TM	Template
BL	Build document for a server or workstation, a specific procedure document
CM	Compliance document, a specific procedure/audit/checklist document
PR	Program, such as the information security program
IN	Incident report, special type of report document
ST	Status report, formatting for all security reports
SB	Service bulletin, notification when there are issues or updates to assets

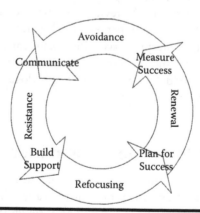

Figure 12 Problems and actions.

the enterprise's mission and goals. This committee will also consist of staff members across varied disciplines to ensure the information security program fits functionally into the enterprise environment and assist in guiding operational activities. Does this team have the final approval for what is implemented from the information security team? Not necessarily. Once the executive team has approved the initial information assurance policy and the information security program, this team will provide guidance in documenting risks while protecting the enterprise assets. The information security team will be the group who looks for solutions for protecting enterprise assets. The ISC's goals can be similar to the following:

- To assure that the concept fits into the mission and objectives of the enterprise
- To perform quality assurance checks for the information security program
- To proactively identify risks and threats to the enterprise environment

The ISC coordinator should be the highest person in the information security team, such as a Chief Security Officer or Director. This coordinator will be responsible for the following tasks:

- Keeping minutes of the ISC meetings
- Keeping records of the incidents within the enterprise
- Keeping track of the proposal and projects of the information security team
- Coordinating the publication of the information security program and activities to the enterprise environment
- Coordinating activities for the ISC

The ISC team members consist of a combination of management and staff for a cross section of the business. There also should be additional delegates when reviewing documents or proposing new ideas for implementation into the enterprise. The management team members of the ISC can include the following personnel (or the equivalent within the enterprise):

- Chief Information Officer
- Chief Financial Officer
- Internal Audit Executive
- Human Resources Executive
- Chief Counsel
- Business Operations Executive

If the enterprise has established business information security officers or a business focused security person, then this person or these people should be members of the ISC. The technical staff members of the ISC can include the following personnel (or the equivalent within the enterprise):

- Infrastructure Specialist (2), Server Specialist, Network Specialist, or Electronic Communications Specialist
- Help Desk/Desktop Support Manager
- Applications Development Director

- Client Community (2) Management—optional
- Technology Services Director—optional

Many times, it is good to also have feedback from members of the user community. An ISC guest would be someone from the business or user community who would like to see what the ISC does or has a vested interest in the topic of the meeting.

The ISC should meet on a regular basis. Depending on the enterprise's activities, monthly meetings may be too often, unless you are getting the program or initiative off the ground. The recommendation would be to have the ISC meeting on a quarterly basis for updates and changes in enterprise business directions and internal projects relating to information protection. The meeting should be coordinated by the ISC coordinator in an advisory capacity to ensure from a broad business perspective and from a technology perspective that the enterprise assets are being protected.

4.7 Initial Approvals for Information Security

Although the information security team develops the initial information assurance policy and information security program, there do need to be executive approvals to support the information security initiative. Depending on the enterprise structure, the following executives should sign off on the initial documents for the information security team:

- Chief Executive Officer/President
- Business Operations Executive
- Chief Information Officer

And the following should acknowledge and not have any issues with the initial documents and direction:

- Internal Audit Executive
- Corporate Counsel Executive
- Board of Directors

With the additional acknowledgement, the information security team has the support of the complete executive team in the enterprise to proceed with a program and policy architecture to protect the enterprise assets.

Chapter 5

Writing the Documents

In this chapter, we will use certain topics to develop a policy, guideline, standard, and password. The topics will be very simple and the concept for development can be expanded depending upon the enterprise topic lists. These samples will be based on the manual of style set up in the previous chapter. Before getting into the actual writing, a project proposal should be completed to ensure management has a clear understanding of what the information security policy architecture will entail. See Appendix F for a sample information security policy architecture project proposal document.

5.1 Policy

A policy is a high level statement of goals, behaviors, and consequences. The most critical policy that any enterprise needs is an overarching information assurance or information security policy. Information assurance and information security can have two different meanings to an enterprise, so first you will need to determine which title will fit into the enterprise culture. Information security is about locking down information, and ensuring privacy and soundness are about security, but this does not bring forward the aspects of assurance through controls, accountability, and measurements. Information assurance depends not only on the soundness of the design strategy but also on the assurance of correctness of the implementation of security controls. Information assurance is about defining standards, controls, and guidelines for maintaining information privacy, protecting information soundness, and ensuring information accessibility by staff. So the enterprise culture and understanding of information security versus assurance will determine the policy title. Policies should be reviewed on an annual basis to ensure they still fit into the enterprise's strategic plans and business requirements.

Title:	INFORMATION ASSURANCE				
Part Number:	**PL00550**	Revision:	**1.0**	Effective:	20050930
Owner:	**CEO**			Last Review:	20070501

This electronic document supersedes all previous electronic and printed documents or oral

statements regarding this policy.

All Company Policies are subject to change at the sole discretion of MYC management.

Figure 13 Sample header.

Based on the manual of style, we can build a document header, as illustrated in Figure 13.

This initial policy is for the whole enterprise, so the scope statement will have to demonstrate that. For example,

> This policy applies to all MYC enterprise information and any MYC staff member who accesses information within MYC locations.

Now definitions of *information* and *staff member* are required not to allow for interpretation. This is where a glossary is nice to have because it keeps the policy short. For this policy, the term *staff member* was defined in Table 2. For a definition of *information* we will use the following:

> The result of processing, manipulating, and organizing data in a way that adds to the knowledge of the person receiving it; organized data which is understood to have significance and meaning; an enterprise asset.
>
> Examples are text, images, sounds, codes, computer programs, software, and databases.

What is the enterprise's statement about information assurance? It could be something like the following:

> Information and information systems are critical and vital to MYC's mission and objectives. MYC has a fiduciary duty to protect, limit risk, preserve, improve, and account for MYC information at all times. MYC must take appropriate steps to assure information protection from risks and threats. MYC's information must be protected

in a manner commensurate with its sensitivity, value, and criticality. Security measures must be employed regardless of the media on which information is stored, the systems which process it, or the methods by which it is moved. Such protection includes restricting access to information on a need-to-know basis. MYC staff must devote sufficient time and resources to ensure that information is properly protected. To properly protect and manage this property, management reserves the right to audit, monitor, and log all data stored in or transmitted by these systems.

The statement may be a little wordy for some enterprises, but it does stand the test of being understandable and easy to read.

When the scope, definitions, and policy statement are completed, next follow the staff responsibilities. The format of how the responsibilities are presented is a matter of style. Bullets or table formats are much easier to read and glance at when looking for particular items in a document; for example:

- Management must make sure that information is protected in a manner that is at least as secure as other organizations in the same industry handling the same type of information and as required by law.
- Information Security will perform regular risk and compliance reviews against MYC information and will coordinate any information incidents.
- Staff must be provided with sufficient training and supporting reference materials to allow them to properly protect and otherwise manage MYC information.
- Information Technology will maintain the technology required for information assurance.

Finally, the consequence if the policy is violated is stated; for example:

Unauthorized access, disclosure, duplication, modification, diversion, destruction, loss, misuse, or theft of MYC information by staff, willingly and deliberately, may result in the loss of computer and/or network resources up to and including termination and legal prosecution. Disciplinary measures are on a case by case basis.

An example of putting all the sections together in a single document can be found in Appendix G. This sample answers the questions of who is responsible, what is being protected, where is the information, when is protection required, and why is the protection needed. The "how" is explained in a guideline, standard, or work instruction.

5.2 Guideline

As we saw in Table 1, a guideline is an outline for a statement of conduct, a guide as to how some or something should perform, such as acceptable use of the Internet. Resources are something that can be used for support or help. Resources are used to access information. Developing a computing resource guideline would be beneficial to any enterprise. What exactly is a computing resource? For this guideline's use, a computing resource is

> Any device or entity that is used to store, transmit, or manipulate information.

That is quite broad, so your enterprise might want to narrow it down to electronic computing resources. This would remove areas such as file cabinets, desk drawers, and human conversation factors. Guidelines should be reviewed on an annual basis to ensure that they still fit into the enterprise's culture, technologies, and business requirements.

Based on the manual of style, we can build a document header based on the standard we set up in Figure 13; we will use the document number of GD00300.

Once again, the scope of the document needs to be defined; for example:

> This guideline applies to MYC staff and all MYC computing resources. Staff are required to be familiar with and comply with this guideline. Issue and questions about the guideline should be directed to the Information Security Manager (ISM).

Definitions of information and staff member are not required because they will be in the glossary. An additional definition of *computing resources* needs to be added to the glossary.

There is a new section in this guideline: references. This guideline is being developed and implemented to support the Information Assurance Policy. There needs to be a reference to the Information Assurance Policy. As the information security policy architecture references higher level documents, the architecture grows and only documents needed to support the information security policy architecture are being developed and implemented.

After the reference section is completed, the actual guidelines need to be documented; for example:

> MYC has a variety of computing resources that store, transmit, and manipulate information. Staff and computing resources introduce a level of risk to the information. Staff access to MYC computing resources is based on business need/justification and on limiting the risk to the information asset.

Table 6 Sample Responsibilities Table

Management	■ At any time and without prior notice, MYC management reserves the right to examine and authorize examinations of electronic mail messages, portable storage devices, files on desktops and laptops, web browser cache files, web browser bookmarks, and other information stored on or passing through MYC computing resources. Such management access assures compliance with internal policies, assists with internal investigations, and assists with the management of MYC information systems. ■ Ensures that staff are performing functions within their assigned rights and permissions.
Staff	■ Staff should ensure compliance with this guideline; ■ Staff are responsible for their own activities; ■ Staff are responsible for reporting violations to all policies and guidelines.
IT Operations	■ MYC logs e-mail, Web sites visited, files downloaded, time spent on the network and Internet/Intranet, and related information. IT Operations ensures that logging and monitoring are constantly enabled/ ■ Ensures supporting documentation for logging and monitoring devices exists and is implemented.

This statement answers who, what, and when. The implied where is from all computing resources. And the how is described in the computing resource areas of the guideline.

Next are the responsibilities, presented in a different style from the sample policy. For this guideline, the responsibilities could be as given in Table 6.

Depending on the enterprise, the areas of computing resources differ, and for this sample the following topics are included

■ Appropriate Behavior
■ Blocking Sites
■ Copyrights
■ Disclosing Internal Information
■ Establishing Network Connections
■ External Representations
■ False Security Reports
■ Inadvertent Disclosure
■ Information Exchange
■ Internet Information Reliability
■ Message Interception
■ No Default Protection

- Notification Process
- Personal Use
- Publicly Writable Directories
- Removal of Postings
- Security Parameters
- Spoofing Users
- Testing Controls
- User Anonymity
- User Authentication, inbound
- Virus Checking
- Web Page Changes

This guideline references the Information Assurance Policy and a noncompliance statement is not required because it would follow the related policy consequence. If the enterprise manual of style is to put a consequence in every guideline, then ensure the consequence wording is identical.

All the sections are put together in a single document and can be found in Appendix H.

5.3   Standard

A standard is a set of rules or procedures that are required. Some enterprises might call this level a standard practice or best practice. Using the term *best practice* in the enterprise implies a recommended set of rules and procedures for the topic. Depending upon the interpretation, *recommended* does not necessarily mean it must be completed. The standard or practice should be used how the enterprise would use these terms. Standards should be reviewed on an annual basis to ensure they still fit into the enterprise's technologies, culture, and business requirements, especially if there has been a change in the enterprise direction or there has been an acquisition or divestiture.

5.3.1   General Standard

There is a sample information assurance policy with a related guideline for computing resources. Moving to the level of a standard, electronic communications is a computing resource. For this standard, electronic communication means

> Any transfer of signals, writings, images, sounds, data, or intelligence that is created, sent, forwarded, replied to, transmitted, distributed, broadcast, stored, held, copied, downloaded, displayed, viewed, read, or printed by one or several computing resources.

This again is a broad definition, so your enterprise might want to restrict it to specific electronic computing resources.

Based on the manual of style we can build a document header based on the standard we set up in Figure 13. But we will use the document number of ST00150.

Once again, the scope of the document needs to be defined; for example:

> This standard is required for and by MYC staff and all MYC computing resources. Questions about the guideline should be directed to the Chief Security Officer (CSO) or Chief Counsel.

Additional definitions can be added to the glossary.

This standard is being written in support of the Information Assurance Policy as well as the Computing Resource Guideline. This continues to build more detailed concepts into the information security policy architecture. A consequence statement does not necessarily need to be written into the document.

A standard normally starts documenting specific technology and details about that technology. This document has been revised a few times, and a version history section has been added to the document. The fictitious MYC company wants to reenforce that there is no implied privacy in the use of its assets and that management has the right to review anything and has added a specific sections on "Persons Subject to Electronic Communications" and "Audit and Review."

The Electronic Communication standard is one of the key enterprise standards. In case there is an older communication system that cannot comply with this standard, there is a documented exception process. If your enterprise is going to have an exception process, ensure that it is documented and the proper approvals are to the level of acceptance within your organization. Exception processes will be documented better later in this text.

The actual standard can then be broken into the specific pieces within the enterprise environment. The following are sample areas to include in the communications standard:

- Network Storage
- Public FTP (ftp.MYC.com)
- E-mail Footer
- E-mail Retention and Storage
- Voice Mail Retention
- BlackBerry Message Retention and Synching
- Cell Phone Retention
- Pager Retention
- Fax Retention
- Fax Footer and Header

Should the enterprise want a standard confidential header or footer attached to e-mails, voice mails, faxes, or other documents, please consult with your Human Resource and Corporate Counsel before implementation.

All the sections are put together in a single document and can be found in Appendix I.

5.3.2 Technical Standard

This standard is for a specific implemented technology and uses a different format for documenting what is required. The production enterprise environment has many Solaris Unix servers and this standard documents required based configurations required by all Solaris servers, including test and development. This format is different from the manual of style displayed earlier, and it fits more into a technical administrator style. A few of the key differences are as follows:

■ Specification, intended use, and rationale instead of a scope and purpose
■ An overview, intended audience, and specific separation of function rather than the general responsibilities

Then the document gets into the specific details of the Solaris operating system for monitoring and specific configurations. The document also lists allowed and disallowed services on the server. And it states that the server will be removed from the network and shutdown until the server is compliance with the standard.

All the sections are put together in a single document and can be found in Appendix J.

5.4 Work Instruction

Work instructions (procedures and processes) are step by step instructions on how to complete a task or a set of tasks. Work instructions should be reviewed on an annual basis to ensure the technology is still applicable and to see if they can be optimized. Depending on the knowledge of the reader or action performer, a work instruction can be setup one of two ways (or a combination of the two ways). The first would be termed a user work instruction where screen shots are used to assist the reader in seeing the outcome of the action (see Table 7). The second would be termed a technical work instruction in which the author merely lists the steps needed to perform the actions.

5.4.1 User Work Instruction

Many times departments will use contracted staff to perform basic functions, and other times they have staff who need instructions with figures so they can validate

Table 7   Instructions with Screen Shots

Create a temporary directory C:\TEMP\SECUREMOTE.	
Install the client software for SecuRemote from the installation software location. You can download the software from http://www.checkpoint. com/techsupport/ freedownloads.html and selecting VPN-1 SecuRemote Release of Version 4.1 (build 4165) with the VPN+Strong version for the specific operating system. The downloaded file will be named something like sr_4165_????_strong.zip into the temporary directory of C:\TEMP\SECUREMOTE.	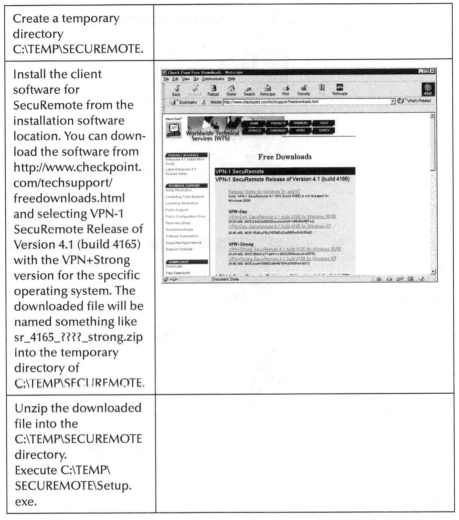
Unzip the downloaded file into the C:\TEMP\SECUREMOTE directory. Execute C:\TEMP\ SECUREMOTE\Setup. exe.	

(continued on next page)

they are working through the instructions properly. When an enterprise develops user work instructions, it will want to include screen shots of prompts or results of activities, along with the information required to perform the activity (see Table 7).

As with any document, a document needs the following sections:

■ Change history
■ Introduction
■ Purpose and scope
■ References

Table 7 (continued)   Instructions with Screen Shots

The setup welcome screen will appear. Click Next.	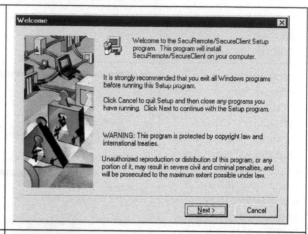
If you wish to change the default location of the install, select Browse and choose a different location. Click Next if you want to select the default installation directory or have selected another installation directory location. The installation process will take over, please wait.	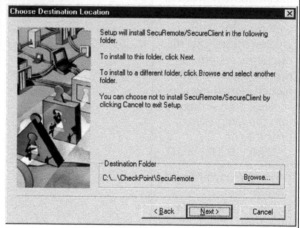

- Acronyms
- Roles and responsibilities

After the basic sections are completed, the document covers step by step instruction to perform the activity described in the purpose and scope of the document. The step by step instruction needs to include details such as:

- Server names
- Directory paths
- File names
- Web sites for reference
- Places to go for assistance or any anomalies

Any staff member or contractor selected to perform the activities should know exactly where to go for assistance, how to perform the activities, and some validation that the instruction is being performed properly. All the sections are put together in a single document and can be found in Appendix K.

5.4.2 IT Work Instruction

An IT work instruction can vary from the user work instruction by assuming the user knows the technology and has previously seen the screen shots to perform the activities. The IT work instruction still gives the detailed steps like the user work instruction, but it only lists the order of the steps to be performed. Another difference between the user work instruction and the IT work instruction is the IT work instruction is for a specific business unit performing regular duties; therefore, some of the preamble of the scope, roles, and responsibilities may not be needed. See Appendix L for a sample of an IT work instruction; the user must have knowledge of the system before being able to perform the tasks.

5.5 Memos

Sometimes the culture of the enterprise is not to use policies and guidelines; instead it uses memos or letters from the executive team to set the direction of how the enterprise should work. Formal policy and guidelines documents irritate the staff and communications are done more easily though a letter. Although there may not be a formal template, a standard letter or memo template can contain the company logo or letterhead with a subject line, date, recipients, and from whom the statement is sent. Very simple and straightforward. The sample displayed in Appendix M demonstrates the consequences to violations of standards, conducts, and policies. A memo can also be a reminder of tips to protect certain enterprise assets. See a sample reminder memo in Appendix N. The memo format can also be used for a tips sheet on a specific application, such as e-mail. The tip sheet should be no more than two pages that describes the use and guideline of the application. See Appendix O for a sample summary e-mail guide. Formal records of these memos should be kept and reviewed on an annual basis, in case the enterprise's position changes or the name in the sender position of the memo changes.

5.6 Forms

Forms are a fact of life in every enterprise in every industry. Forms are used for requesting information to setup access, terminate access, review settings, perform assessments, and myriad other items. Forms, just like every other document, should have a standard format for staff to follow. Forms can be in hard copy or electronic. One thing to remember with an electronic copy of a form is how the recipient is to validate the authenticity of the requestor. Is an e-mail electronic signature validation enough? This question will need to be answered by the enterprise before the implementation of any forms. Using the manual of style for the font, pitch, header, and footer, the base form outline can be defined. Depending on the form owner and the topic, the actual content structure will vary. As with all other documents in the information security policy architecture, versioning and an annual review should be completed on the forms. See Appendix P for a sample form document.

5.7 Cautions

The tables, figures, and appendices referenced for samples are just samples. As was stated previously, the information security policy architecture wording or declarations need to be acceptable to the enterprise's culture and business requirements. Specific wording or disclaimers need to be reviewed by the enterprise's Human Resource and Corporate Counsel departments to ensure compliance with the other standards within the enterprise.

Chapter 6

Additional Key Policy Topics

Until now, the focus of this book has been on information security topics. If the security team goes beyond information security, then topics such as physical security, personnel security, privacy, and third-party security must also be included within the security policy architecture. If the security team does not go beyond information, the security team may want to participate with the groups who are developing these topics within the security policy architecture. Using the manual of style content, these topics can be developed in the same way. The topics in this chapter are developed using guides to think about for the enterprise location(s).

The topics within this chapter need to be developed and reviewed by staff within Legal, Facilities, and Human Resources departments because these discussions are based on generalizations and the requirements within specific industries and locations will vary.

6.1 Miscellaneous Items

As with all enterprises, definitions and acronyms mean different things to different people. For example, in the security triad CIA means confidentiality, integrity, and availability, yet those in the government sector regard CIA as the Central Intelligence Agency. Within an enterprise sometimes the enterprise technology department is referred to as IT, Information Technology, or IS, Information Systems, and IS can also refer to Information Security. A glossary and acronym reference ensures there is no misinterpretation within the security policy architecture. The glossary and acronym references need to include everything within the enterprise, so there is a common ground for any documentation written.

6.2 Physical Security

The physical security topics can range from building or office security to background checks to guiding users on business travel. This group of topics is just as important as the information security topics. All business units must work together to ensure that the staff are protected physically because they are considered enterprise assets also. Some of the questions that should be answered with physical security policy topics are as follows:

1. Is the exterior of the building reviewed on a regular basis for protection deficiencies, such as cracked windows or unlocked doors?
2. Is there a process to identify vendors, contractors, and visitors before they enter the business area?
3. Is the lighting adequate to illuminate critical interior and exterior areas?
4. Are the entranceways blocked enough to block intruders and efficient enough for staff?
5. Are badges and keys audited on a regular basis? Who is permitted to receive a badge or key?
6. Are combination locks changed on a regular basis?
7. Are cameras angled and monitored to effectively and efficiently protect all enterprise assets from compromise?
8. Are enterprise assets inventoried on a regular basis?
9. Are the building, server room/data center, and key office areas marked for locations, so a visitor can get around without an escort?

At a minimum, physical and environmental security controls for the enterprise should address the following:

■ Barriers and procedures establishing controlled areas around the building
■ Access controls which prevent unauthorized entry into those controlled and sensitive areas
■ Access controls to prevent access to hard-copied files and media libraries
■ Controls to lessen natural disaster impacts
■ Controls to prevent or minimize the environmental impact

Before modifications are done to improve or reduce physical safeguards, a risk assessment should be performed on the probably of compromise and as with information security-layered physical protection should be a mandatory requirement.

Every enterprise location has at least one entryway, and the building/office is the shell that protects the staff and assets of the enterprise. No matter what the location in the world, the building needs some basic protection, at a minimum locks and lighting (power and environmental controls). The location will determine how much protection is required. It is very important to protect the building perimeter to detect and defend against unwanted intruders. If you can determine the threat before it enters the building, the enterprise has a better chance to avoid the risk. Many times, the building security can include the following topics:

■ Guards
■ Bordering
■ Environment
■ Locks, keys, badges
■ Cameras

All of these physical security features are methods of access control. The more sensitive the enterprise asset, the more selective the access control mechanism should be. One thing to remember is that no staff member should ever be granted access to or knowledge of a sensitive asset or asset area based only on rank or position within the enterprise. This is a restatement of the need-to-know principle.

Security guards are one of the oldest forms of physical security. Security guards are human and can make decisions that automated systems cannot. Security guards are normally placed where there is an unlocked entryway. Security guards can see and pick out people or objects that are out of place better than any automated systems. By contrast, security guards, being human, have drawbacks that should be addressed with security policy topics.

■ *Reliability.* Just as with staff and contractors, guards need to have pre-employment screening. Pre-employment screening is not foolproof, and security guards can have issues outside work that might reduce their productivity and produce a security risk. See the personnel security section for some pre-employment screening requirements.
■ *Availability.* Whether the security guards are in-house staff or outsourced, they cannot be everywhere at all times and need to be supplemented by other forms of automated security.
■ *Training.* Although security guards are trained in physical protection for building compromises, security guards also need to receive information security training, especially in social engineering.* If a security guard can

---

* Social engineering attacks are based on deceiving people. Social engineering attacks can be performed by telephoning users or operators or by pretending to be an authorized staff member attempting to gain access to an enterprise asset.

be tricked and bypassed, the enterprise risk may be higher than a network compromise.

■ *Rotation.* After a while, security guards may become complacent because they have gotten to know the staff. Rotating security guards will ensure some of that complacency will not happen. If the security guards are outsourced, then rotation may be a contract requirement. These security guards will be sterner about following the security policies and will not become involved with office politics.

Bordering can be many things, for example, fencing, gates, mantraps, or turnstiles. Depending on the location, bordering can assist with crowd control and deter the casual trespasser by controlling entrance access. By contrast, bordering is not necessarily eye-appealing and can be cost prohibitive. Bordering requirements should be developed and implemented by facilities and a building designer. The security policy topic should include not bypassing or avoiding the bordering when entering the enterprise location.

Implementing environmental controls will protect the environment from environmental hazards. These controls may include but are not limited to temperature, humidity, power, and lighting controls; smoke detectors; and fire suppression systems. Of these, lighting is the most important external building element for seeing the traffic and people who are approaching the property and building. Although bright lights after dark will discourage the casual intruder, the enterprise must balance the power expense. As enterprise networks expand, the requirements to maintain a data center or server room increase. Cabinets, network equipment, and servers all require power and cooling requirements. UPS (uninterrupted power source) systems need to be included in the data center or server room requirements in case the building should have a power issue. Lighting and power requirements should be developed and implemented by facilities and a building designer. Power requirements should be developed jointly with information technology (for the amount of equipment in the server room or data center), facilities, and a power contractor. Although temperature and humidity controls, smoke detectors, and fire suppression systems are key for the building, they are even more important for a data center or server room. The networking and server equipment need the environmental controls to ensure they are running in the proper environment. The security policy topic should include environmental controls for the building, which should not be tampered with, and it should include regular checks and testing of the data center or server room environmental controls.

Locks, keys, and badges are only effective when they are used and a security topic sets the standard for no piggybacking into a building. Within a building, areas such as Human Resources, the server room/data center, and executive offices may require additional access restrictions. There are two standard types of security mechanisms for entranceways:

- Preset locks. This is the typical door lock, which requires some sort of hard key.
- Programmable locks. This can be mechanical or electronic. The cipher lock with a combination is considered mechanical. A badging or biometrical system is programmable for passing an item over a reader.

Many buildings today have closed circuit television (CCTV) or cameras placed on the building interior and exterior. CCTV systems enhance the coverage that a security guard can monitor. The greatest benefit of CCTV is the integration with other alarm systems. Multiple cameras throughout the building can be used to track on intruder or to follow the trail of a missing asset.

6.3 Personnel Security

Personnel encompass the largest amount of enterprise assets. Enterprises must protect personnel while at work and while on business travel.

6.3.1 Badging

The easiest way to identify a valid staff member versus a contractor/consultant or a visitor is colored badges. The security policy architecture must contain statements about the badging process:

- The where, when, and how badges are to be acquired, worn, displayed, and disposed of;
- The request process for adding or removing additional access;
- Badge replacement or carrying more than one badge;
- What type of person is required to have a badge: staff, visitor, onsite contractor or consultant, or vendor;
- What type of person is required to sign in at the front desk and what are the escort procedures;
- What areas within the building are public versus secured for badge access;
- Does the person have to badge in and badge out;
- What color badge should each badged person wear, such as green background for staff members, blue background for authorized contractors and consultants, yellow background for vendors, and possibly red for visitors.

6.3.2 Staff

Simple checks can assist with some of the basic enterprise personnel risks. In today's environment, employers must ensure the following for candidates, contractors, and consultants:

■ Ensure a signed disclosure from candidates authorizing the potential employer to obtain relevant background (and, potentially, financial) information. The documents need to be developed to ensure enough latitude with the investigation.
■ Use reputable firms that are experts in reviewing potential candidates. This is especially important when candidates, contractors, and consultants can be placed or are coming from locations around the globe.
■ Besides reference checks, additional information should be provided. The last seven years of residence and ten years of employment can be a strong base. With that information, state driving records, county civil and criminal records, state criminal records, and federal civil and criminal records can be more readily reviewed for history. At least a drug screening should be performed, along with a possible physical. Past issues of DUI or bankruptcy filing can point to future problems within the enterprise.

Escalating costs of employee discharge (including legal fees and replacement costs) and concerns about workplace security and sabotage have spurred enterprises to implement background checks on regular staff, as well as contractors and consultants.

One major enterprise risk that background checks may not determine is workplace violence. Much workplace violence can be prevented if management and staff watch for major changes in behavior that can include a combination of some of the following traits:

■ Unreasonable. No matter how hard someone tries, the staff member is never happy or the staff member starts making personal attacks against others.
■ Controlling. A staff member considers himself superior to all others and constantly forces his opinions on others. Or he has the opposite controlling effect by being paranoid and do not letting others enter into the area.
■ Irresponsible. A good worker all of a sudden turn irresponsible about her actions and behaviors.
■ Angry. A staff member blows situations out of proportion or has hate and anger issues on and off the job.
■ Odd. A staff member excels at job performance and details, but possibly lacks people skills. His presence makes other feel ill at ease.
■ Unhealthy. A staff member might start having sleep disorders, fatigue, sudden weight loss or weight gain, or other health related problems. Addictions, such as alcohol or gambling, can fall into this category.

Businesses may require staff to travel outside their area. Security policy topics should be in place to guide staff travel behavior and to protect staff while on business travel. This is primarily for the protection of enterprise assets, rather than for acts of terrorism. Topics that should be documented within the security policy architecture are as follows:

- The travel department should be on global alert lists for areas that present a travel risk.
- Executives should not travel using the same method at the same time as other executives, in case there is an accident.
- There should be crisis plans for emergency access to travel arrangements and rearrangements.
- Safe travel tips for modes of transportation, luggage, hotels, identity information and meeting others should be emphasized.
- Tips for system and accessory power requirements should be advised.
- Tips for import/export requirements for enterprise assets or encryptions should be offered.
- Health precautions are needed for particular situations such as food, water, and disease.

A potential risk for every organization is nonstaff who do not have company badges and are free to roam the building and access the network unrestricted. This category includes unescorted visitors.

6.3.3 Authorized Non-Employees

Enterprises will always have contractors or consultants in place for staff augmentation or special project support and regular vendors who access equipment for maintenance. Security policy architecture statements need to be in place for contract support, see the Third Parties section below. Security policy architecture statements need to be in place for the following topics:

- Building access including days of the week and time schedules
- Direct connect network access and required permissions
- Remote network access and required permissions
- Who is responsible for the activities of the contractor or consultants
- Acknowledgment of the security policy architecture, just as if an employee

6.3.4 Visitors

Enterprises have visitors who arrive on a daily basis for business and nonbusiness purposes. As with the authorized nonemployees, visitors must have rules or guidelines to be followed while accessing enterprise assets, such as:

- The location of public areas within the building
- Staying with their escort
- What they can and cannot access
- Wearing a visitor badge
- Acknowledging basic enterprise security rules, including the right to search the visitor's bags and containers being brought onsite and taken offsite

Visitors should be required to sign a log book (hard copy or electronic). This log book can help if there is a breach or an incident and all people must be accounted for. Basic visitor log entries should contain the following legible information:

- Name of visitor
- Visitor business affiliation
- Person being visited
- Reason for visit
- Citizenship
- Date and time of entry
- Date and time of exit
- Signature of the escort
- The type of equipment the visitor is bringing onsite
- Acknowledgment of basic security, confidentiality, and privacy statements

As with every other company record, the visitor log also must be included in the records retention statements. If the visitor log can be maintained in electronic form, reporting and trending can be performed for research and access.

6.4   Privacy

Another special topic that needs to be covered within a security policy architecture is privacy of data, customer, and staff. If the enterprise collects any data, then the topic of privacy needs to be included in the security policy architecture. If the enterprise collects data on an external Web page, then a privacy notice should be posted on the external Web page. Some of the questions that need to be answered for the topic of privacy within the policy architecture are as follows:

- Who will be entering (or giving up) information?
- Who is doing the information collection?
- Who will receive the information after (and during) collection?
- What regulations does the enterprise have to be compliant with for privacy?
- What will be done if there is a compromise?

- What information is being collected, stored, destroyed, and manipulated?
- What is going to be done with the information?
- What privacy requirements are included in contracts?
- When is the information going to be released and destroyed?
- Where is the information going to be stored and processed?
- Why is the information being collected?
- How does the enterprise define *vendor, third party,* or *affiliate*?
- How is a breach notification done?
- How does the enterprise ensure privacy is considered in all business initiatives?

The privacy topic within the security policy architecture must answer who, what, where, when, why, and how, and this should be included within every level of the security policy architecture.

6.5 Third Parties

Enterprise environments, at times, need staffing for projects, need to contract specialists, and need to augment their existing staff or are dependent on external resources. Although employees may present a risk to the enterprise, there is the potential of higher risk when third parties access an enterprise asset. Third parties can include vendors, visitors, contractors, consultants, and partners, that is, any party who is not a direct hire to the enterprise. The enterprise scope of third parties can include, but is not limited to, the following:

- Perform functions on behalf of the enterprise.
- Provide and maintain customer access to the products and services.
- Provide support to internal staff.
- Third-party risks can affect the following business processes.
- Strategy. Advisement on business directions or implementation of decisions and technology that can affect the future direction of the enterprise.
- Compliance. With the number of increasing regulations, activities performed or not performed by a third party could place the enterprise in a non-compliant state.
- Reputation. Dissatisfied customers when using third-party support can affect how potential customers view the enterprise.
- Financial. Third parties that do not deliver the appropriate customer service or product can affect the return on sales. Or something happening to the third party as a result of contractual obligations may affect the enterprise finances through litigation or insurance.

- Unauthorized access. Third parties may be granted excessive access to enterprise resources because of the scope of activities that are being performed and the enterprise has no way of monitoring the activities.
- Loss of information control. When a third party leaves the enterprise, how can the enterprise guarantee intellectual property, proprietary, or confidential information has not left the enterprise?
- Increased information technology risks. With enterprises not wanting to pay travel costs, many enterprises are granting remote access to their corporate networks globally. External connections to the enterprise network are opened and sometimes not isolated.

When engaging a third party with services or products, a risk assessment should be completed before the contract is signed.

Controls for authentication, authorization, and access should be defined before an enterprise enters into a third-party contract. The following are samples of controls useful when engaging third parties:

- Third parties should agree to any acceptable use, security, and standards documents that apply to enterprise access and information prior to access being granted or when entering into a contract.
- Third-party contracts should include enterprise security policy architecture violations that can lead to removal of system privileges up to and including termination of third-party contract.
- It should be ensured that the enterprise has security standards as high as, if not higher than, the third party. Security is only as strong as the weakest enterprise link. The enterprise needs to agree on base security levels before permitting access to enterprise assets.
- Third-party access should be reviewed and audited on a regular basis to ensure permissions are still valid and the contract is still within the valid operational period.

Within the security policy architecture, the topics that need to be considered for third party access are as follows. (possibly a checklist of controls):

- In what role is the third party participating for the enterprise?
- What are the authorization procedures for granting access to enterprise assets and who must provide that authorization?
- What is the business need for the access to be granted and can the access be restricted or limited?
- What is the defined period of time for the third-party access?
- What monitoring procedures are in place based on the legal and regulatory requirements?

- What is the procedure for disabling third-party access? How can it be verified?
- Does the enterprise have to provide equipment for the third party or what end point security procedures are in place when third parties use their own equipment to connect to the enterprise network?

Appendix Q displays an enterprise third-party service provider standard. Please ensure you consult with Counsel before implementation of this standard.

6.6 Application Requirements

Whether an enterprise internally develops an application for sale or internal use or purchases a third-party piece of software, there should be documented application security requirements or guidelines when performing a review. Ensuring applications are compliant with the security policy architecture can assist in limiting risk to enterprise assets, as well as limiting the customizations and exceptions that will be needed when the application is implemented. The document or documents that support the security application requirements should include a matrix that states

- What the requirements are?
- Whether the requirement is required, a practice, or not applicable?
- If the application complies?
- If the application does not or cannot comply, what the compensating control is?

As with any application the requirements need to include the areas of passwords, administration, logging, authentication, and networking requirements. Table 8 and Table 9 display some of the basic requirements that all applications should have, as they apply to the enterprise security policy architecture.

Table 8   Sample Application Requirements Matrix (1)

Requirement	Configurable?	Compliant?	Comments/ Compensating Control(s)
General Processing			
Host administrative access is not required to maintain the application or supporting files			
Separation of administrative, monitoring, and user duties			
The application uses integrated authentication with MYC's native LDAP or directory structures for authorization and authentication. If not compliant, the application is configurable to require regular password changes and account administration to match the enterprise password standard			
Authentication is exchanged in a secure method; for example, user IDs and passwords are not passed in clear text. Two-factor authentication will be used where possible and especially for remote access			
The operating system should participate in time synchronization using the enterprise NTP server for transactional processing			

Table 8 (continued)   Sample Application Requirements Matrix (1)

Requirement	Configurable?	Compliant?	Comments/ Compensating Control(s)
No sensitive files, data, or transactions are transmitted in the clear outside the internal network; for example, customer contact file information copied from an external source needs to be encrypted during transport to a file server within the DMZ or internal environment			
The user/system is required to change the password at various intervals as specified by the Network Security Policy; for example, if the Network Security Policy states that passwords must be changed every 90 days, can the application accommodate the policy?			
The application operates with two-factor authentication including SecurID or PKI			
Are there varying levels of user access (e.g., read, read–write, grant access)?			
Database configuration complies with the enterprise database standards			
Accounts can be disabled, locked out, or end dated			

Table 8 (continued)   Sample Application Requirements Matrix (1)

Requirement	Configurable?	Compliant?	Comments/ Compensating Control(s)
Anonymous access can be disabled without losing application functionality			
Layered security exists within the application and data file access			
All application ports and protocols are documented for Internet access and compliant with enterprise standard port access			
System physically separates application and database layers			
Security features comply with applicable federal, state, and international privacy and security regulations for data integrity, confidentiality, auditing, and availability			
System supports secure transmission of data to external parties or sites, if enterprise requires data transfer			
Secure inter-host communication exists; for example, data entry from an external source to a host within the DMZ is done through an encrypted session, then the host within the DMZ needs to encrypt the data to the internal server for storage			

Table 8 (continued)   Sample Application Requirements Matrix (1)

Requirement	Configurable?	Compliant?	Comments/ Compensating Control(s)
Account ID Information			
Application user accounts can easily be disabled without stopping the functionality of the application; for example, if a single application user account becomes disabled or locked out, all other application users can continue to use the application without interruption			
Assesses password strength, assesses password formatting to match the Security Policy format, and reports invalid password formats and matches the requirements of the enterprise password standard			
Application user ids do not require extra system privileges; for example on Windows NT, the application users do not require a user right to log on locally to the host			
Restrict application user accounts to specific application functionality			
Identify application accounts which do not have a password			

Table 8 (continued) Sample Application Requirements Matrix (1)

Requirement	Configurable?	Compliant?	Comments/ Compensating Control(s)
Identify application accounts which have been expired, inactive, or not logged into			
Application accounts locked out or disabled, and login times can be identified through reporting			
Application can report on specific or all groups used within the application			
Perform the above functions with wild cards and wild card searches			
Access Control			
Application user access is limited to the application, database, data set, data element level, and application function; for example, a user who enters client location information cannot view client financial information			
The application runs as a non-root or non-administrative user with limited system access			
Specify specific accounts, groups, or combination with read, change, full control, and write access to the application			

Table 8 (continued)   Sample Application Requirements Matrix (1)

Requirement	Configurable?	Compliant?	Comments/ Compensating Control(s)
System Monitoring			
All logging must be centralized			
Successful and failed login attempts are logged			
Failed function attempts are logged			
Account record maintenance on all—including add/remove groups, revokes/resets, account information			
Successful and failed attempts on application and data file configuration changes can be logged			
Log files can be exported to readable format and into other applications for review; for example, the log file can be exported into tab delimited format and imported into an SQL database			
Log files can be viewed real-time			
Log files can be automatically archived			
Each of the above records requires at least the following information displayed with it: date, time, type, success/failure, account performing action, target of action, change to/from			

Table 8 (continued)   Sample Application Requirements Matrix (1)

Requirement	Configurable?	Compliant?	Comments/ Compensating Control(s)
Perform searching on the above items using a wild card			
Reporting			
Reports can be archived			
Reports can be customized for key information			
Data collected for the reports can be archived			
A routine to remove archived data after a specified amount of time exists			
The tool can perform active monitoring, not merely scheduled data collection			
The reports can be scheduled to execute at specified times			
Administrative ID Access			
Administrative account access complies with enterprise password and password change requirements			
Segregation of duties for administrative access between reset passwords without being able to create new application accounts			
Built-in administrative ID can be renamed to something other than the default			

Table 8 (continued)   Sample Application Requirements Matrix (1)

Requirement	Configurable?	Compliant?	Comments/ Compensating Control(s)
System allows for patching and updating of platform technologies immediately upon patch issuance (e.g., MS Security Updates)			
System automatically logs users off after a specified period of inactivity			
System provides the capability to place security controls on each system module and on confidential and critical levels within each module			
Administrative access to the application does not require administrative access to the system file server or domain and does not require any special privileges			
Access Control			
Application administrative access is restricted by selected IDs or IP addresses?			
Vendor does not require remote access to the application or the application database for maintenance or issues			
If the vendor requires access, limitations are placed on the vendor access and how the vendor gains access			

Table 8 (continued)   Sample Application Requirements Matrix (1)

Requirement	Configurable?	Compliant?	Comments/ Compensating Control(s)
Logging/Auditing			
Logging is enabled by default within the application. If the logging is configurable, then what type of events can be logged?			
No independent application logs exists and can be integrated into the enterprise logging standard			
Log files can be locked down for read-only access for monitoring and auditing			
Application must log failed login attempts to the application			
Application must log the administrative access to the application log and changes to the application system and data			
Vendor Access			
When help is requested from the vendor, does the vendor need access to the application? If so, what level of application and operating system access?			
There is a process for testing security and performance of interfaces			
Vendor notifies customers of application vulnerabilities			

Table 8 (continued)   Sample Application Requirements Matrix (1)

Requirement	Configurable?	Compliant?	Comments/ Compensating Control(s)
When administering systems, personnel from vendor will follow MYC privacy and security policies			
When administering systems, vendor actively monitors system and will notify MYC promptly of potential security incidents			
When administering systems, vendor maintains access, maintenance, and security audit logs for a reasonable time and will make those available to MYC upon request			

Table 9   Sample Application Requirements Matrix (2)

Requirement	Configurable?	Compliant?	Comments/ Compensating Control(s)
Basic Application Requirements			
Information security and privacy and protection of data are of pivotal importance in any business. This security checklist provides guidance on configuring application in a security manner.			
Only install required platform applications and no additional third-party applications. Additional third-party applications may render the Tekelec product inoperable.			
Upon successful application, install lock and expire most default application accounts, including the guest account.			
Disable any services that are not used by the application.			
Rename the default administrator account or make it inaccessible.			
Disable all debugging features.			
Edit error messages to provide a meaningful message, but do not disclose any information for a possible compromise.			

Table 9 (continued)   Sample Application Requirements Matrix (2)

Requirement	Configurable?	Compliant?	Comments/ Compensating Control(s)
Application			
Tekelec products use application-level, techniques for authorization.			
Application has only one entry and exit point.			
Application run time has excluded any software libraries, routines, or other resources that are not explicitly called by the application.			
Application executes under the absolute minimum privileges assigned to access the data or call the processes it needs.			
Application consists of multiple small, simple, single-function modules instead of one large, complex module that performs multiple functions.			
Each application module is self-contained, so any module can be disabled when not needed or if found to be vulnerable or in error without affecting the operation of any other modules.			

Table 9 (continued)   Sample Application Requirements Matrix (2)

Requirement	Configurable?	Compliant?	Comments/ Compensating Control(s)
Application is designed to prevent users from bypassing any user interface software to directly access application data or process or the operating system.			
Application does not include command-line or shell escape codes.			
Application does not include escape codes that invoke system level or device level functions.			
Application clears own cache frequently.			
Aliases, pointers, links, caches, and other objects are named consistently throughout the application.			
Application does not trust operating system environment variables but passes every argument in an application environment variable.			
Application does not contain any hard-coded credentials.			
Application requires the user to type in the password every time an attempt is made to initiate a new processing session.			

Table 9 (continued)   Sample Application Requirements Matrix (2)

Requirement	Configurable?	Compliant?	Comments/ Compensating Control(s)
Application requires the user to explicitly log out of the application to terminate the session.			
Application has a configurable session time out for inactivity; the default is 15 minutes of inactivity.			
When a session is terminated due to inactivity, the session time out information is logged within an application log.			
Application explicitly defines URLs and path names within the application code.			
Application does not accept relative path names or URLs input by the user.			
Before application shutdown, the application deletes/erases all temporary files, caches, data, and other objects it created during its execution.			
Application does not process the transaction until all input has been received and validated.			
Application explicitly initializes all variables when they are declared.			

Table 9 (continued)   Sample Application Requirements Matrix (2)

Requirement	Configurable?	Compliant?	Comments/ Compensating Control(s)
Authentication			
Anonymous account access is disabled.			
Identity information is passed by signing/encrypting from one part of the application to another.			
Application ensures users are authenticated before granting access to resources and role-based activities.			
Application prevents the backend system from authenticating users or interference in any way with the authentication process.			
Authorization is performed in the UI tier such that controls are hidden/shown based on application account authorization.			
Authorization is performed in the UI tier such that flow of UI is changed based on type of account.			
Authorization is performed in the UI tier such that authorization check is carried out each time a new page is loaded.			
Authenticate clients properly; authenticate logins only over secure connections.			

Table 9 (continued)   Sample Application Requirements Matrix (2)

Requirement	Configurable?	Compliant?	Comments/ Compensating Control(s)
Account lock out for invalid password attempts during a certain period of time is configurable. The default is to lock the account after three invalid password attempts within 15 minutes.			
Password Management			
The most trivial method by which an application can be compromised is a default account which still has a default password associated with it even after installation. This includes changing the default password of administrative and regular users.			
Apply basic strong password management rules (such as password length, history, and complexity) to all account passwords. All accounts must be required to change their passwords periodically.			
Password expiration is configurable. The default is to force a password change at a maximum of every 90 days.			
Password history is configurable. The default password history is 5.			
Default passwords are configurable to be changed immediately by the account owner.			

Table 9 (continued) Sample Application Requirements Matrix (2)

Requirement	Configurable?	Compliant?	Comments/ Compensating Control(s)
Passwords should be transmitted in a secure manner.			
Passwords should be stored in a secure manner, such as a one-way hash.			
The administrator is the only account that can change other account passwords.			
Application does not authenticate an account with an expired password until the account password has been changed.			
Practice Principle of Least Privilege			
Grant necessary privileges only. Do not provide accounts more privileges than are necessary. In other words, principle of least privilege is that an account be given only those privileges that are actually required to efficiently and succinctly perform his or her job.			
Restrict permissions on run-time facilities. Do not assign "all permissions" to any object or module.			
There exists a clearly defined matrix defining access permissions on resources by different user roles and processes.			

Table 9 (continued)   Sample Application Requirements Matrix (2)

Requirement	Configurable?	Compliant?	Comments/ Compensating Control(s)
Access to sensitive and system resources is restricted to documented and selected roles only.			
Tekelec products use ACLs (in addition to other) techniques for authorization.			
Accounts, excluding the application administrator, are forbidden to change their own privileges, roles, and access.			
Application prevents any account from performing any function the account is not authorized to perform.			
Restrict Operating System and Network Access			
Do not permit the application to abort into the host operating system.			
Limit the number of operating system users.			
Limit the privileges of the operating system accounts/ (administrative, root-privileged) host (physical machine) to the least privileges needed for the account's tasks.			
Use a firewall within the operating environment, keeping the Tekelec product behind a production firewall.			

Table 9 (continued)   Sample Application Requirements Matrix (2)

Requirement	Configurable?	Compliant?	Comments/ Compensating Control(s)
Application does not use nonstandard ports for operability.			
Encrypt traffic to and from the application.			
Application administration does not change operating system configurations.			
Application can verify operating system configurations and detect failure conditions in the underlying operating environment.			
Session Management			
Authentication cookies are protected in transit by using SSL.			
The contents of authentication cookies are encrypted.			
A session timeout has been factored into the design of the application and the time out is configurable.			
Session IDs generated for tracking sessions should not be guessable numbers (e.g. . First user who visits the site gets session no. 1, the second user gets 2, and so on).			

Table 9 (continued) Sample Application Requirements Matrix (2)

Requirement	Configurable?	Compliant?	Comments/ Compensating Control(s)
Design supports an elaborate mitigation for session hijacking attacks.			
The system does not rely on persistent cookies.			
Guards are present for confidentiality and integrity of cookies.			
Auditing and Logging			
Ensure the log entry information contains the following: date, times, initiating process, process owner (account), and description.			
The audit facility used by the application allows the administrator to select the events to be logged and the information to be captured about each event.			
The audit facility used by the application allows the administrator to view the application's audit records and to report against them.			
The administrator is notified of all security related events.			
The design has a standardized approach to exception handling across the application.			

Table 9 (continued)   Sample Application Requirements Matrix (2)

Requirement	Configurable?	Compliant?	Comments/ Compensating Control(s)
In the case of an exception, minimum amount of information is returned to the user. Lowest level exceptions are encapsulated into a relevant exception for the benefit of the above tiers of the application.			
When account actions are being logged, private data is not written to the log. (e.g., changed passwords, critical settings).			
The key parameters to be logged and audited have been identified.			
Log all administrator activity.			
Log the deletion of any data.			
Log all authentication and authorization events—logging in, logging out, failed logins.			
Log any modifications to data characteristics: permissions, location, field type.			
Application has levels of auditing and logging.			
Application logs have been protected from tampering.			
Application logs have been protected from unauthorized access.			
Utilities have been factored in for interpretation of log files.			

Table 9 (continued)   Sample Application Requirements Matrix (2)

Requirement	Configurable?	Compliant?	Comments/ Compensating Control(s)
Log files should be centralized and secured.			
Log files should be archivable.			
Data Handling—General			
All data along with its criticality has been identified.			
A matrix indicating the data and the means to secure it is available in the design document.			
All data required to be kept confidential is encrypted.			
Database connection information such as account name and password are not stored in plaintext on disk.			
No sensitive data is stored in persisted cookies.			
Sensitive data is not transmitted using GET as It can be directly seen in the browser address bar.			
Sensitive information is not being sent in the HTTP headers as these can be easily changed.			
Data input is validated by type, length, format, and range.			
Data input is sanitized.			

Table 9 (continued)   Sample Application Requirements Matrix (2)

Requirement	Configurable?	Compliant?	Comments/ Compensating Control(s)
All data input through the UI is pre-pended and appended with a quote.			
Database and file updates are implemented as discrete transactions.			
Application bounds checks all arrays and buffers every time the arrays and buffers are accessed.			
Data updates are date and times stamped within the database or file storage.			
When viewing data, the displayed data includes the date and time stamp of last modification.			
Data Handling—Encryption			
No custom-built algorithms are being used to encrypt data.			
If standard algorithms are being used, then the library used to implement them is tested sufficiently. There is a documented rationale for chosen algorithm key sizes.			
The encryption key is stored in a secure manner.			
There is a provision in the application for changing the keys used for encryption.			

Table 9 (continued)   Sample Application Requirements Matrix (2)

Requirement	Configurable?	Compliant?	Comments/ Compensating Control(s)
There is a provision in the application for rolling over data (i.e., data encrypted with "old" key is to be re-encrypted using "new" key).			
There is a provision in the application for handling scenarios such as "lost key," "lost password to key," and "key compromise."			
The crypto algorithm being used will be easily replaceable. Hard coding is not being done. It is easy to upgrade the algorithms in the future.			
Encryption provides replay protection. This is protection against techniques that can be used to prevent a previous message from being replayed to recreate the desired operation. This is done with a combination of message digesting and timestamps.			
Data Handling—Error Handling			
Documentation exists to state which errors should trigger a user response.			
Log unhandled errors to the centralized event log to include date, time, user ID, error code, and if possible, the code line.			

Table 9 (continued) Sample Application Requirements Matrix (2)

Requirement	Configurable?	Compliant?	Comments/ Compensating Control(s)
Ensure the application does not abort to the command line or operating system.			
Temporary Files			
If possible, avoid temporary files altogether.			
If temporary files are used, then ensure temporary file name uniqueness. The filename of the temporary file must be unique. This ensures that the application does not end up clobbering any existing data on the disk. If a file having the same name already exists on the disk, the logic of file name generation should generate (see next point) a new file name and use that instead.			
If temporary files are used, then ensure file name randomness. When generating the file name of the temporary file ensure that the name is not guessable. Typically, the default APIs that are supplied by the operating system for generating temporary files create filenames containing monotonically increasing integers. Therefore, it becomes possible to predict the filename of the next temporary file that the application will generate.			

Table 9 (continued)   Sample Application Requirements Matrix (2)

Requirement	Configurable?	Compliant?	Comments/ Compensating Control(s)
If temporary files are used, then ensure proper permissions for the temporary file. Ensure that the temporary files have the appropriate ACLs (access control lists) set on them. Avoid publicly writable temporary directories if possible. If using a publicly writable directory, make a directory within the publicly writable directory for temporary files, with read and write permissions for the application only. Temporary files are often used to hold intermittent state information about the operation in progress and may contain confidential information.			
If temporary files are used, then ensure secure cleanup of temporary files after usage. One of the most common attacks on applications that use temporary files is the recovery of previously deleted temporary files from the disk. This is trivially possible with the help of software available on the Internet. In order to mitigate against this operation, shred temporary files. Depending on the sensitivity of the information contained in the temporary file, ensure that the cleanup is commensurate with the security levels desired.			

Table 9 (continued)   Sample Application Requirements Matrix (2)

Requirement	Configurable?	Compliant?	Comments/ Compensating Control(s)
If temporary files are used, then prevent covert access. Sometimes the application's temporary files containing sensitive information may be indexed by the underlying operating system service that may be active on the user system.			
If temporary files are used, then avoid storing very sensitive information in temporary files. As a rule, avoid storing sensitive information in temporary files.			
If temporary files are used, then rely on absolute file paths and file handles. When building the file paths of the temporary files, use absolute paths. Do not use relative file paths.			

Chapter 7

Putting It Together

The manual of style has been created, the list of initial topics has been put together, and the initial documents have been drafted. Now comes the hard part: the approval process and the actual implementation of the initial information security policy architecture.

We know from previous chapters that the cornerstone of an effective information security policy architecture is the well-written policy statement. This is the source from which all other policy architecture documents are written. That initial information security policy is the executive team's directives to create an information security program, establish its goals and measures, and target and assign responsibilities. The current task is to take these documents, decisions, common practices, or folklore and fashion them into an approved published information security policy architecture that is used as the basis for protecting information resources and guiding employee behavior.

7.1 Topics to Start With

Many times, the hardest thing is to figure out the first set of topics or priorities for the security policy architecture and the second hardest thing is to get through the reviews and approvals. Before an enterprise can determine the top security policy architecture priority, the enterprise needs to have a statement from the top endorsing the need for security or assurance of enterprise assets. If a risk assessment has been performed, then you can start with the high risk areas. That choice will depend on the organizational structure and the amount of staffing you have. The higher-level topics were talked about in a previous chapter, so if the security policy architecture is being started from the beginning, then the highest level security policy topic needs to be completed.

Another way to start the security policy architecture is the enterprise can start with lower level process documents after the top management endorsement. These documents are the device and software security configuration standards and the security work instructions, procedures, processes, or standard operating procedures. These types of documents normally do not need to have approvals all the way up the management structure. Therefore, these documents can be written and implemented more easily than a policy statement or guideline. These lower level documents give the security policy architecture a strong hold for being implemented within the organization. This option does contradict the statements in Chapter 3 and Figure 10 for building a security policy architecture from the ground up. By contrast, an enterprise knows that there need to be configuration standards and standard operating procedures. Therefore it does fit together in the end.

The last option for priorities is addressing problem areas that have been happening within the enterprise environment. If social engineering is an issue, then maybe user awareness takes priority. If virus and worm infections are an issue, then enhancing and developing preventative documents and training take priority. If Internet surfing and downloading are an issue, then the user awareness and additional monitoring and reporting take priority. The priorities depend upon the enterprise and the direction that management wants to take.

No matter which way the security policy architecture is going to be initiated or reviewed, the information security team needs to gather the following information to ensure an understanding of the enterprise:

- Organization charts
- Network diagrams
- Existing policies
- Application list enterprise and departmental to include function
- Management tools
- Network device list to include function, vendor, and version
- Production server list to include function, operating system, and version
- Enterprise strategic plans
- Compliance and privacy requirements
- Threat, concern, risk matrix for the most precious enterprise assets or a definition of enterprise assets

7.2   Reviews

Before getting any approvals for the documents, the documents need to be reviewed. Because electronic forums are the best way to initially review documents, start the document review process with a task to the review team. A review team consists of an author who controls the review cycle, reviewers who will make comments on the document, and an observer, a staff member outside the policy team, who will review the document, but will not have a vote to move forward with the document.

The initial review team should be no more than five subject matter experts. These subject matter experts should understand risk, the operating environment, and the business requirements. With smaller organizations, the team should be about three people. As the author, you need to ensure that the document will fit into the enterprise culture.

If the review team includes staff from other countries or areas in different time zones, the review process will need to accommodate different time zones. The size of the document also determines the estimated review time for the document. Listed below are some guidelines for estimated document review times, but this does not include estimated times if the document needs to be translated before someone can review the document:

- Initial Document Review
  201 pages or more in length: 80 business hours of review time
  101–200 pages in length: 60 business hours of review time
  51–100 pages in length: 40 business hours of review time
  0–50 pages in length: 24 business hours of review time
- Subsequent Document Review
  201 changed pages or more: 40 business hours of review time
  101–200 changed pages: 32 business hours of review time
  51–100 changed pages: 16 business hours of review time
  0–50 changed pages: 8 business hours of review time

These estimated time frames take into account that staff are working on other projects and are not full time to the review team. If the members are 100 percent dedicated to the review team, then the times can be cut by at least one third.

What is the actual document review cycle? It is simple. It is just like a project requirements review:

1. Create a central point to store the information security policy documents for review. Ensure that the review team has access to the document storage. Documents should not be emailed because the team may not remember who has the most current version.
2. Publish information security policy document(s) for review. The author places the information security policy document in the central location.
3. The author sends out a notice to the reviewers. A sample email is documented below.

> *Subject: Review Requested: Information Security document XXX*
>
> *You have been selected to be on the review team for the XXX information security policy architecture document. The purpose of this document is XXX and is to apply to the whole enterprise. The document is located XXX. Please review the document for accuracy, content, grammar, completeness, and how it would fit into the enterprise. You have full editorial liberties when reviewing the document. If there are any questions, please do not hesitate to contact me. The review comments are due by close of business on XX/XX/XX. Thank you.*

4. The reviewers will edit the appropriate documents making revisions and comments and asking questions.
5. The author sends out a reminder to complete the information security policy document(s) reviews.
6. When the reviewers have completed the document review, the author will review all of the input and comments.
7. The author will merge all of the revision.
8. Repeat the review cycle with the review team if the author decides not enough changes have been made to the information security policy document(s). If there are only grammatical changes or items to better clarify statements, then the document may not need to be re-reviewed.

As the reviewer reviews the information security policy document, he or she needs to ask the following questions while reading the documents:

- Is there applicability and completeness for business requirements, compliance, and regulatory requirements?
- Can the requirements within the document be tested and have documented results?
- Does the document have correctness/accuracy?
- Does the document employ correct grammar?
- Dos the document have technical adequacy, where applicable?
- Business requirements
    Have integrity and evidential value of information been maintained?
    Is information available to properly authorized personnel?
- Is the information security policy document long enough or too long?
- Does the roles and responsibilities section cover the enterprise?
- Is the information security policy document customized enough to meet business requirements? Has the enterprise done its due diligence?
- If we give the policy to a high school student, could the student understand it and state the meaning of the document?
- Does the information security policy document state how the enterprise feels about risk and how risk will be handled?
- Would a staff member state that the information security policy document is reasonable and realistic? Will it impact their day-to-day activities?

After the review team completes and accepts the document, and then the document needs to be forwarded onto the management team for the formal approval sign-offs.

7.3 Project Approval

In preparation for getting signature approvals, electronic communication, namely e-mail, is one of the better methods to communicate with the executive team.

Many executive teams will give staff members no more than 15 minutes to make a presentation to get a point across, catch their attention, and get their agreement or approval to move forward. When you are dealing with an information security policy architecture, the issue is not whether security is necessary, but whether it is recognized as an urgent need. The executive team understands that the enterprise environment is characterized by more complex computer environments, multiple computer platforms, multiple levels of information users, and vast conglomerates of integrated computer networks. Some executive team members may not understand information security in detail, but they will understand information risk to the enterprise.

When an executive presentation is performed, the presenter needs to keep in mind the limited time that is available and remember to answer these four questions:

1. From a strategic point of view, is the enterprise doing the right thing by writing an information security policy architecture?
2. From an enterprise architecture point of view, is the enterprise approaching limiting asset risk in the right way?
3. From a value point of view, will the enterprise achieve benefits from the implementation of an information security policy architecture?
4. From a delivery point of view, is the implementation plan being done well for the benefit of the enterprise?

With these four questions, two slides with four balloons each can be the high-level presentation for getting approval to move forward with a project to develop or review an information security policy architecture. The first set of four balloons would be for project goal, project objectives, the core project team, and using the project approach, which present the business case for the information security policy architecture. Sample balloons can be found in Figures 14, 15, 16, and 17.

The second set of four balloons would be to discuss keys to project success, project assumptions, project and policy architecture metrics, and a recommendation to move forward, which present the executive summary for moving forward with developing and implementing an information security policy architecture. Sample balloons can be found in Figures 18, 19, 20, and 21.

These balloons provide the executive summary and business case to move forward with building an information security policy architecture.

Goal

Establish an information security policy architecture that provides accountability and reliable protection to limit enterprise asset risk.

Figure 14   Sample project goal.

Objectives
- Ensure the confidentiality, integrity, accountability, and availability of enterprise assets
- Protect against anticipated enterprise asset risk
- Protect against unauthorized access or use of enterprise assets

Figure 15   Sample project objectives.

Core Project Team
- Executive Sponsor—CEO
- Project Sponsor—CSO
- Project Manager—Sandy
- Business Lead—Michael
- Reviewers—Mary, Bill, Stan, Mark, Kevin

Figure 16   Sample core project team.

Policy Architecture Approach
- Planning
   - Perform risk assessment
   - Identify gaps with existing policy architecture
   - Document key business requirements for asset protection
- Phase I
   - Identify a matrix of required topics
   - Present findings to executive team
- Phase II
   - Develop top level information security policy architecture
   - Develop second tier information security policy architecture

Figure 17   Sample project approach.

Keys to Success
- Implementation of an enterprise information security policy architecture to limit enterprise asset risk
- Standardization of device configuration, monitoring, and implementation
- Guides for acceptable use when evaluating business requirements

Figure 18   Sample keys to success.

Assumptions
- Risk assessment and gap analysis started within the next month
- Information Assurance policy approved and published by year end
- Information Security Program approved and published by year end
- Consultant budget approved by EQ02

Figure 19   Sample project assumptions.

Key Financial Metrics
- Availability–$250k annual cost avoidance relating to lost intellectual property through access control
- Productivity–$150k annual productivity increase across company (IT & Business) through better secured access control
- Control–$300k annual cost avoidance for asset loss

Figure 20   Sample project and policy metrics.

Recommendation
- Develop information security topics for policy architecture
- Use internal resources where possible
- Limit the use of external consultants to save costs
- Develop an awareness program

Figure 21   Sample recommendations.

7.4 Document Approval

To be ready for the approvals, you need to have that 60-second elevator speech ready and be ready to respond to any type of question that may be asked. Consider the following when a 60-second elevator speech is being developed.

- Believe in yourself and the mission. Go in thinking success. This is a given and this is a gentle reminder to yourself.
- Never give up. You do not know what you can achieve. Many times, the first answer is "no" or a conditional yes with caveats.
- Have a strategy before; meeting with anyone. You know the direction you want the enterprise to take, ensure you also understand the business.
- Know the sound bites—important, high-risk, business-related. Read the trade rags to know the risk, threat, compliance, privacy, and security headlines, especially if there are ones for your industry.
- Know who, what, where, when, why, how. Being able to answer these six questions will lessen the questions and potential resistance to implementation.
- Be flexible and adaptable. There is no such thing as totally secure and zero risk. Ensure that there are options to present to the enterprise. What is the level of risk acceptance?

What approvals do you need for what levels of documents within the enterprise? First, you need to determine the information security policy architecture document levels before you can determine who needs to approve them. The levels within an enterprise for the information security policy architecture document could be as follows:

- Enterprise
- Country
  - Location
  - Site
- Business unit
- Technology

The level of the document will be determined by the document scope and the roles and responsibilities. As mentioned previously, the information security policy architecture document levels are policy, guideline, standard, work instruction, memos, and forms. Then the information security team needs to determine the highest position in authority for the area for approval and enforcement. With this determination, the information security policy architecture approval matrix can be developed. See Table 10 for a simple approval matrix sample for an information security policy architecture.

Match the titles within the sample approval matrix to the highest level possible within the enterprise that can promote and endorse the information security policy

Table 10 Approval Matrix

Document Type[a]	Dept. Mgr.[b]	Dept. VP[b]	Highest Site Position	CIO[c]	CSO[d]	CFO[e]	COO[f]	CEO[g]	Counsel/HR	Board of Directors
Enterprise Policy				X	X	X	X	X	X	Awareness
Enterprise Guideline				X	X	X	X	X	X	Awareness
Enterprise Standard				X	X	X	X	X	X	Awareness
Enterprise Work Instruction	X			X	X		X		Awareness	Awareness
Enterprise Memo						X		X	X	Awareness
Enterprise Form	X			X	X		X			
Location Policy			X	X			X			
Location Guideline			X	X			X			
Location Standard			X	X			X			
Location Work Instruction	X									
Location Memo			X							
Location Form	X									
Business Unit Policy		X	X	X	X		X			
Business Unit Guideline		X								
Business Unit Standard		X								

Table 10 Approval Matrix

Document Type[a]	Dept. Mgr.[b]	Dept. VP[b]	Highest Site Position	CIO[c]	CSO[d]	CFO[e]	COO[f]	CEO[g]	Counsel/HR	Board of Directors
Business Unit Work Instruction	X									
Business Unit Memo		X								
Business Unit Form	X									
Technology Policy	X	X		X						
Technology Guideline	X	X		X						
Technology Standard	X	X		X						
Technology Work Instruction	X									
Technology Memo		X		X						
Technology Form	X									

a The document type approval is dependent on the topic of the document for the additional approvals.

b This could be the information security person, if the document is related to information security.

c Chief Information Officer or the highest position level that leads information technology or the technology of the enterprise.

d Chief Security Officer or the highest position level that leads the enterprise security.

e Chief Financial Officer.

f Chief Operating Officer or the highest position level that leads the operations portion of the business.

g Chief Executive Officer or highest level in the enterprise.

architecture. For example, if the highest security level position is a Director reporting to the Chief Information Officer, then the Chief Information Officer should be the initial level to sign off on the policy architecture document and then move higher up the enterprise organization chart.

After the approval matrix has been developed, the information security team can start a marketing campaign to get the signature approvals. If you have been in an enterprise for a while, you should be able to determine the best communication method for the executive team. With all the electronic communication methods available, many executive teams prefer the electronic communication method for review over a face to face meeting. You will need to ensure that the executive approval team understands that protecting enterprise assets and meeting business requirements is the fundamental reason for the information security policy architecture. As the author for the information security policy architecture information, you need to meet face to face with each of the executives for signatures and final approval. This meeting with the executives will allow the executives to ask any last minute questions or voice any concerns. A video conference will also work when a true face-to-face meeting cannot be set or the executives are in various locations.

7.5 Support

Let us dispel some myths about getting information security support from the enterprise.

1. Executives only care about their company. Executives and management have goals and objectives to support and expand the enterprises market share or to produce new products. With either goal, the executives need to keep in mind protecting the enterprise assets in order to make that bottom line.
2. Stories and anecdotes waste time. When someone lectures and reads the slides, do you remember? Or do you remember better when someone tells an incident or story that relates to the topics on the slides, especially if the incident had severe consequences or wonderful outcomes?
3. Executives only want the numbers. The almighty dollar, the dashboards, and the scorecards play an important role in the progress of meeting a goal and objective. Within information security there is also an attitude and awareness toward asset protection, which cannot have a number put on it.
4. Executives hate auditors. Auditors are our friends. Auditors can bring good and bad news. It is when auditors bring news of issues and noncompliance that executives have issues with the enterprise and business unit methods and not the auditors themselves.
5. Executives want a return on investment (ROI). Within information security, this is return on security investment (ROSI). If asset protection is integrated into every process and into everyone's daily job, the concern over ROSI goes away and the ROI across the enterprise goes up. If information security is

only considered an insurance policy for the enterprise, then the message of integrating confidentiality, integrity, and availability is not being promoted to the benefit of the enterprise.

Paul Revere was the messenger of the revolution and the famous saying "the British are coming out!" That message is really not too far off from today's compliance with the copious regulations. Why was Paul Revere such a good communicator? He had a specific message that needed to be spread about the risk that was entering the environment. Community lives were in jeopardy because an external force was going to invade. He ran into British road blocks and through various communication skills either talked his way through the road blocks or ran them. At the one road block where he was interrogated by British officers, Paul Revere stated what his mission was by telling the British officers more than they knew about their mission. Risky? Yes. In the end, the British talked among themselves, released the prisoners and began a slow retreat. What limited that threat? Telling the British they were going to run into resistance in their take-over. And the British decided the invasion was not worth the risk. Paul Revere's warning to the communities allowed them to prepare (and add controls) to limit the risk of the invasion. As information security professionals, we need to take the lead from Paul Revere in spreading the message about business risk and ways to mitigate that risk. We need to know our own strengths and weaknesses and increase our influence within the enterprise. We can increase our influence understanding by the following:

- Being a central role in the enterprise. This does not mean the center of the enterprise's attention. This does mean active participation in projects and activities within the enterprise.
- Skill substitutability. Yes, you are an information security professional. You also have skills to perform requirements gathering and defining, facilitating meetings and projects, and understanding how information security can be integrated into the business functions.
- Dealing with unexpected situations brings influence. You are performing daily activities and a denial of service attacks takes down the corporate network work segment. Using your incident response skills, you can activate the incident response plan and take control of the situation, including updating management on the status. You write up the post mortem, present the document, and get back to your daily routine without the expectation of a bonus or a promotion.
- Resources, information, and expertise bring influence. You should be able to face a group and say, "I do not know, but let me get back to you with additional information" (and you actually follow up). Let's the group know you are human and do not know everything. If there is an Oracle database issues that is being discussed and you do not know Oracle security but you know what questions to ask, you then call your Oracle database reference and ask for assistance.

- Building a base of support. As we continue through our careers, we add people to our list of associates, contacts, and references that we can call on for advice and assistance.
- Associating with influential people. This does not mean to take up the sporting event of the executives or join an elite club. This means taking the time to meet with various managers to learn issues and concerns. This is the old theory of "managing by walking around."
- Image-building. You come into an organization and the people do not know you and you do not know them. You need to build credibility without being a bull in a china shop. You need to be known for understanding and speaking in business requirements, for having active listening skills, for being dependable, for completing requests on time, for not speaking techno-babble, and for not lecturing about the missing security controls within the enterprise.
- Creating obligation to reciprocate. This is not blackmail. This is, I assisted you in enhancing your business requirements to protect our intellectual property, and this is how you can assist me in understanding your business direction.

As the information security group starts the promotion and implementation of the information security policy architecture, start the information dissemination early to let the staff voice their concerns. Sir Isaac Newton stated, "a body at rest tends to stay at rest" and enterprises that do not embrace change do not move ahead in the industry. Therefore, make sure the information security team has commitments for support from executive management for change to embrace the concept of information protection. Find a sponsor within the enterprise to ask advice and to test concepts, and become an insider to build your personal credibility. If staff are not responding, go out into the business environment to see if there is any resistance, and use active listening skills to seek out how the environment can be improved together.

After getting business unit support for an information security policy architecture, the complaints start rolling in:

- We cannot be impacted by security.
- We have project deadlines and security interferes with it.
- We do not have time to read those additional security documents or the staff to dedicate to the project.
- It's not my job to review and keep up with the security stuff.
- Because information technology does monitoring, do we really need more information security?
- This is going to take too long to implement and we will not see any benefits.
- By whose authority do I have to follow what you say?
- We have processes to do our jobs and we do not need anyone interfering with our jobs.

The first thing to remember is, do not take the questions and issues personally. This is a theme in many organizations. This theme is changing with the myriad regulations and regulating bodies imposing compliance and requirements on the business. The key to reducing the questions and the resistance is to perform marketing about the information security policy architecture as the project task gets started. The key is knowing the enterprise, the business, and the business requirements from the executive team down to the administrative assistant level. The marketing means using the business requirements and bringing out the risks that are present every day, such as visitors walking around unescorted or permitting contractors and consultants to plug into the corporate network for access with non-standard equipment. As with the executives, the following four questions need to be promoted:

1. From a strategic point of view, is the enterprise doing the right thing by writing an information security policy architecture?
2. From an enterprise architecture point of view, is the enterprise approaching limiting asset risk in the right way?
3. From a value point of view, will the enterprise achieve benefits from the implementation of an information security policy architecture?
4. From a delivery point of view, is the implementation plan being done well for the benefit of the enterprise?

Knowing the business requirements, a set of basic answers could be as follows:

1. MYC is a global company and must comply with over 10 global regulations. Some of the global regulations, for example, privacy, state that MYC must provide a strategic plan for protecting customer and employee information. Executive management has previously stated that enterprise assets must be protected to the level of their importance to the business. We need to identify safeguards and controls to protect the enterprise assets from threats.
2. Executive management has been presented with the results of an enterprise risk assessment. The external consultants reviewed the various risk areas within the enterprise and stated that MYC needs to strengthen its policy architecture before implementing additional technology to limit the risk to the enterprise assets.
3. One of the benefits of implementing the information security policy architecture and tuning the network and technology architectures currently implemented is that MYC will be able to expand its partnerships overseas with other development companies.
4. The implementation of the information security policy architecture will be a gradual process to ensure that no business unit is shutdown by the implementation of this architecture. Before implementing additional information security policy documents or technology, meetings will be held and presentations will be done to ensure that business requirements are met and the implementation impact is very limited.

Talk to the business units about their existing threats, some of which could be used to base the information security policy architecture. Threats and risks to the business should be viewed from an enterprise point of view with potential associated costs. Business unit threats could be presented in terms of incidents that have occurred over the last year within the enterprise, such as some of the threats seen in Table 11.

Explain to the business units (and management) how the information security policy architecture and the subsequent technology tweaking will reduce risks and may not even impact the current business unit processes. Speaking with business units in terms of business risk and business requirements will assist the information security policy team to receive support for the approval and implementation of the information security policy architecture. Remember that the recommended information security policy architecture must be approved by decision makers and representatives who are business unit stakeholders.

As the information security policy architecture is presented to the business units, the presentation can focus on confidentiality, integrity, availability, and accountability in business requirements.

- Confidentiality of data. Can the business unit document that customer and staff information is protected from unauthorized access, disclosure, and use?
- Integrity of data and systems. Can the business assure executive management that they can confidently state that information has not been altered in an unauthorized manner and that information is free of unauthorized access and manipulation?
- Availability. Can the business unit ensure prompt and accurate access to information or systems to authorized users? Does the business unit know if the critical information is backed up regularly and can be recovered?
- Accountability of data. If the business unit has a compromise, missing data, or unauthorized alteration, can the business unit trace the actions back to the source?

As support presentations are made, the information security group needs to focus on the business requirements and the threats and risks to the business information, and to lessen the fear, uncertainty, and doubt about the impact of implementing an information security architecture. When using the 60-second elevator speech and speaking with business units on their requirements, the difference between great and average is how often you take risks. That is, calculated risks that temporarily force you outside your comfort zone often result in big wins. Most of us succeed because we are determined to succeed, not because of destiny.

Start with staff who understand risk and want additional guidance on protecting their information. These staff can be the group that the information security policy architecture documents and concepts can be tested against for applicability and usability. This group will give the honest feedback on the proposals and

Table 11   Risks Threats Costs and Controls

Threat	Sample Situation	Probability of Occurrence	Possible Control	Estimated Loss	Risk Reduction
Unauthorized data modification	In the last year, the customer technical request database became corrupt when our Brazilian partner tried to upload over 50 product enhancements.	30%	Strong access controls	$150k	45%
Denial of service on corporate network	In testing our new product, the engineer misconfigured routing protocols and when load testing was performed, the corporate network was impacted by a flood of network traffic.	10%	Firewall/switch access control lists	$50K	80%
Virus	The executive administrator downloaded a presentation for the CEO. The video presentation contained a worm and because she disabled the anti-virus software, the worm spread through the management network segment.	20%	Internet filtering, centralized anti-virus software, user awareness training on downloading executables	$45k	80%
Authorized data modification by an untrained user	Last month Eric moved to a new position in finance, transferring from manufacturing. Eric's manufacturing access was not removed and Eric was able to order and receive equipment. Eric had not been instructed that he was not permitted to perform both functions.	25%	Strong access controls, segregation of duties training	$10K	75%

directions. The information security group will know this staff because they will be ones who invite the information security group to their meetings, projects, and requirements sessions. They will be the ones who ask for help and listen and hear what the information security group is saying about risk and threats.

When the presentations start with other business units, throughout the meetings remember to

- Hear their questions
- Hear their needs
- Hear their expectations
- Hear their business requirements
- Hear their responsibilities
- Watch for hidden agendas

As the meeting proceeds, determine

- What are the information security goals and objectives and how can you assist the business unit to accomplish their goals and objectives?
- How can the goals and objectives be merged to assist the business unit?
- How do both sets of goals combine to make a stronger business?
- What is most productive way to accomplish the goals and objectives?
- By knowing the business, you can list past accomplishments (or key failures) that can assist both groups.
- Is there a way to start small and non-impacting, for all to reach their goals? Is there a way to start incorporating some of the information security rules in daily activities and responsibilities?
- Also, be sure to remember you are promoting asset protection and you are not selling anything to the business units.
- Good communication skills with the business unit by avoiding jargon, staying focused, and establishing your credibility.

In summary, remember to actively listen to the enterprise for business requirements and merge the information security policy architecture into those business requirements.

7.6 Publishing

The information security team has developed the information security policy architecture and received the executive team approval and support in writing. That was the easy part. The next piece of the architecture is to publish the information security policy architecture and ensure that the enterprise understands the document set. Publishing the information security policy architecture at an enterprise level provides a framework for the business units to easily access and on which to develop their business practices. Publishing the information security policy architecture to all staff is a critical component of the information security program. Initially this can be distributed at new hire orientation, but it must also be distributed to existing staff through user awareness training throughout the year. The publication of an information security policy architecture is critical. The main questions that will need to be answered before publishing your information security policy architecture are as follows:

- Who within the enterprise is responsible for publishing security policies and procedures?
- How are the information security publications reviewed and validated before publication?
- How are document updates published to everyone?

It is hoped that within the enterprise, there is a communications or publications group. If such a group exists, then go to that group for suggestions on enterprise publications and time frames for publishing. If not, then the information security team will need to establish its own criteria for the responsibilities of publication. In this and the previous chapter, we talked about reviewing the documents for approval. What is needed also to know who is going to validate the format for publication. Again that would go back to the communications or publications groups or to a technical writer. Someone needs to have the responsibility that the current document format can be reformatted into the appropriate media for publication. As with software versioning, there needs to be an enterprise document management system for version control of documents. The author is not endorsing a third-party or a home-grown system; the author is endorsing the business requirement of document versioning. If there is no document versioning or document management system, how is the enterprise to know which is the most current and active set of documents?

When it comes down to the actual question of what options are available for publishing documents, the answer is two: print them in hard copy or publish them electronically.

Hard copy. Information security policies are not interesting. Volume sets are space consuming and can quickly become obsolete. By contrast, short paper documents can be carried around for easy reference and can be quick read. So an implementation technique for the information security policy re-enforcement could be summary sheets, reference cards, posters (or advertisements), buttons, or stickers. These types of media will enhance the information security awareness training programs. On the downside, there may be so many printed copies that it will be difficult to find and update every copy. The question also becomes one of finding the page or section to print and insert, rather than just reprinting the whole document. And many staff do not have the time to stick pages into a manual. If a new employee violates a policy and the printed copy is an older or mis-updated copy, it may be difficult to justify dismissal for wrongdoing and could become a legal nightmare.

Electronic copy in today's technology advancements and the work style of staff make electronic publication more conducive to the enterprise environment. Electronic publication has a huge administrative advantage if it is centrally managed and a statement is made about the master source location for the information security policy architecture and that any additional copies (electronic or printed) are not to be used. There are various formats of electronic publication: hypertext markup language (HTML), rich text format (RTF), proprietary word processing format, portable document format (PDF), and help file format. Depending on the enterprise, a combination of electronic publication formats may be implemented. In the electronic format, the enterprise needs to ensure that only the publishers have read–write access to the document areas and that all other staff (including contractors, consultants, visitors, vendors, and partners) have read-only access. Hypertext is the most valuable contribution to the enterprise's electronic publications because hypertext permits the reader to jump to sections and return easily. More importantly, hypertext within the information security policy architecture can provide definitions and acronyms without the need of having the reader go to another reference location. The following are some pros and cons of the various methods.

- HTML. It is one of the most widely used formats today. A simple and quick mouse click and a person can jump to another page. This format permits a person to move freely from page to page and text to text within a page. A new window can be opened to view documents simultaneously. The main con is that you need to understand HTML coding to have an efficient HTML page. Word processing and other applications will convert documents to HTML pages, and this can make it a potential nightmare for quick tweaking of a document.
- Rich text or proprietary word processing format. Linking documents and using hypertext with word-processing files will work as long as all parties use the same word-processing software. Depending upon the word-processing software, pop-ups may display by clicking or just mousing over. But some obscure (or old) software may display nothing or you get an information balloon to display. Would every person be able to communicate what they saw and read?
- A combination of HTML and word process format would be hypertexting and PDF. Adobe Acrobat's PDF provides the benefits of hypertexting while giving the effect of a word processing document. PDF documents can be locked down from an access control point of view on the network, as well as within the PDF document itself. The PDF document can have hyperlinks to other documents, definitions, or acronym explanations.

Help files. Help files can provide hypertext capability, but many help file utilities are not centrally managed and updates will need to be pushed out. With help files, you will need to know the operating system that a person is using to customize the help file format.

Publication in a non–home country's language or for a sight-impaired person adds to the complexity of the information security policy architecture. When translating the enterprise's information security policy architecture into another language you need to ensure that it is translated almost word for word. The enterprise cannot afford to have the document translated into another language only to have the translator interpret what the document was trying to state and change the wording. Work with an enterprise translator who is proficient in both languages and work with the translator to ensure the meaning and intent have not been changed in translation. There can be some proficient staff members who are sight-impaired and cannot directly read text or the words on a screen. The enterprise needs to decide how it will handle the publication of the information security policy architecture to those staff. Braille would be one way or digitally recording the information security policy architecture. Whatever publication methods are used by the enterprise need to cover everyone who accesses an enterprise asset.

7.7   Updates—Effective Versioning

A central document repository or document library is a location where a collection of files is stored. There are many applications that can assist with maintaining a central repository. Document versioning—allowing the enterprise to keep multiple versions of documents—can cause complications. With document versioning, if an enterprise change needs to be reversed, the document can be reverted to the previous version and the enterprise can continue to work. An automated document management system enables an enterprise to

- Standardize on document version numbering
- Know who has checked out/in a document
- Know who made the changes
- Know when a document was initially created
- Know when the document is/was obsolete
- Know who is the owner of the document
- Automatically create a backup of the previous version when a document is checked back in

Based on business requirements, the enterprise needs to evaluate and implement a document management system to work productivity, to free server space, and to streamline document management processes by providing a centralized location for documents, as well as methods for tracking changes from members of a work team.

7.8 Acknowledgment of Understanding

Confucius said, "What I hear, I forget. What I see, I remember. What I do, I understand." Normally an enterprise has a new hire document that acknowledges a new staff member has received the Employee Handbook. If the Employee Handbook includes the documents from the information security policy architecture, then the new hire process may be completed for acknowledgment. Every enterprise should have a new hire process that specifically includes information assurance training and acknowledgment. This can be done the day of new hire or within a week of the start date, but it needs to be standardized and formalized.

As part of the information security architecture, the enterprise should have an annual acknowledgment of the information security policy architecture. This annual acknowledgment would be attendance at a training session, completing a computer-based training session with a set of questions at the end, or sending a notice to everyone and trusting them to review and return the acknowledgment document. The method needs to fit into the enterprise culture and each mentioned method has a pro and con. For example,

- Having everyone attend, in person, a training session would cause scheduling and logistic issues, but, by contrast, the information security team would be able to meet everyone in the enterprise.
- With the computer-based training, you will have people start it, not know there are questions at the end, and say they completed it, or some will skip to the end and just answer the questions, but you also will be able to track who performed the training, how long they were in the program, and how many questions they answered correctly.
- Using the signed or e-mail accepted acknowledgment means trusting in all of the staff to complete the review and acknowledge on their own, but again you will be able to track receipt and acknowledgment and know if they really reviewed the information security policy architecture documentation.

The enterprise needs to determine the best method for new hire acknowledgment and for the annual reacknowledgment.

The enterprise also needs to determine how far this acknowledgment goes—contractors, consultants, vendors, visitors, customers. If there is an extended need, the information security team needs to ensure the information security policy architecture documents are available to all classes of people and needs to have a documented method for acknowledgment by these people. For non-employee types, there may be a different set of policy architecture documents that include the topics such as

- Business ethics
- Intellectual property

- The overarching information security policy
- Exceeding or attempting to exceed granted access
- How to request access through business point of contacts
- How and to whom to report issues

See Appendix R, Appendix S, and Appendix T for three sample acknowledgment forms—hard copy, electronic, and nonstaff.

7.9 Exceptions to the Information Security Policy Architecture Documentation

Although it would be extremely nice, cost effective, and efficient to have every information system and every business unit in compliance with all documents within the information security policy architecture, that may be a dream. Every enterprise has situations for a specific period of time when something or someone will be noncompliant with a policy, guideline, standard, or work instruction. The information security team needs to be able to respond when those situations occur and be able to monitor and reassess the environment.

An enterprise must have an exception process for documenting an exception to compliance with the published information security policy architecture. The scope of this document will apply to all publishing information security policy architecture documents that are owned and maintained by the information security group. The enterprise will need to describe the circumstances for which an exception may be requested:

- Accidental noncompliance. The business unit was unaware of the published information security policy architecture. A new hire was unaware of the location of the information security policy architecture.
- Another acceptable solution is available. The business unit is recommending a solution with better information assurance controls and the exception can be granted until the published documented has been updated.
- A legacy system is being allowed to go to end of life. This would be a managed risk with a definitive end date.
- Lack of resources. A new piece of software is being implemented, there are not enough available resources for the segregation of duties, and this risk needs to be managed.

Then the process document will define what the business unit needs to perform to be granted the exception. If the noncompliance is due to anything other than a better solution, the enterprise needs to document what must be in the exception request, such as

- Description of the noncompliance
- Anticipated length of noncompliance, no more than 12 months
- Risk assessment associated with noncompliance
- Plan for alternate means of risk management or compensating controls
- Method for monitoring and evaluating the risk
- Review date to evaluate progress toward compliance

If the noncompliance is a result of a superior solution, an exception will automatically be granted until the information security policy architecture document is updated with the new information.

Many times an exception cannot or will not be granted and sometimes saying that no is difficult. Saying no means that the team has set limits on the enterprise acceptable risk, and it also means that that team may need to assist the business unit in offering a different option or creating compensating controls for the risk. When the team says no, the whole team needs to be in agreement in both verbal and nonverbal communications. When an exception cannot be granted, as part of the exception process the team must

- Acknowledge the other person's request by repeating it
- Explain its reason for declining it

Regardless of the decision, the information security team needs to keep a record of all exceptions, whether they were granted or not, the actions performed for each exception, and when the next review for each exception is being performed. The information security team needs to be proactive in maintaining the exceptions to the information security policy architecture and be able to report to management at anytime what exceptions exist.

See Appendix U for an exception request work instruction and form.

Chapter 8

Crafting Communication for Maximum Effectiveness

The information security team is ready to implement, promote, and train staff on the documents produced by the information security policy architecture. The information security team creates a mental image of the objective(s) to be accomplished in getting the information disseminated. That mental image is transformed into words and actions for presentation to the enterprise staff. We need to remember that communication is a two-way process between a sender of information and a receiver of information. We communicate by talking, watching, listening, observing activity. The majority of our communications are written and the words become ambassadors to the enterprise.

- They are either success or failure for the information security policy architecture.
- They tell staff what the enterprise believes about the executive team's direction for information security.
- They open or shut doors for future development and communication of the information security program.

We have been communication since we were very young. And after all those years of communication, we have many situations where the message is lost in translation between the sender and receiver. Although most of our presentation communication is verbal, the recipients also see and hear the nonverbal communication, body language and tone. Sometimes this is more important than the verbal communication, and some are more effective in delivering a message than others. Common research states that in verbal exchanges:

- Words are about 7 percent effective.
- Tone of voice is about 38 percent effective.
- Nonverbal cues are about 55 percent effective.

So whenever we verbally communicate, what we say may not be as important as how we say the message. Long time presenters have asserted that audiences make up their minds about the presentation within two minutes of the beginning. Other presenters assert that first impressions are made in thirty seconds.

8.1 Barriers to Effective Communication

As an effective communicator, we need to present a certain image. As a communicator need to consider the following:

- Do I have the credentials to be doing this job properly? Credentials do not necessarily mean a bunch of certifications after your name. Credentials can be "I have been actively participating in the industry and community for years."
- Are we perceived as competent and trustworthy? Do I have the background and knowledge to present this topic? Is my enterprise track record one of honesty, integrity, and understanding? Do I make an effort to not limit my scope of knowledge on the topic?
- Are we perceived as dynamic? Am I a leader more than a follower? Do I actively perform within the enterprise?

We need to be creditable before we can actually promote any of the information security policy architecture to the enterprise. Whether we choose the written or verbal communication method, we need to avoid the following to limit the chances of the message, being misunderstood:

- Slang or local dialect words
- Word associations that cause different meanings to different people
- Emphasis or specifying certain words
- Incorrect or inappropriate usage of words and phrases
- Homonyms or words with the same spelling and sounds, which have different meanings, for example, *their* or *there*

So, before the message is given to staff, it is important to take time to consider whether staff who receive the message will be able to understand what the information security team means because the information security team relies on the staff's perception or interpretation.

As we communicate with each other sometimes there is interference, which could be background noise in the environment or distractions during the conversation. Other causes for interference can include the following:

- The choice of words or language a communicator uses can cause interference. Someone might use slang and everyone might not know the correct meaning of the slang.
- Selective hearing can interfere with message communication. You are sitting in an office area not paying attention to the conversation until subconsciously you hear the term *hack* and you start listening because something interested you.
- Language, in general, can have different meanings in different cultures. A *slave drive* in English refers to a secondary drive within a computer, but in another language *slave drive* may mean something derogatory.
- Many times assuming the audience knows the background of something causes the sender to skip information.

We need to be straightforward in communication our message on the information security policy architecture. We, as information security professionals, need to develop our most effective communication skills through understanding questions and comments, telling people what to do, asking someone to do something, listening to responses and questions, observing, and being convincing in what we believe in. Each skill has pros and cons, depending on which situation the presenter is in. As information security professionals we are effective communicators when we succeed in persuading staff to act in the way that is documented within the information security policy architecture and continue to enjoy doing it. It is the author's opinion that some of the information security team should spend about 75 percent of their time communicating directly with enterprise staff.

8.2 Listening

Before, during, and after the presentation, we need to solicit information from others. Some effective listening tips are as follows:

- Listen openly to the whole statement of the other person. Look at the person making the statement and be patient for that person to complete the whole statement.
- Listen to the content; do not judge the other person and delivery.
- Ask questions, ask for more detail, repeat the responses through rephrasing to ensure you heard what was stated.
- Try to ensure distractions are not in the area, such as cell phones going off.
- See if there might be a different root cause for statements and questions.
- Ask others for their opinions on the communication being given.

- Respond to actions and not feelings, such as telling a person his or her cell phone going off is interrupting the presentation and not getting angry at the person.
- Do not totally control communication, remember communication is a two-way process and you need to acknowledge what is stated by others.
- If necessary, take notes while listening so that all points can be addressed.
- Be respectful, courteous, and polite to everyone in the session.

8.3   Know Your Audience

Before any communication is disseminated, the author or presenter needs to understand who will be in the audience and why they are receiving the communication. Although the topic may not change, the way it is communicated may change depending on the audience. The presenter knows the audience from working with them on a regular basis or knowing who they work for and the function of the business unit. The audience will come in with various attitudes, for example:

- I am coming because I have to
- I am coming because I want to learn more
- I am in agreement with the concept being presented
- I am totally opposed to the concept
- I do not care one way or another, just get it over with

With a varied audience, the presenter has a challenge and can relate to the audience in three different ways:

1. Being oblivious. I have this point to get across, I am going to tell it like it needs to be, and no questions will be asked.
2. Adapting to the audience. I will get the point across in a way they will all understand.
3. Respecting and understanding the audience and their interpretations. I need to get the point across and want to facilitate the audience's questions and concerns so the information security policy architecture document is accepted and implemented more smoothly.

Depending on the enterprise culture, the presenter could do additional research and seek out questions, concerns, and additional business requirements to ensure the audience will understand the concept of the information security policy architecture document that will be presented. The presenter needs to use materials and examples that are concrete and apply to the business requirements. As an example, in Figure 22 we perform an initial business link with the enterprise values for information assurance.

Continuing with the example, in Table 12 we link current enterprise issues to the enterprise values.

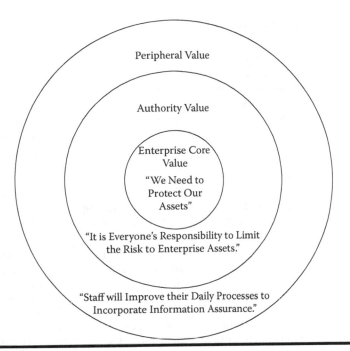

Peripheral Value

Authority Value

Enterprise Core
Value

"We Need to
Protect Our
Assets"

"It is Everyone's Responsibility to Limit
the Risk to Enterprise Assets."

"Staff will Improve their Daily Processes to
Incorporate Information Assurance."

Figure 22   Connecting with the audience.

8.4 What Is the Enterprise Standard Method of Communication?

There are many methods of communicating: speaking, watching, listening, or observing the activity of others. There are many channels of communication: face to face, telephone (land line and mobile), fax and e-mail, text messaging, computer-based training, video conferencing, memos, and reports. The primary method may change as technology systems become more sophisticated. In this author's opinion, the most effective method by far is face to face because you can see, hear, and listen as the message is being communicated. Although this is the most effective, it may not be the most practical in many instances. What constitutes effective communication?

- **Appropriate method.** Knowing and determining the appropriate or best method to disseminate information to the intended staff assists the information security team in specifying the importance and key points of the information security policy architecture. For some announcements, e-mail may be the best communication, and for specific topics, other methods (meetings, one on one, newsletters, online postings, etc.) may be more effective in reaching the staff.

Table 12   Linking Values and Issues

Issue	Peripheral Value	Authority Value	Enterprise Core Value
Financial database corruption	We need to ensure proper field editing for data enter.	We need to ensure proper access control to the data.	We need to validate access and data on a regular basis through monitoring and reporting.
Laptop theft	We need to ensure the staff is physically aware of the risks around them.	We need to implement strong authentication to ensure that only authorized users access mobile devices.	We need to have a valid and complete asset management and tracking system to limit the losses to the enterprise.
System or application downtime	Business continuity procedures should be in place to ensure customers can be responded to when applications or systems are down.	Each business unit needs to understand its processes and be able to perform them manually or have a work around.	Business continuity and disaster recovery plans will ensure the enterprise can continue business during a major event.

- **Content of communication.** When communicating to a diverse staff, it is likely that some staff will not need or want the information. Complaints from a large number of staff can temporarily overload a specific communication method, such as e-mail.
- **Perceived importance to staff.** If staff do not care to get unsolicited communications of the type the information security team is sending, this may persuade them to ignore future communications from the information security team.
- **Segmenting intended staff.** Targeting a pre-defined or a specific level in the enterprise will have better results than sending the communication to the whole enterprise.
- **Repeated or frequent contacts.** If the information security team makes repeated informational communications, it may be more effective to have an opt-in and opt-out for general information security communications. And keep the high priority information security communications for the whole enterprise.

When coordinating communications, ensure that the information security team has the authority to communicate to the enterprise. Access to an enterprise distribution list or method does not necessarily imply permission to use.

Trying to coordinate a meeting with multiple groups is a hard task in itself. At times, meetings are scheduled weeks in advance and it is hard to get much face time with staff members and executives. With a limited amount of time, an effective meeting structure is required and you need to know the audience, as was mentioned earlier in this chapter. The higher the organization structure, the less a staff member knows about any one issue and the less he or she can focus on one issue. And each staff member has his or her own style for interpretations and decisions based on instincts, trust of others, homework, and good questions. The information security team's objective is to provide the best available information and master complex and substantial issues in a short period of time.

Through past experience in the enterprise, the best way to determine the most effective and efficient communication to the staff is by asking questions or going to the secretaries or administrative assistants to see what the best method is for which group. Whether it is a face-to-face meeting (one to one or one to many) or written communication, an announcement of the event needs to be developed and sent to the staff members. The announcement should contain the following:

- To-the-point subject line
- Purpose of the meeting, explaining the importance of the topic and why you need to meet
- The topic broken down into essential facts with a course of action
- The final recommendation using sound reasoning

With any communication, the information security team presenting information needs to provide a reasonable connection for the enterprise as to why the information security policy architecture document is required. Let us walk through an example of requiring two factor authentication for staff remote access to the enterprise network.

1. Evidence. We know that some staff require off-hours access to the enterprise network to support customers. We know that many passwords can be cracked quickly. We know that hackers sometimes use key stroke loggers to catch user IDs and passwords going across the network.
2. Reasoning. When a house is secured using a simple door lock, it makes it a little harder for an intruder to break into the house. When the house has a deadbolt lock and an alarm system, the intruder has another layer of security to avoid before being able to break into the house. This implies that layered security lowers the risk of compromise to a network access.
3. Claim. Using two-factor authentication (two-factor authentication is based on something a user knows plus something the user has or something the user is) will lower the unauthorized access risk to the enterprise assets. Based on

business requirements and product evaluations, the enterprise will implement X with the following user instructions for remote access.

8.4.1 Lunch and Learns

When a lunch and learn is held, the presenter normally prepares a logical method to communicate to the group. The audience knowledge and structure of a lunch and learn session enables the information security team to be able to present the session in three ways:

- Tell and sell. This is most effective for new employees. This involves the presenter lecturing the audience on what is being implemented and trying to sell the concept to the audience. This is where the presenter may be expecting defensive reactions or requires acceptance from the audience for the concept.
- Tell and listen. This is more effective when presenting a new topic or implementation. The presenter introduces new concepts and wants feedback from the audience as to how to improve or make the implementation easier, such as solving a joint business requirement.
- Fulfilling the business requirement. This is effective for formal implementations where the goal is to let the audience know why they need to comply with the information security policy architecture document, what they need to do, and the results of compliance.

Throughout the presentation, questions will be asked and the presenter will be asked to think on his or her feet. When we have to think on our feet, we can feel pressure when not prepared. Here are four things to assist with thinking on your feet:

1. Look at the person requesting information, listen to what is being stated, and ask questions or rephrase to ensure that you understand what is being asked.
2. It is okay to pause and gather your thoughts, then repeat the question.
3. Focus on the response to one point and support it.
4. Then summarize the response and stop. Do not ramble and do not apologize.

8.4.2 Written

If we use memos to communicate, before we distribute the following questions, we need to ask ourselves:

- What is the main message to be disseminated and what tone am I going to use?
- Does the first paragraph contain all the key information?

- What do we want the group to remember and take action on from this memo?
- Are the statements convincing and feasible, and what do we want the group to do?
- What other risks are we missing with this memo?

In Chapter 4, there was a review of basic writing skills required to write an information security policy architecture. Those same skills are applied when communicating with the enterprise in implementing the documents from the information security policy architecture. A reminder of tips to achieve an effective writing style:

- Choose simple and straightforward words to state what is needed and required.
- Sentence structure needs to be "active"; also avoid phrases such as "there are" or "it is."
- Proofread or have someone else proofread carefully before dissemination. Do not distract your readers with poor spelling or grammar.

The memo or written document to announce information security policy architecture should contain the following clear and concise information while avoiding jargon:

- Heading
    To: Name and title
    From: Name and title
    Subject: Specific topic of the document
    Date: Date that it is being sent
- Summary
    The issue
    Why a decision is needed
    What key information is contained in the memo
    What course of action is recommended
- Background
    Brief, essential points
    How this issue has evolved or become a concern
- Body
    Business requirements and key issues
    No more than four points including risk of nonimplementation and
        noncompliance
    Position of the policy document
    Where to go for answers to questions

One last check before sending the mass communication should include answering "yes" to each of the following questions:

- Is this the best, most appropriate method to get information security policy architecture information to the intended staff?
- Have you clearly identified the intended staff and the appropriate distribution list to use to reach the staff?
- Is the message relevant to the information security policy architecture and the enterprise's core missions?
- Is contact information present, in case there is a question, comment, or complaint about the message?
- Have you included only plain text in the message body (and no attachments), in case there is a nonstandard mail application in the environment?

8.4.3   Employee Handbook

The employee handbook is normally one of the items that a new staff member receives on his or her first day and it gets placed on a book shelf. For the most part, it is a static document until there is a major change within the organization, such as an enterprise acquisition or divestiture. An information security policy architecture cannot reside within an employee handbook because it is a living architecture document and it changes depending upon the enterprise growth. Within the employee handbook, the information security policy architecture should be mentioned with the mission and objectives of the information security program and policy architecture, the location of specific documents, and a generic contact, such as a general e-mail box or position title. The information security staff should be part of the new hire orientation and show the new staff where the information security policy architecture is located, who to contact on issues, and what business uses for the enterprise assets are.

8.4.4   Intranet

The information security Web site, like the employee handbook, can become static if not maintained properly. Although the information security policy architecture may only change when there is a change in the enterprise or business requirements, the information security Intranet site should be a place to keep all staff up to date with information on protecting the assets of the enterprise, with announcements of information security projects, tips, and tricks for the home networking environment, and for getting to know the information security team. The information security Intranet site needs to be dynamic and updated regularly. The information security team cannot keep static information on a Web site and think that staff will not get complacent about information security. Because the information security policy architecture is a living architecture document, it changes depending upon the enterprise growth and the enterprise need to be updated on potential risks and threats to the enterprise assets.

8.4.5 Informal Training

Traditional classroom training is declining as a result of increased costs and e-learning's increasing popularity. The information security team needs to look at the staff we are trying to serve for awareness training and design the best method for access. The information security team needs to develop flexible and responsive sessions for the enterprise environment. Informal training needs to be relevant and immediate, possibly using the current work environment. Informal training needs to be short and valuable, so staff can be involved without taking time away from enterprise projects.

One of the most common informal training methods is e-communities. E-communities comprise frequently asked questions, message boards with moderators, Web sites, and chat rooms. Many enterprises know about these options for projects but have not extended them to the information security awareness environment. Superusers and subject matter experts assist in keeping the material responsive, relevant, and current.

Another method of promotion of the e-learning is "brown bag" lunches or "meet the experts." These sessions are information sharing and displaying of critical awareness that staff need to protect the enterprise assets. "Meet the experts" will permit staff to ask questions on how information security pertains to their work environment or to ask for better explanation of the existing information security policy architecture. The "brown bag" lunches and "meet the expert" sessions will also allow the information security team to mentor staff in becoming more familiar with the information security team and becoming more comfortable with the information security policy architecture.

8.4.6 Death by PowerPoint

We have seen PowerPoint presentations during which the presenter reads the slides and we also have seen PowerPoint presentations that contain so many slides and graphics that the message gets lost. Earlier in this chapter, there were guides given to know your audience and in using these principles PowerPoint presentations can be developed to enhance training. As we develop a PowerPoint presentation, we need to consider the size of the room for the presentation and the size of the audience. Many people like to sit in the back of the room and you need to consider whether your voice is loud enough to carry or audio equipment if required. We also need to consider what goes into the PowerPoint presentation. When creating a PowerPoint presentation, the following questions should be considered.

- What is my audience and where is this being presented?
- What is the objective of the presentation and why do I need to present these objectives?
- What business requirements relate to the presentation objectives?
- When during the day is the presentation being given, because depending on the time of day, the delivery may have to be modified?
- How can we integrate confidentiality, integrity, availability, liability, privacy, and due diligence within the presentation?

As the presentation is put into electronic form, you need to consider how it will look and work in printed form. Things to consider for easily read presentations in written form as are follows:

1. No more than six lines per slide
2. No more than six word per line
3. No major distractions on the slides
4. High level, no details
5. Straight to the point

Using this format will permit the presenter to talk to the audience using examples and permit the audience to see the slide no matter the size of the presentation room. By keeping the slide at a high level, the same presentation slides can be used for different audiences by providing more or less detail in the examples. Using many moving graphics, movie clips, or sounds can distract the audience from hearing what the presenter is saying or stray the presentation to other topics.

PowerPoint is just another form of communication and knowing the audience and the business requirements and understanding the subject matter will increase the efficiency and effectiveness of the PowerPoint slides.

8.4.7   No Such Thing As a Stupid Question

"What gives you the right to tell me how to do my job?" "What is intellectual property?" "What do you mean by confidentiality?" "What do you mean by secure?" Are you laughing? Or do you think these are valid questions that have to be answered? If you are in a hurry to answer these questions or you even ignore these questions, you are limiting how much you want the enterprise staff to understand and be comfortable with the information security policy architecture. If one staff member has these questions, there is a high probably that others will have the same questions in mind. You need to realize that staff need to understand why they must comply and with what they have to comply. If you ignore these types of questions, are you implying that you are too good to answer the questions or the staff is so stupid you should ignore their questions? Go back and remember your first day in the information security field, you were the novice and possibly asked these same questions. Staff need to understand the who, what, where, when, why, and how. The more the information security team can make the staff understand how information security fits into their business requirements, the more easily and readily the information security policy architecture will be accepted into the enterprise.

8.5 Attention Spans

When we are young, our attention spans are not very long, maybe 20–30 minutes. As we go through school, our attention spans grow to match class times. When we start our careers and grow older, our attention spans change depending on the situation in which we find ourselves. We need to use a variety of communication techniques to keep everyone engaged in the communication session.

- Focus the discussion on the information required and then relate it to business.
- Use a variety of questioning techniques to keep the attendees involved:
    Use open-ended questions to expand the discussion. Use closed-ended questions to prompt for specifics.
    Use redirection where a question is framed in such a way to elicit multiple responses.
    Use probing to get the attendees to validate that they understand how to apply the information security policy architecture document content in their working environment.
- Encourage dialogue through eye contact and expression. Restate the question or comment to show that you understand what you are hearing.
- To end the session, summarize the key points and get agreement on the next steps and where to go for assistance and show appreciation for the audience effort.
- Use reality, that is, references to specific and concrete events that relate to the business requirements for the implementation of the specific information security policy architecture document.
- Use novelty facts, which are startling facts or unusual combinations of events that relate to the business requirements for the implementation of the specific information security policy architecture document.
- Use humor sometimes, such as playful remarks or exaggerated images. Be careful with humor because it may also present itself as a demeaning or sexual comment to an audience member.

8.6 Constructive Feedback (AKA Do Not Take It Personally)

"I don't know how to make them listen; they are constantly installing unauthorized software; I don't know why this is happening and what to do." This information security person is dealing with one of the most important yet trickiest and most difficult tasks when providing communication to the enterprise. As an information security manager, how would you respond? Effective feedback is absolutely essential to the information security team's effectiveness; people must know where they are and where to go next in terms of expectations and goals. The information security team needs to remember to not take criticism, misunderstanding, and noncompliance with the information security policy architecture personally. Feedback taps into the need to improve, to compete, to be accurate; people want to be competent. If feedback is given properly, feedback will motivate people to improve. There are many reasons people are hesitant to give feedback, including

- Fear of causing embarrassment
- Fear of a reaction, a staff member becoming defensive
- Fear that feedback is based on opinion and not on concrete information

As with all communications, when giving and receiving constructive feedback, we need to observe some key items:

- Use open-ended and closed-ended questions appropriately to talk about alternatives and understand the feedback
- Use eye contact, encouraging gestures, and other nonverbal communication skills, such as active listening
- Continue constructive relationships with staff, peers, and managers
- Ensure that the feedback is summarized
- Ensure that you lead by example

We need to realize how critical feedback can be to overcoming our difficulties; feedback can be rewarding but it requires skill, understanding, courage, and respect for yourself and the information security team. Without feedback, we continue to send the information security team out to bake a cake without a recipe.

Constructive and effective feedback will

- Be descriptive (not evaluative) by providing specific examples and details about a situation.
- Describe your own reactions or feelings with objective consequences that might occur. Focusing on the action (behavior) and not the individual information security team member, so the team member can change the action.

- Suggest more alternatives or be prepared to discuss alternatives.
- Share information, as giving advice does not allow the information security team member to make his or her own decision.

When we receive feedback on a communication, security policy architecture or another topic, we should

- Try not to be defensive or overreact
- Check on possible misunderstanding by restating what you understood was said or asking for clarification
- Gather information from other sources or other information security team members

Communicating with the enterprise is the most important piece of an information security policy architecture. Knowing the culture and style of the enterprise will allow the security policy team to communicate more easily with the enterprise, keep the misinterpretation to a minimum, and keep the constructive feedback from being personalized.

Chapter 9

Security Monitoring and Metrics

It has been implied throughout this book that a security policy architecture document should not be written unless it applies to protecting an enterprise asset and unless executive management is willing to enforce it. Another thing to remember is as a security policy architecture document is written, how is it going to be monitored and enforced? Therefore, what specific items or activities can be monitored that are documented within security policy architecture document. The details from the security policy architecture documents are what the enterprise can use to develop and document security metrics or the return on security investments (see Figure 23).

A metric is defined as the quantitative standard of measurement that coincides with a specific method, procedure, or analysis, or it can be a set of related measures that facilitates the quantification of security characteristics. Security metrics can be tracked for costs and benefits. The security metrics can answer questions such as:

- What is expected from the technology and security teams?
- How much is my security team costing the enterprise?
- How much is being spent on asset protection relative to costs and time? (This will enable better decisions for risk and security technologies.)
- How protected are the enterprise assets? Is management enabled to make better risk decisions on enterprise assets?
- What security metric information should be presented to assist the business?

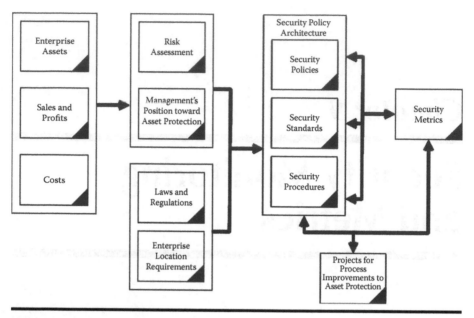

Figure 23 Feeding Metrics.

9.1 Monitoring for Enforcement

The policy architecture enforcement can be a problem, especially if a physical security policy states there is no piggybacking for building entrance. Unless the enterprise has mantraps for building entrance, how is the enterprise going to enforce that physical policy statement unless there is a security guard who watches everyone and every building entrance. Or if there is a logical policy statement that nonenterprise devices cannot connect to the enterprise network, who will enforce this? Although scripts for every network switch and router in the enterprise can be written and implemented, is it practical for the enterprise to perform this type of monitoring? There is the option of network access control and unless the baseline traffic has been defined, there may be many false positives reported. Enforcement is sometimes the hardest part of the security policy architecture. Security policy architecture monitoring cannot be done as a project. It must be done as an ongoing business process. The enforcement needs to be measurable and repeatable.

As policy architecture documents are being written, the writer needs to consider enforcement of the document. How is compliance going to be monitored? How is the reporting of a violation going to be performed? Who is going to be performing the enforcement? A security professional reports the facts and does not put any emotions into what is being reported or done by a user. In a rare incident, the security professional may have to report an executive for a policy violation. The security professional must have the supported documentation to formally report the incident. This comes through routine monitoring and metrics. For policy architecture documents that cannot be automatically monitored, such as logical security, routine walk-throughs need to be conducted and regular user awareness training needs to be conducted. The more the enterprise builds security into the culture the easier anomalies will stand out for irregular policy monitoring. In an earlier chapter various forms of user awareness training were discussed. As walk-throughs are performed for policy architecture compliance, the security professional needs to document the following items:

1. Date of the review
2. Name of the reviewer
3. Enterprise location of the review, such as which facility, department, or building area
4. Topic of the review
5. Name of staff talked to
6. Findings and areas of risk

Many executives know that the enterprise cannot be managed if there is nothing against which to measure. Before regular monitoring takes place, baselines for the security policy architecture compliance need to be documented.

In many countries, privacy laws require enterprises to disclose what is being monitored and logged with regard to employee activities. The security team needs to document business reasons for monitoring employee activities. Basic business reasons for monitoring various business areas are as follows:

■ Business transactions or to ensure processes are being followed
■ Regulatory compliance
■ Enterprise systems functioning effectively and preventing unauthorized access
■ Training and service standards
■ Preventing criminal activity

An enterprise needs to remember that assets are being monitored and the monitoring cannot invade an employee's privacy. Enterprises need to define monitoring with specific limitations, such as:

■ Track data, rather than communication contents, unless filtering for the loss of intellectual property
■ Use periodic checks, rather than continuous monitoring, such as system configurations
■ Target enterprise areas that are high risk

The enterprise needs to define monitoring. For example, monitoring can be defined as communication interceptions, validation of systems and their configurations, or the logging, recording, reviewing, and auditing of data. A simple monitoring document can comprise a few statements, such as:

> There are legal, privacy, and regulatory requirements and conditions with which the enterprise must comply. There is also a business requirement for monitoring because the enterprise must protect all of its assets. The XXX department may monitor and record communications to establish existence of facts for regulatory and legal practices, to prevent and detect crime, to detect and investigate unauthorized use and access to enterprise systems, and to secure the use of all enterprise assets. Monitoring will be conducted and documented with business and legal requirements. Note that monitoring and logging without authority may be a criminal offence, so such activities must be agreed to by the management team.

After enterprise monitoring statements have been defined to assist with security policy architect enforcement, defining baselines and metrics is the next step.

9.2 Baselines

A baseline is a standard by which things are measured or compared. Establishing a security baseline will give enterprises benchmarking for the progress of asset protection. Before the baseline can commence, the following types of questions must be answered.

- What specific information/data will be collected and why?
- What are the business drivers/requirements for the collected information/data?
- When and how will that information/data be collected?
- Who will be responsible for the collection and disbursement of the information/data collected?
- What is the team attempting to show with the collected information/data?
- Who will receive the information/data collected and in what format will it be presented?
- Can the team ensure the presentation is simple and clear?
- Whether a third-party application is going to gather the data or a home-grown script basic application, requirements needs to be established for the gathering and processing of the baseline.

A sample listing of the metrics that can be collected can be seen in Table 13.

Table 13 Sample Baseline Metrics

Topic	Metric
Results	Viruses stopped
Results	Spam messages filtered
Results	System patches implemented
Results	New accounts created per operating system/application/remote access
Results	Accounts removed per operating system/application/remote access
Results	Accounts disabled per operating system/application/remote access
Results	Number of Internet/internal probes logged
Results	Number of Internet/internal port scans
Results	Summary of firewall rule usage
Results	E-mail messages processed
Results	Account and passwords reset per operating system/application
Results	Certifications maintained by staff
Results	Number of unauthorized wireless access points
Results	Number of new network devices (workstations, routers, switches, firewalls)
Results	Number of retired network devices (workstations, routers, switches, firewalls)
Results	Number of new wireless devices (cell phones, BlackBerrys, personal digital assistants)
Results	Number of retired wireless devices (cell phones, BlackBerrys, personal digital assistants)
Results	Top 10 hosts for source/destination port scanning, network probing, e-mail
Results	Number of administrative/root accesses to operating systems/applications
Costs	Estimated costs of a virus infection per hour of downtime, including recovery time
Costs	Estimated costs of a breach of customer information, including recovery time

Table 13 (continued)   Sample Baseline Metrics

Topic	Metric
Costs	Estimated costs of an internal network breach, including recovery time
Costs	Estimated costs of breach of staff personal information, including recovery time
Costs	Estimated cost per person for security administration, including recovery time
Costs	Estimated cost of vulnerability exposure being compromised, including recovery time
Costs	Estimated cost per operating system and application for each patch for security vulnerabilities
Costs	Estimated costs to perform compliance and security controls (monitoring and auditing)
Quality	Number of security incidents
Quality	Number of remediated security vulnerabilities
Quality	Number of compliance controls
Quality	Number of control deficiencies
Quality	Number of privacy incidents
Quality	Total number of employees, contractors, consultants, and partners
Quality	Number of new hire/termination/transferred employees, contractors, consultants, and partners
Quality	Number of staff (employees, contractors, consultants, partners) who have attended security awareness training
Quality	Number of visitors and vendors onsite

9.3   Routine Metrics

Once the baseline is established, regular metric processes needs to be performed. The security team needs to establish specific procedures or work instruction on how the information and data will be collected and where it will be distributed on what specific schedule. This will allow management to see standard progress in asset protection. The regular metrics will give the security the foundation for justifying additional security software and additional staff for the security program. The regular metrics also can be used when presenting user awareness training. Metrics can improve accountability through collection, analysis, and reporting of relevant performance-related data. The procedures should be a step-by-step document on how and where the scripts or applications are executed. The security metrics program can be set up on a repeatable cycle.

1. Define metrics and thresholds
2. Document the source from which the metrics are gathered and determine how accurate the data is
3. Collect and transform the data using automated or manual tools
4. Report on the results and ensure the results can be duplicated with the data
5. As the environment or situations change, review and revise what metrics are being monitored and reported on

See Appendix V for a sample security monitoring work instruction and see Table 14 for a sample security monitoring schedule.

Table 14   Sample Monitoring Schedule

Security Monitoring Task	Frequency	Time Period	Duration
Server, domain, and NT security issues	Alert/D/W/M		
Firewall and IDs log	Daily/Alert		
Review network device logs for security violations by accounts	Daily/Alert		
Review network device logs for security violations by superuser accounts	Daily/Alert		
SQL server log	Daily/Alert		
Virus activity	Daily/Alert		
Attend Change Management meetings	Weekly	1, 2, 3, 4 W	M
Attend IT department staff meetings to monitor critical project status reports and decisions, provide control guidance, etc.	Weekly	1, 2, 3, 4 W	M
Exchange database—authorized user review	Weekly	1, 2, 3, 4 Q	M

Table 14 (continued)   Sample Monitoring Schedule

Security Monitoring Task	Frequency	Time Period	Duration
Exchange e-mail security issues	Weekly	1, 2, 3, 4 W	M
MS Security Configuration Tool/ SecEdit	Weekly	1, 2, 3, 4 Q	M
Oracle database	Weekly	1, 2, 3, 4 W	M
Oracle server log	Weekly	1, 2, 3, 4 W	M
SQL server database	Weekly	1, 2, 3, 4 Q	M
Monitor third-party security compliance for access to information assets	Monthly	1, 2, 3, 4 Q	M
Provide Information Security Status Reports to the management	Monthly	1, 2, 3, 4, Q	M
Review administrative password changes for network and application accounts	Monthly	1, 2, 3, 4 Q	M
Review inactive account activity for network and application accounts	Monthly	1, 2, 3, 4 Q	M
Internally run external network audit/security analysis tools— NMAP, NESSUS	Quarterly	1, 2, 3, 4 Q	M
Maintain and distribute Employee Emergency Contact Cards	Quarterly	1, 2, 3, 4, Q	L
Provide summary security status reports about Information Security program for reporting to the executive team	Quarterly	1, 2, 3, 4 Q	M
Review physical security	Quarterly	1, 2, 3, 4 Q	L
Review to ensure user account password changes—systems and applications	Quarterly	1, 2, 3, 4 Q	M
Run DBMS security analysis tools	Quarterly	1, 2, 3, 4 Q	M

Table 14 (continued)   Sample Monitoring Schedule

Security Monitoring Task	Frequency	Time Period	Duration
User group privileges for privileged groups and IT-owned groups—final tools to be determined	Quarterly	1, 2, 3, 4 Q	M
Validate contractor and remote user access to network	Quarterly	1, 2, 3, 4 Q	M
Collect and review disaster recovery test records and report to management	Semi-annually	1st and 3rd Q	M
Data classification processes	Semi-annually	1st and 3rd Q	M
Maintain, monitor, and test the business continuity planning	Semi-annually	2nd Q and 4th Q	H
Maintain, monitor and test the disaster recovery planning	Semi-annually	2nd Q and 4th Q	H
Monitor IT disaster recovery testing and support IT Audit's review of IT disaster recovery plans	Semi-annually	1st and 3rd Q	M
Annual internal information security awareness	Annually	3rd Q	L
Maintain information security templates, guidelines (e.g., data/information security)	Annually	2nd Q	M
Maintain the corporate information security policy architecture	Annually	2nd Q	M
Password strength testing	Annually	2nd Q	M
Review business unit business continuity plans	Annually	3rd Q	L
Review business unit disaster recovery plans	Annually	3rd Q	L

Table 14 (continued)   Sample Monitoring Schedule

Security Monitoring Task	Frequency	Time Period	Duration
Review the IT and security job functions/descriptions and match to production access for separation of duties test	Annually	End 1st Q	M
Scrub network, application, e-mail, voicemail, and wireless account information	Annually	End 2nd Q	H
Support the coordination of the annual network security/risk/ vulnerability review	Annually	2nd–3rd Q	H
Maintain and coordinate network incident response	On-going	As needed	M
Monitor the implementation of system patches, configuration management	On-going	1, 2, 3, 4 Q	M
Monitor compliance with the enterprise information security policies and procedures among employees, contractors, alliances, and other third parties, and refer problems to appropriate department managers or administrators	On-going	1, 2, 3, 4 Q	M
Audit logs (system, application, security, registry)	Troubleshoot	As needed	
Coordinate incident response investigations	Troubleshoot	As needed	M
Internet gateway	Troubleshoot	As needed	
VPN access	Troubleshoot	As needed	
Architecting network design changes	Ad hoc	As needed	M
Monitor IT measurements "audit certifications" of work completed by areas: Database Management, Help Desk, Network, Operations, Telecommunications	Ad hoc	As needed	M

Table 14 (continued)   Sample Monitoring Schedule

Security Monitoring Task	Frequency	Time Period	Duration
Provide Information Security Training to new employee classes	Ad hoc	As needed	M
Review the security features of new computing systems to ensure that they meet the security policy requirements	Ad hoc	As needed	M

Notes:

- All * items are currently reported on a monthly basis to IT Management
- Blank items are not being done and are possible gap items
- Time Period: D, W, M, A = Daily, Weekly, Monthly, and/or Annually
- Reviewed by: NA = Not Applicable. These items do not require any further review

Duration:

- L (Low) = A few hours per occurrence (unless the frequency is high then it is considered a Medium duration)
- M (Medium) = Up to one week total commitment
- H (High)—Anything greater than one week

9.4   Reporting

Metrics reporting can be classified as operational and business metrics, because metrics serve different audiences. Operational reporting can include the following:

- Number of security policy violations by risk
- Number of devices deviating from enterprise security configuration standards
- Number of abandoned accounts
- Number of different types of attacks against the enterprise from external sources
- Number of viruses, worms, and Trojans that were blocked

Business reporting includes items such as the following:

- Amount of downtime and cost caused by misconfigurations or wrongful implementations
- Dollars overspent or underspent in security projects
- List of outstanding or accepted risks

The enterprise culture will determine if the metric reporting will be done through spreadsheets, power point presentations, or executive dashboards. The key to all the presentations of data is that they are in summary form and relevant to the objective of the presentation. Spreadsheets and PowerPoints need planning for their presentation. Many times, it is just a process of gathering the summary information from multiple points and putting them into a centralized location. By contrast, dashboards can be used for up-to-date ad hoc reviewing of metric reporting. Dashboards can be used by management to get a quick view of the security metrics within the organization.

Most metric reporting is a combination of operational and business and is presented in various forms, depending on the audience. The security team needs to define the methods for reporting and what information will go into each type of presentation when the security metrics program is being developed.

Chapter 10

Continuing to Mold Your Style Through Experience

Every organization has good things about the environment, and there are always issues. The good things include a dedicated staff, enough staff, adequate budget, adequate tools, and support from the management team. All of these good items also can fall on the issue side of not enough staff, no budget, no tools, and sometimes little support from the management team. As a security professional, you continue to grow as a leader through the development of an effective policy architecture. This last chapter reveals tips to building longevity into the security policy architecture and finding assistance outside the enterprise environment. These techniques can be applied in any sized organization. Security professionals adapt to their situation and know there is no silver bullet to developing and implementing a security policy architecture. There are good times and rough times for the security professional, and sometimes, the security professional needs to take advantage of the small wins and personal growth over being the security professional to continually get recognized or the security professional who is constantly written up in articles.

10.1 Building for Longevity

Although security is normally stated as a process, the security policy architecture is providing a service to protect the enterprise assets. The security team needs to look at the security policy architecture life cycle servicing the enterprise, as seen in Figure 24.

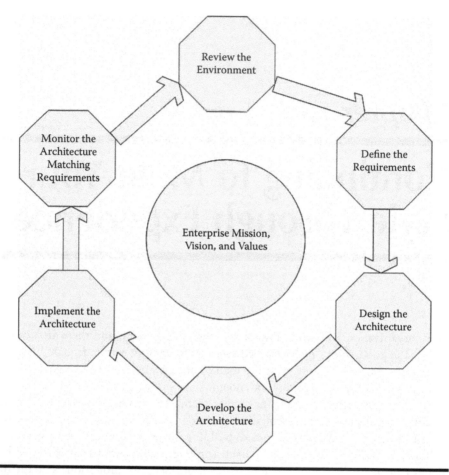

Figure 24 Policy Service Process.

The development or review of the security policy architecture is similar to the system development life cycle for software development. Software will always have an end-of-life. The security policy architecture continues to evolve as the enterprise grows and expands.

A leader accepts challenges by using his or her vision and a mission to move something into the future. As a security professional, the enterprise mission and vision assists in the development of the appropriate security policy architecture.

10.2 Basic Leadership

At times, most organizations are tangled bureaucracies with many competing goals. Key decisions are based on factors that are not strictly objective and analytical. Important actions are taken that cannot be explained by the workings of the formal organization. What does one do when it appears as if someone is sabotaging security efforts? What does one do when the formal organization does not know how to get done what needs to be done to protect the enterprise assets? Effective security professionals find a way to get things done—to help smooth the path, to resolve conflicts, to gain support, to build sound working relationships, to move forward—and minimize risk in doing so—through leadership.

Throughout this book and other sources, you have learned that the security professional needs to be a leader when working through the challenge of protecting enterprise assets. Howard Gardner stated, "A leader is an individual who significantly affects the thoughts, feelings, and/or behaviors of a significant number of individuals." A security policy architecture does that through the leader who develops, implements, communicates, and maintains that architecture. A good leader uses the formal and informal organizational structure for gaining support of the security policy architecture. The formal organizational structure is for the approvals and support for building the strength of the security policy architecture. The informal organization structure is to determine where roadblocks may exist for the development and implementation of the security policy architecture. The informal organization structure assists in dealing with potential politics for the implementation of the security policy architecture.

Leaders build a set of resources that can assist with the following types of questions:

- Who can give good advice on moving the security policy architecture forward?
- Who can act as a sounding board for ideas in building, promoting, and implementing the security policy architecture?
- What are the enterprise business areas that I do not fully understand and who can assist me in learning?
- Who else within the enterprise understands the business risk?
- Which business units have the most to lose should an enterprise asset be compromised?
- Who can assist in the marketing of the security policy architecture?
- Who do I respect within the enterprise and who has resistance to the security policy architecture?

Leaders huddle with their resources. Huddling is brief, intimate, work-oriented conversations among two to three people. The huddling can happen inside or outside the office and before, during, or after standard business hours. Huddling is spontaneous, so real reactions can be obtained.

Leaders build their personal credibility through integrity, confidentiality, and key characteristics, including:

- Being a central resource when it comes to security, the go to person or the consultant to the enterprise
- Being able to adapt to different and unexpected situations and not panic or turn away
- Having a set of resources to call upon when information is not readily available
- Being able to say, "I do not know, but I will get back to you," then following up with the requested information

Leaders build their influence through the following types of activities:

- Building a base of support. Discovering which people who align with the same goals and personal characteristics.
- Associating with influential people. Some people in the enterprise have influence in getting things accomplished throughout the enterprise, even if they do not necessarily have the upper management title.
- Looking and acting the part. Many people judge on appearance and communication. Many enterprise environments have the casual dress code, which makes looking and acting the part a more important task.
- Taking on a support, rather than a leading, role. It is nice when someone is in the spotlight for successfully accomplishing something. It is also nice to have someone take the information given to them and expand and promote, taking on the supportive role.

A leader uses good negotiation skills to accomplishing the development and implementation of the security policy architecture. Don Corleone, of Mario Puzo's *Godfather* saga, said, "Never get angry. Never make a threat. Reason with people." A security professional does not need to take the reasoning with people as far as Don Corleone did, yet they do need to understand the business requirements and negotiate how much the risk can be limited for enterprise assets. Crucial elements of any negotiation are time, influence, and information. As a security professional, the information for negotiation is a strong suit. Many times, the security team does not have the necessary time to develop and implement everything that is needed. The security professional takes as much time as it is reasonable to develop and implement a security policy architecture.

When a security professional is negotiating how detailed the security policy architecture will be or how secured the secure configuration will be, the security professional should not take the tactic of succeeding at all costs. The succeeding or winning at all costs can leave the enterprise with a negative impression of security. The security professional needs to use mutual satisfaction in limiting the risk to the enterprise assets through a win–win situation. The security professional negotiates process topics and configurations to meet the needs of the enterprise while building trust with the enterprise and limiting the risk to the enterprise assets. For example, do not judge a business unit for the ultimate requirement of needing to meet deadlines, just document the facts and risks without personal opinion. This does not imply compromise; it does imply collaboration in defining and understanding the risks to the enterprise assets. Look for ideas and methods that will implement the security policy architecture correctly the first time.

10.3   Find a Mentor

A mentor describes a teacher in a teacher–student relationship. In fact, Mentor is the name of the person to whom Odysseus entrusted the care of his son, Telemachus, when he went on his wanderings, which is now called an odyssey. Mentor was Odysseus' wise and trusted counselor as well as a tutor to Telemachus. Mentors are wise, knowledgeable, and trusted counselors for a mentee. A mentee is a person receiving the advice and support from the mentor. A mentor's knowledge, experience, encouragement, and skills offer the growing leader guidance, advice, and small amounts of training. A mentor can direct a mentee toward the right direction to meet the mentee's potential and goal. A mentor cannot and should not attempt to force changes against the will of the mentee.

A security professional should have a mentor and a mentee because the security professional needed assistance in gaining his or her skill level, and as he or she grows in leadership that information can be passed on to others who are new in the security profession. When a security professional is looking for a mentor, he or she should look for someone with the following types of knowledge or skills:

- The person should have a wealth of experience on which guidance can be given based on past experience, not reminiscence. This needs to be handled sensitively based on the security mentor's background.
- The person should have similar personal characteristics that you believe in, live by, or want to grow into.
- The person should have respect of his or her peers and the industry.
- The person should have integrity in his or her work and the work of others.
- The person should be able to create a positive and open environment for communication in developing relationships. It is important to not treat the mentee as incompetent, and it is important to create a genuine interest in the mentee role.
- The person should not micromanage or be seen as "checking up" on the mentee. This means mutually agreed-upon contact times.
- The person should be able to brainstorm in assisting the mentee to identify issues and potential solutions. Helping the mentee find the root cause is more important than just looking at the issue symptoms.

- The person should be able to lead the mentee through the problem-solving process using open- and closed-ended questions, letting the mentee come to solution by empowering him or her to use his or her own experiences.
- The person should offer constructive criticism in a supportive way, without making things personal.
- The person should be able to show strengths and weaknesses with the mentee and how they work in different situations.
- The person should be able to say "I do not know" and then refer the mentee to others.
- The person should also get feedback from the mentee. Mentoring is giving and receiving, so the mentor can also continue to develop his or her own skills.

A mentor looking for a mentee should look for the following in the person being guided:

- The person should be a self-motivator
- The person should have confidence in him or herself or need just a little push
- The person should have good problem-solving skills
- The person should be able to work with little direction
- The person should have some set of resources, however small, of his or her own

Whether you are the mentor or mentee, the experience will improve confidence, leadership, communication, and workplace skills. If you are looking for a mentor, try the local or regional security, risk, and audit organizations for people who have skills sets and knowledge that you would like to acquire through experience. If you are looking to become a mentor, try the local or regional security, risk, and audit organization to see where you can volunteer and use your experience to help others grow in their experiences.

10.4   Find Opportunities to Expand Experience

Whether you are in a small, medium, or large business, as a security policy architecture is developed and implemented, questions will come up and it is possible that outside advice will be needed. Using the local and regional security, audit, and risk organizations as reference points or joining in their activities assists in expanding your experiences and resources. Volunteering to be a trainer within or outside your enterprise will assist in bettering all communication skills. Volunteering in nonsecurity, nonaudit, and nonrisk events will broaden your resources and contacts when working on the enterprise security policy architecture. Attending local vendor presentations can provide opportunities for ideas on improving areas within the enterprise. List serves, user groups, and electronic versions of security magazines can provide options, ideas, and solutions to possible issues and projects within the enterprise.

The point here is, if there is a chance to work on a project, with a specific business unit, with a specific group, take the opportunity to grow your network to get a different perspective on security and how others perceive you, your work product, and the security policy architecture that you are developing, reviewing, or implementing.

10.5 Summary

Most enterprise executive management realize the need for a security policy architecture and believe in the requirement to protect the enterprise assets. And most executives give their support to the development of a security policy architecture. The challenge for the security professional is to ensure that building the security policy architecture remains a priority for the enterprise. The security policy architecture needs to be flexible, scalable, and manageable so that it fits into an everyday practice of the enterprise. Security professionals cannot build and implement a security policy architecture alone; security professionals need a team. This team can consist of people within the enterprise or outside acquaintances and mentors. And do not forget to include a few contrarians to ensure the security policy architecture is validated. Internally the team needs to set priorities and adjust as the business requirements change. The security professional should be able to write down the top priorities in a few paragraphs of less than 150 words. The priorities should advance the business and be simple. The security professional should then be able to address the priorities with action items. As Winston Churchill said, "Of all the talents bestowed upon men, none is so precious as the gift of oratory." Use the security policy architecture to inspire the enterprise to secure enterprise assets, not to provoke fear and anger, and provide strong security leadership by using all your resources and skills.

Appendix A

Department	Corporate
Owner	CSO
General Area	Assets
Topic	Information Assurance
Policy Number	PR00100
Effective Date	09/30/06
Last Review	05/01/07

1.0 Information Security Program Update Log

Date	Modifier	Section	Description of Update
06/30/06	Sandy Bacik	Whole document	Initial proposal and publication of the Information Security Program.

2.0 Information Security Program

2.1 *Mission*

The Information Security Program (ISP) and its policies, processes, and account-abilities establish accountabilities and provide reliable protection against threats including virus attacks, improper activity of employees, and accidental damage by authorized personnel. This extends to providing reliable information security and security awareness education to staff, guests, clients, and third parties within My Company (MYC). The ISP administrators will be thoughtful stewards in helping MYC protect all of its information assets through access control.

The ISP will accommodate all regulatory requirements and best business prac-tices with response to information security and is designed to assure a high degree of protection for the technology environment. This program establishes a baseline of policies, standards, and procedures that apply to all MYC-wide and Information Technology (IT) systems and services, both operational and administrative.

This program is intended to be distributed throughout MYC and therefore contains no information which could be classified as sensitive or business proprietary, or that would pose a threat to the security of the MYC information resources. Where necessary, organizations and titles are referenced rather than individual names.

The Corporate Security Officer (CSO) is responsible for the development, management, and maintenance of this program.

This document describes the vision of what we would like to have included in our ISP.

2.2 Scope

This program applies to all current and future MYC information technology resources for all organizations, regardless of business line association or information resource subsystem. Due to their inter-connectivity, inter-reliability, and inter-operability, MYC information resources include but are not limited to all computer hardware and software, printers, FAX machines, network routers, hubs, gateways, switches, controls, telecommunication system, cabling, and all operating systems applications, databases, and data stores. Additionally, this plan applies to all connections, modes, or methods of connection, access, or utilization of any and all MYC information resources.

Business Services has primary responsibility for physical security, and the ISP will help support and enhance the physical security requirements and needs of Business Services.

This plan applies to all persons who, in any way, connect to or make use of MYC information resources for any reason, including but not limited to MYC full- and part-time employees, MYC contract employees, business partners, vendors, and others.

2.3 Security philosophy

Information security is the management of information technology risk in pursuit of business objectives. Within our day-to-day function we may perform the following:

- Handle sensitive client information that we are expected to keep in confidence
- Handle information that we have legislative obligations to protect
- Rely on Information Systems for a significant part of our business processes

Prolonged failure of the business process can cause significant disruption and may affect long-standing relationships with clients and partners. An even more significant risk would be the unauthorized disclosure of information given in confidence. Information security will allow us to better understand the risks to our business and put in place strategies to mitigate the risks we feel are unacceptable. Therefore, an ISP needs to be a critical part of any business architecture.

Security is an important component of business as the lack of a properly implemented and up-to-date security policy can result in the loss of valuable information assets. The ISP will implement a program governed by the following ideas:

- Release or improper use of confidential information can be disastrous
- Access to MYC computing environment is given on a need-to-know basis
- Having access to data on the MYC network does not qualify one as being authorized to access that information
- Proactive identification of important assets, security threats, and how the threats could be realized will allow MYC to minimize the risks of those threats
- It is better to minimize the damage that could be inflicted by realizing a threat than to catch the perpetrator of the security breach
- Committing an act out of ignorance does not relieve responsibility for the action or the outcome

2.4 Updating the program

This plan will be reviewed and updated annually by the MYC Chief Information Officer (CIO). This plan will be reviewed on an ongoing basis by the CSO and MYC Information Security Committee, defined below, and will be subject to change at any time to ensure it is consistent with MYC's mission, business requirements, organization structure, applicable laws and regulations, or changes in technology. All revisions to the plan require the approval of the CIO. A revised, approved plan will be forwarded to the MYC Executive Team and Board annually.

3.0 Information Security Responsibilities

Information security is the responsibility of all persons who access MYC information systems. All persons who are granted access to MYC systems are responsible for being familiar with, understanding, and acting in accordance with this plan. No person shall, through intentional action or inaction, place MYC information resources in jeopardy. All persons are required to immediately report any known or suspected illegal, improper, or hazardous situation or violation of the information security program to the CSO.

3.1 Chief Executive Officer

The Chief Executive Officer (CEO) is ultimately responsible for ensuring that an effective information security program is established and carried out. This responsibility is delegated to the CIO.

3.2 CSO

The Corporate Security Officer is a management official, who is knowledgeable of both computing and information security methodologies and practices. The CSO is responsible for the following activities for the ISP and information security initiatives:

- Development
- Implementation
- Management
- Monitoring

3.3 MYC Management

MYC management, at all levels, is responsible for the implementation of all corporate policies, guidelines, standards, processes, and procedures including the ISP within its respective organizations.

3.4 Information Security Committee

Information security committee (ISC) is a group of staff and executives through which the information security program will be guided. This committee will consist of executive team members who will assist the ISP in following MYC's mission and goals. This committee will also consist of staff members across varied disciplines to ensure the ISP will fit functionally into the MYC environment and will not drastically impact trends and operational activities. The ISP does not represent the functions or duties of the SWAT or incident response teams within MYC. This committee may be presented the findings of incidents on a need to know basis.

3.4.1 Goals

- To develop, implement, maintain, and perform quality assurance for the ISP
- To offer proactive identification of security threats for the MYC environment
- To provide a fast, efficient, and knowledgeable response to the realization of a security threat

3.4.2 Lead

The lead and coordinator of the ISC will be the responsibility of the CSO. This lead will be responsible for the following tasks:

- Keeping minutes of the committee meetings
- Keeping record of the incidents within MYC
- Coordinating the publicizing of the information security program and activities to the MYC environment
- Coordinating activities for the ISC

3.4.3 Management Team Members or Delegate

The management team members of the ISC will advise the Information Security Program in ensuring that we are meeting the MYC goals and business needs within the whole organization.

The executive team members will include the following personnel:

- CIO
- Chief Financial Officer
- Senior Director Business Services
- Human Resources Officer
- Chief Counsel
- Executive VP Operations

3.4.4 Technical Staff Members or Delegate

The technical staff members of the ISC will recommend and help develop projects for ensuring that business needs are met while implementing a strong information security program. The technical staff members will include the following personnel:

- Infrastructure Specialist (2) to include a Server Specialist, Network Specialist, or Electronic Communications Specialist
- Help Desk/Desktop Support
- Applications Development personnel
- Client Community (2)—optional
- Technology Services Directors—optional
- CIO—optional

3.4.5 Guests

A guest to an ISC meeting is anyone besides a committee member or delegate who

- Would like to see what we do
- Is the focus of our meeting discussion

3.4.6 Meeting Times and Structure

The ISC staff members will meet on a monthly basis to see if any issues have been presented.

The complete ISP Committee (Management and Technical Staff Members) will meet on a quarterly basis for updates and changes in business directions of MYC and internal projects. This quarterly meeting will coincide with the monthly meeting of the ISC.

Should an incident arise, any ISC (Management or Technical Staff) member may call an emergency meeting.

This whole committee functions in an advisory capacity to ensure from a broad business perspective and from a technology perspective that the information security program is achieving the MYC mission and protecting enterprise assets.

4.0 System Security Plans and Security Controls

All systems must have security controls that reflect the true importance of the information processed on the system and/or MYC's investment included in the components of the system. A security plan should be prepared and submitted to the CSO for all MYC applications, and systems that have been identified as mission critical and mission essential. The CSO will work with system and data owners to define the sensitivity level of all information systems and technology. Assessments will be done for each system based on the sensitivity of the data processed or the importance of the system to mission accomplishment.

4.1 Governing Policies

There are several governing policies that directly influence the content of MYC's Information Security Program. This listing is by no means all-inclusive but does discuss some of the more basic direct influences.

4.1.1 Information Security and Responsibility Policy

This policy will govern what types of information will be protected within the MYC network environment and who will be responsible for keeping MYC information assets protected.

4.1.2   Electronic Communication Policy

MYC provides all authorized personnel with electronic communications systems ("Systems") to improve productivity and communication between individuals, divisions, regions, and headquarters. The Systems include, but are not limited to, e-mail, voicemail, cell phones, facsimile, laptops, palm pilots, Intranet, and Internet. The Systems also enable MYC to communicate with persons outside MYC, such as clients, partners, and other professional contacts.

The Systems, and all messages, information, conversations, or other data ("Data") created, transmitted, and stored on them, are the property of MYC. There is no right to expect privacy in the Data. MYC reserves, and will exercise as it deems necessary, the right to review, audit, intercept, access, and disclose the Data, including messages received, sent, or forwarded by the Internet. Notwithstanding MYC's right to retrieve and read the Data, such Data should be treated as confidential by other System users and accessed only by the sender(s) and the intended recipients.

4.1.3   Internet Acceptable Use Policy

Our Internet Service Provider has specific terms and conditions by which MYC must abide when using their service. MYC is not allowed to reproduce or transmit copyrighted or trademarked material without the permission of the owner, MYC is also not to transmit threatening, lewd, lascivious, indecent, or obscene material; or transmit material protected by trade secret; or make, create, solicit, or transmit any obscene or indecent material to or from any person under eighteen (18) years of age.

4.1.4   Personnel Guidelines

- Harassment
- Ethical business conduct
- Standards of employee conduct
- Protecting proprietary and confidential information

4.1.5   Risk Management

The Risk Management Department at MYC works to prevent losses affecting our staff, clients, and partners, as well as our business property and equipment. We also buy insurance to help reduce our exposure to loss. In addition to the administration of MYC's property and casualty insurance program, Risk Management provides safety and emergency preparedness training, workers compensation oversight, Safety Committee support, ergonomic evaluations, and assistance reporting and tracking insurance losses. They are also available to consult with divisions and regions regarding program development and community collaborations.

The Risk Management Department has primary responsibility of records retention policies for paper and electronic records, as well as business continuity and disaster recovery. The ISP will be in place to help support the Risk Management Department.

4.2 Supporting Documentation

When developing a security architecture, there are several topics that need to be included in the supporting documentation and be accepted by various levels of management. The following describe the varying levels of support documentation.

4.2.1 Board of Trustees (BOT)

Two critical aspects of the company's security policies will be to clearly define to the entire organization the corporate assets and appropriate uses of the company's information systems. The corporate assets must include tangible and intangible assets. In order to hold employees accountable for their actions and to have effective enforcement mechanisms, employees must clearly understand what behaviors and uses are acceptable or unacceptable. Without a clear definition of what inappropriate behavior is, employees cannot realistically be held accountable. The BOT should review and, possibly, reapprove the following policies approximately every 2–5 years:

- Client security
- Corporate assets and resources and expected level of privacy
- Software licensing
- Software piracy
- Corporate authority and responsibility
- Asset responsibility and criticality matrix
- Information/data classification
- Acceptable use of corporate assets and resources
- Record retention and control
- Equipment and transmission monitoring and auditing
- Disaster recovery and business resumption(corporate/high level)
- Public information and media
- Asset management
- Intellectual property
- Business ethics
- Third party/partner access

4.2.2   Executive Team (ET)

Once the corporate level security practices are in place, then the ET can take over to create a more detailed set of security architecture policies. These policies have to be supported by management and highly visible, but are the responsibility of Technical Services. The ET should review and, possibly, reapprove the following policies on an annual basis:

- Group, account, and password management
- Access control and authorization for all company assets
- Computing resource and network security
- Remote access
- Anti-virus
- Change management
- Media and material disposal
- Incident response/handling
- TCP/IP and other protocols (protocols permitted in-/out-bound from network)
- Physical access (badges/keys/combinations, building(s), floor(s), data center, data closets)

4.2.3   Technology Services

These documents will expand as new technologies and software are implemented within the company's environment. This phase will take the longest to develop and implement, due to the individual department responsibilities. The following is an initial list of security procedures and best and standard practices that would apply to each type of operating system and device defined by the company assets. These should be reviewed on an annual basis.

- Account and password management, protection, reset, and change on all devices
    Routers/switches
    PBX
    Wireless devices (access points, PDAs)
    Windows servers
    Firewall(s)
- Account addition, change, deletion, and reset procedures
    Routers/switches
    PBX
    Wireless devices (access points, PDAs)
    Windows servers
    Firewall(s)

Group addition, change, and delete procedures
PBX
Servers
Firewall(s)
■ Share, data set, device, file and directory permission addition, change, and delete procedures
Servers
Workstations
■ Administrative account security and access control procedures for all devices
Routers/switches
PBX
Wireless devices (access points, PDAs)
Servers
Firewall(s)
Workstations
■ Operating system security guideline or standard practice or best practice
Routers/switches
PBX
Wireless devices (access points, PDAs)
Servers
Firewall(s)
Workstations
■ Disaster recovery for department
■ Incident handling
■ Information and media disposal
■ Remote access security
CarbonCopy
Remote access server
VPN Access
Terminal server
■ Individual application security
Remote control
E-mail
Anti-virus
Database
Remote access
Personal firewall
Application/document versioning
■ Operating system audit procedures
Routers/switches
PBX

    Wireless devices (access points, PDAs)
    Servers
    Firewall(s)
    Communication lines (type—analog, digital, frame relay, T1, DS3)
    Workstations

■ Operating system monitoring/logging and log review procedures
    Routers/switches
    PBX
    Wireless devices (access points, PDAs)
    Servers
    Firewall(s)
    Communication lines (type—analog, digital, frame relay, T1, DS3)
    Workstations

■ Operating system monitoring procedures
    Routers/switches
    PBX
    Wireless devices (access points, PDAs)
    Servers
    Firewall(s)
    Communication lines (type—analog, digital, frame relay, T1, DS3, MPLS)
    Workstations

■ Access control procedures—add, modify, delete, archive
    Accounts for all operating systems
    Groups for all operating systems
    Shares/directories/data sets for all operating systems
    Groups for all operating systems

■ Application/service requests

■ Data center operational procedures
    Access to data center
    Server (new/remove)
    Backup/restore
    Incident response (network, fire, water, earthquake)
    Disaster recovery
    Alarm responses (fire, humidity, temperature)

5.0 Security Reviews

At this time, it is unknown what the review process and schedule will be for application and systems.

5.1 Policies, Standards, Procedures, and Practices

The ISP policies, standards, procedures, and practices will be reviewed on an annual basis. The ISP policies, standards, procedures, and practices can be modified by the ISC at any time at the request or with the consent of the CSO.

5.2 Risk Management

All system owners will perform periodic risk assessments on existing systems and on all new systems prior to implementation at MYC. Risk assessments must document known risks and their respective impacts on the system. Risk assessment categories are defined in the section below. Risks should be identified as acceptable or unacceptable, and mitigation measures should be documented for all unacceptable risks. The risk assessments must factor in the sensitivity, criticality, and value of the systems as well as their impact on other systems.

5.3 Risk Assessment

The purpose of a risk assessment is to ensure that appropriate, cost-effective safeguards are incorporated into new and existing systems. The object of the risk analysis is to provide a measure of the relative vulnerabilities and threats to applications or information resources so that security resources can be effectively distributed to minimize the potential for future loss. Risk analysis may vary in form, from an informal, documented review to a formal, fully quantified risk analysis for a large single or multiplatform system. A risk analysis will be performed

- Prior to the approval of design specifications for new systems
- Whenever a significant change occurs to the system
- At least every two years

Some of the topics that should be included in a risk assessment are as follows

- Physical security
    To be performed by Risk Management
- Security management practices
    Security policies, standards, guidelines, and procedures, for example, asset ownership, corporate assets, acceptable use, remote access, third parties, privacy, configurations, due diligence, anti-virus, record retention, and media disposal
    General user security awareness
    Employment practices (hiring and termination processes for security awareness and network accounts)

Configuration and change management
Data classification and responsibility matrix for assets
■ Telecommunications and network
Access control
Current network device configurations
Configuration management
Logging, auditing, monitoring, encryption practices
Anti-virus
Backups and recovery
Administrative practices and separation of duties.
Third party remote access and connectivity through various methods
LAN/WAN architecture
Internet/Intranet/Extranet access
■ Application and system development
Application controls over source code development, testing, and implementation
System development controls such as application life-cycles, system testing, requirements development, and review processes
■ Business recovery
Disaster recovery (corporate and departmental levels)
Business impact statements
Backups and recovery strategies
Incident response

5.4 Audits

Formal audits will be performed on a regular basis as documented by the state and federal regulations that govern MYC's business processes.

5.5 Regular Monitoring

Network management tools such as sniffers and scanners and monitoring, auditing, and reporting tools may be installed and operated only by agents designated by the CSO and the ISC.

To ensure regular compliance with security policies and standards, regular monitoring will be implemented in the following areas:

■ Badge, computer room, and building access
■ Internet access
■ Web site/content filtering
■ E-mail filtering
■ Intrusion detection

- Production server configuration
- Production server system and application log files
- Workstation configuration
- Network device configuration

5.5.1 Windows-Based Servers

The following are the items that will regularly be monitored on the Windows-based servers:

- Security eventlogs
- Account policies
- Audit policies
- Built-in group memberships
- User/application group memberships
- Organizational unit
- Domains
- Shared accounts
- Administrative accounts
- User rights
- Services
- Share/file/directory permissions

5.5.2 Remote Access

The following are the items that will regularly be monitored for remote access:

- Webmail successful logins
- Failed Dial-up attempts
- VPN failed and successful attempts.

5.5.3 Internet Access

The following are the items that will regularly be monitored for Internet access:

- Top 50 Internet site hits
- Number of hits per standardized category

5.6 Other Testing and Monitoring

To ensure regular compliance with security policies and standards, varied interval testing will include the following areas:

- Asset matrix of information and systems
- Incident response
- Business continuity and disaster recovery

6.0 Incidents and Violations

All MYC organizations will establish and implement a process that provides procedures to minimize the risk associated with violations of information security and to ensure timely detection and reporting of actual or suspected incidents or violations. Incidents and violations are to be reported to the CSO using an out-of-band communication method, non-e-mail or nonpager. The CSO will coordinate all official responses to management, the executive team, legal, technical services, and Human Resources.

Incidents are to be documented including the following information:

- Name and contact information of the person making the report
- System(s) affected
- Nature of the incident (details)
- Damage/impact of the event
- Cost estimate
- Names of all persons involved
- Names of all contacts made
- Changes to be made as a result of the incident (lessons learned)
- The CSO will maintain a record of all violations of information security.

7.0 Security User Awareness Training

In order to ensure personnel compliance with the MYC ISP, user security awareness training will be a mandatory process. Attendees will be required to understand and acknowledge the MYC security policies. The following will be the proposed structure for user security awareness training using varied media:

- New hire training
- Information security awareness
- Policy acknowledgement
- Acceptable use acknowledgement
- Annual security awareness training
- Technical services, including directors
- Executive team/board
- All personnel
- Third parties/temp/part-time
- Termination refresher

- Privacy
- MYC assets

8.0 Contingency and Disaster Recovery Planning

System owners, in cooperation with those who are dependent on their technology and systems for the support of essential business functions, are responsible for the development and maintenance of contingency plans for these functions. For mission-critical systems, contingency and disaster recovery plans should be tested annually. The contingency planning process will address

- Backup and retention of data and software
- Select of a backup or alternate site operations strategy
- Emergency response actions to be taken to protect life and property and minimize the impact of the emergency
- Actions to be accomplished to initiate and effect backup or alternate site
- Processes for resumption of normal operations in the most efficient and cost-effective manner

Contingency/recovery plans are to be maintained in hard copy by the system owners and the CSO and Senior Director of Business Services is to have access to them for review, and use in emergency circumstances. Because of the sensitive nature of these plans, they are not distributable documents. Each page of this documentation will be clearly labeled "For Official/Departmental Use Only."

9.0 Personnel Security

All MYC business units shall comply with personnel security policies and procedures including, but not limited to, these minimum requirements:

- Individuals will be granted only the least possible privileges necessary for job performance. Privileges, which have not been specifically granted, will be specifically denied.
- Where feasible, a separation of duties will be maintained to preclude any one individual from graining the opportunity to personally benefit from or adversely affect the operations of critical and essential systems. Procedural checks and balances must be defined and enforced so that accountability is established and security violations are detectable.
- All individuals are to be held personally accountable for their own proper use of and security practices while using MYC information resources.

- All users are to be provided with periodic security awareness briefings and copies of system rules and are to be properly trained to fulfill their information security responsibilities.
- Access privileges are to be immediately disabled upon suspicion of illegal or improper use or where there is a threat to MYC information resources.
- Access will be removed or modified as appropriate to accommodate changes in access requirements (e.g., transfer, resignation, retirement, changes in job descriptions).

10.0   Hardware Security

All IT hardware configurations must be approved by the ISC prior to use within MYC. For all hardware not already approved and listed on the IT approved hardware configurations, MYC business units shall ensure that appropriate security requirements are included in specifications for the acquisition and/or operation of new equipment. These specifications shall be reviewed by the ISC to ensure compliance with standards.

10.1   Connection of MYC Hardware to the MYC Network

Direct connection of any device to the MYC network is to be performed only by qualified IT staff. No devices may be connected to the network that have not been approved for connection. A device connected to the network is a device that uses resources outside the local resource. Examples of a network connected device are computers that access the Internet, devices that transmit traffic and information from one location to another, computers that receive e-mail, or computers that access files on another computer.

10.2   Connection of Non-MYC Hardware to the MYC Network

Any device not purchased or leased by MYC is not to be connected to the MYC network. Any non-MYC hardware found connected to the network will be immediately disconnected and the personnel will be disciplined. A device connected to the network is a device that uses resources outside the local resource. Examples of a network connected device are computers that access the Internet, devices that transmit traffic and information from one location to another, computers that receive e-mail, or computers that access files on another computer.

10.3 Remote Connections to the MYC Network

Remote connection of any device, to the MYC network is to be performed or directed only by qualified IT staff. No devices may be remotely connected to the network that have not been approved for connection.

11.0 Software Security

Software acquired for use at MYC, whether purchased off the shelf or developed in house or under contract, must be capable of providing the level of security protections required by the processes and data for which it was acquired.

11.1 Applications Software

Any application that processes sensitive data or that requires protection because of the risk and magnitude of loss or harm that could result from improper operation, manipulation or disclosure must be provided protection appropriate to the risk. The following will be considered as the minimum controls to be applied to systems which process sensitive data, with additional controls and safeguards imposed if appropriate:

- A documented software development and testing methodology must include a change management process for moving software into production and application security reviews throughout the requirements gathering and testing phases.
- Security requirements will be defined and security specification approved by the data/system owner prior to acquiring or starting development of applications or prior to making a substantial change in existing applications or the environment upon which they reside and operate.
- Design reviews will be conducted by the system owner at periodic intervals during the development process to assure that the proposed design will satisfy the function and security requirement specified by the user and appropriate to the system.
- New or substantially modified applications shall be thoroughly tested prior to implementation to verify that the user functions and the required administrative, technical, logical and physical safeguards are present and operationally adequate. Live production data or files will not be used to test applications software until software integrity has been reasonably assured by testing with test data or files. Application software will not be placed in production status until the system tests have been successfully completed and the application has been properly certified.

- Current copies of critical application software, documentation, databases and other materials required for its operation will be maintained at a secure off-site location to be readily available for use following an emergency.
- Application software documentation should be provided the same degree of protection as that provided the application itself.

11.2 Operating System Software

Operating system software for systems that provide multiuser access to resources must have the capability to control user access to those resources where necessary. They shall have the capability to identify and log all functions performed or attempted by users, and to deny user access to capabilities or resources which have not been authorized.

11.3 System Management or Diagnostic Software

All software classified as systems management or diagnostic software is to be strictly controlled because of the high level of access and control this software affords the user. With the exception of system administration staff, purchase and distribution of this type of software requires the written approval of the CIO for appropriate authorized use. Some examples of this classification of software are as follows:

- Network packet sniffers
- Password crackers
- Network instruction detection tools
- Network security diagnostic tools
- Network auditing and monitoring tools

11.4 Software Installation Authority

Only officially authorized and licensed software technicians may install software on MYC systems. The IT organization are the only individuals authorized to install properly licensed and approved software onto MYC systems.

12.0 Telecommunications Security

MYC telecommunication systems are information resources and are to be protected as other technology systems.

12.1   Telephone Switches

MYC telephone switches shall be configured to provide the maximum protection to MYC and its resources.

12.2   Telephone Lines

MYC uses both analog and digital telephone systems. In general, analog lines are assigned for connections to equipment such as modems, fax machines, and environmental control systems.

12.3   Modem Controls

Modem purchase and use will be managed. Modem purchases will be allowed only where there is a documented business requirement. Modems may be connected only to assigned analog telephone connections. No digital modems or digital converters may be connected to an MYC digital telephone connection. No cellular modem may be installed on any system that maintains a standard network connection to the MYC network.

13.0   Physical Security

The Risk Management Department has the responsibility of maintaining physical security of the MYC owned and leased buildings. Please see Risk Management for the detailed requirements of physical security.

The ISP will be responsible for the following on a regular basis:

- Unscreened visitors, contract maintenance personnel, and others not authorized unrestricted access, but who are required to be in controlled areas, must sign in and out, and are to be escorted by an authorized person at all times when within controlled spaces
- Access control procedures are to be reviewed annually for compliance with this plan and to determine that existing procedures are being followed
- Data center will conduct physical access log reviews and authorized access reviews

14.0   Environmental Security

Adequate environmental safeguards must be installed and implemented to protect information resources as deemed appropriate for the criticality of the system as determined by a risk analysis and as defined in the system requirements. At a minimum, the following safeguards are required

- Fire prevention, detection, suppression, and protection
- Water hazard prevention, detection, and correction
- Electrical power supply protection
- Temperature control
- Humidity control
- Natural disaster protection from earthquake, lightening, wind, and flood
- Electrical and magnetic field protection
- Good housekeeping, protection against dust and dirt

15.0   Glossary

Acceptable Risk	The level of risk that management finds acceptable to a particular asset. Acceptable risk is based on empirical data and supportive technical opinion that the overall risk is understood and that the controls placed on the asset or environment will lower the potential for its loss. Any remaining risk is recognized and accepted as an accountability entity.
Access	The ability or the means necessary to read, write, modify, or communicate data, or otherwise ensure the availability of any system resource.
Access Authorization	The granting of privileges to an individual or system, to perform specific functions on data or other computing resources.
Access Control	The prevention of unauthorized use of a computing resource.
Accountability	The property ensuring that the actions of an entity can be traced uniquely to that entity.
Administrative Information	Information relating to the administrative operational functions, e.g., personnel, human resources, student systems, and library systems.
Application Program	A computer program—written by a computer user, for computer users—that causes a computer system to satisfy defined requirements.
Application Programmer	One who designs, develops, debugs, installs, maintains, or documents application programs.

Asset	An asset is a valuable quality, resource, or thing. Some assets are physical in the instance of a computer while others are not, for example, an organization's public reputation. Assets are what allow a company to achieve.
Audit	Performance of an official, independent review and examination of system records, operational procedures, and system activities to test the adequacy of system control, to ensure compliance with established policies and procedures, and to recommend necessary changes in controls, policies, or procedures.
Audit Trail	A system of record-keeping. The audit trail tracks activities sufficiently to enable a reconstruction, review, and examination of the sequence of environments and activities surrounding or leading to each event in the path of a transaction, from its inception to output of final results. The audit trail must be designed to meet the legal record-keeping requirements of such transaction activities.
Authentication	The act of verifying the identity of a terminal, workstation, originator, or individual to determine that entity's right to access specific categories of information. Also a measure designed to protect against fraudulent transmission by verifying the validity of a transmission, message, station, or originator.
Authorization	The granting of a user's right of access to a terminal, transaction, program, or process. Authorization is generally used in conjunction with the concept of authentication. Once a user has been authenticated, he or she may then be authorized for different types of access within a process, transaction, or program.
Availability	The condition that a given information resource will be accessible to authorized persons or programs in a timely way, in the form needed, and that the information it provides will be of acceptable integrity.
Backup Procedures	A documented plan, to be used for the recovery of data, software, and hardware following a system failure or other disaster resulting in the loss of systems, services, or data.
Best Practice	A combination of high level statements and operational steps that are recommended for proficiency.
BOT	Board of Trustees.
CIO	Chief Information Officer.

Classification	Separation of information into two or more categories, each having different protective requirements.
Computer Security	The protection of a computing system against internal failure, human error, attack, and natural catastrophe, with the goal of preventing improper disclosure, modification, destruction of information, or denial of service.
Confidentiality	A condition ensuring that information is not made available or disclosed to unauthorized individuals, entities, or processes. Also, the degree to which sensitive data, about both individuals and organizations, must be protected.
Contingency Plan	A documented strategy for emergency response, backup operations, and post-disaster recovery, maintained as a part of the unit security program. The contingency plan ensures the continued availability of critical resources and facilitates the continuity of operations in an emergency situation.
Custodian	A person or entity designated to have access to, and possession of, authorized information. The custodian is responsible for providing proper protection, maintenance, and usage control of the information in an operational environment.
Data	A representation of information, knowledge, facts, concepts, or instructions that is being prepared or has been prepared in a formalized manner and is intended to be stored or processed, is being stored or processed, or has been stored or processed in a computer. Data may take many forms, including but not limited to, computer printouts, magnetic or optical storage media, and punch cards, or it may be stored internally in computer memory.
Data Dictionary	A file, document, or listing that defines all items or processes represented in a data flow diagram or used in a system.
Data Integrity	The assurance that computerized data is the same as its source document form—that is, that it has not been exposed to accidental or malicious modification, alternation, or destruction.
Database	An organized file of related data.
Delegate	A person or position specifically granted authority to perform duties that are normally outside of job responsibilities.

Denial of Service	The prevention of unauthorized access to resources. Also, the unauthorized delay of time-sensitive operations.
Dial-Up Access	Access to a computer system using telephone lines and a modem.
Distributed Processing	A form of system-to-system communications in which an application is divided among two or more systems in a fixed design. The decision as to where work will be done is made during the design stage and is bound during implementation. The system itself is designed for multiple users and provides each user with a fully functional computer. Distributed processing is designed to facilitate communications among the linked computers and shared access to central files. In personal computer environments, distributed processing takes the form of local area networks (LANs).
Electronic Data Interchange (EDI)	The interchange of electronic business documents (e.g., purchase orders, invoices) among multiple organizations' computers.
Encryption	The transformation of data by cryptographic techniques to produce ciphertext.
ET	Executive Team.
Event Logging	A collection of information, generally of machine and user activities, that tracks a sequence of electronic transactions.
Federal Privacy Act	A federal law that allows individuals to request and view any information on file which pertains to them, and to know how that information is being used by government agencies or their contractors.
File Protection	The processes and procedures established to inhibit unauthorized access to and contamination or elimination of a file.
Guidelines	An outline of a policy, conduct, or procedure.
Identification	The recognition of users or resources as those previously described to a computing system, generally by using unique, machine-readable names.
Information	The communication or reception of knowledge. This can include, but is not limited to, intelligence, news, facts, data, messages, and notes.

Information Asset	Valuable or sensitive information in any form (i.e., written, verbal, oral, or electronic).
Information Security	The practice of protecting information from accidental or malicious modification, destruction, disclosure, or denial of service. Similar to Data Security, but Information Security implies a broader scope, encompassing both electronic and traditional, non-electronic forms of information.
Information Security Incident	Any event or suspected event that could pose a threat to the integrity, availability, and confidentiality of MYC's systems, applications, or information. Incidents may result in the possession of unauthorized knowledge, the wrongful disclosure of information, embarrassment to MYC, the unauthorized alteration or destruction of information or systems, or violation of federal or state laws or regulations or MYC business requirements.
Integrity	The condition of maintaining data, processes, or information resources in such a way that they are not improperly altered or destroyed.
ISP	Information Security Program.
Least Privilege	An access principle requiring that each entity be granted the most restrictive set of privileges needed for performance of authorized tasks. The application of this principle limits the damage that can result from accident, error, or unauthorized use.
Liability	Refers to the quality or state of being liable, obligated by law or equity, or exposed or subject to some usually adverse contingency or action.
Local Area Network (LAN)	The linkage of personal and other computers (work-stations, front-end processors, controllers, switches, and gateways) within a limited area by high-performance cables, so users may exchange information and programs, share peripherals, and draw on the resources of a massive secondary storage unit (file server).
Mission Critical Systems	Are defined as those information systems and technology that support the real-time control of business systems.
Mission Essential Systems	Are defined as those information systems and technology that have a significant effect on the reliability and efficiency for the operation of MYC.

Network Connected Device	A device connected to the network is a device that uses resources outside the local resource. Examples of a network connected device are computers that access the Internet, devices that transmit traffic and information from one location to another, computers that receive email, or computers that access files on another computer.
Nonsensitive Data	Public data, which has no protection requirement for confidentiality or integrity, and the mission of MYC can be accomplished without it.
Off-Site Storage	A secondary storage location that is not adjacent to or within the primary computing/business facility.
Password	Confidential authentication information in the form of a string of characters. The password is used as proof of identity.
Policy	High level statements intended to provide guidance to those who must make present and future decisions. Policies can be thought of as generalized requirements on which management should focus attention. Policies typically include general statements of goals, objectives, beliefs, ethics, and responsibilities. Policies are often implemented or enforced by the general means for obtaining these things, such as procedures.
Privacy	An individual's or organization's ability, or right, to determine whether, when, and to whom personal or organizational information is released. Also, the right of individuals to control or influence information that is related to them, in terms of who may collect or store it, and to whom that information may be disclosed.
Procedures	Specific operational steps that employees must take to achieve a certain goal. A policy describes only the general means for addressing a specific problem; a procedure provides the solution. For example, a policy may state that all router access must be authenticated; this states what should occur. A procedure will provide the solution for authentication; this states how it occurs. Standard or best practices can be part of procedures.
Resource	Any function, device, or collection of data in a computing system that can be allocated for use by users or programs.

Security Controls	Techniques and methods set in place to ensure that only authorized users can access a computing system and its resources, and by which the IS environment ensures the integrity, availability, and confidentiality of system resources.
Security Policy	The set of laws, rules, and practices that regulate how an organization manages, protects, and distributes sensitive information.
Sensitive Information	Information that must be protected because its unauthorized disclosure, alteration, loss, or destruction may cause substantial damage.
Separation of Duties	A control separating a process into component parts. Each component has an authorized user, who must perform his or her part in the process in order for the process to be completed. This approach requires collusion among those who control the component parts, in order for security to be breached.
Standard Practice	A combination of high-level statements and operational steps that are required for proficiency.
System Administrator	A person, a group within a unit, or a consultant who acts for a unit, with responsibility for implementing a level of security consistent with that defined by the data custodian.
System Integrity	A condition in which a computing system can provide complete assurance of the logical correctness and reliability of the operating system and the logical completeness of the hardware, software, and firmware that implement the protection mechanisms and data integrity.
System Owner	A person or organization for whom a system exists. Thus inputs, storage, and outputs of the system are primarily designed in order to accommodate the business needs of these persons or organizations, and the loss of the system would directly impact them. System owner's, with applications support personnel, design system requirements and are responsible for defining any changes to the existing requirements for the system.
Test Data	Nonoperational data that simulates operational data in form and content, used to evaluate a system or program.

Threat	Any person, object, or event that, if realized, could potentially cause damage to MYC assets. Threats can be malicious, such as the intentional modification of sensitive information, or accidental, such as an error in a calculation, or the accidental deletion of a file. Threats can also be acts of nature, i.e., flooding, wind, lightning, etc.
Update	The process of altering master records to reflect the current business activity contained in transaction files.
User	People or processes accessing an information system either directly (e.g., data entry at a terminal) or indirectly (e.g., receipt of output data or preparation of software).
Violation Reports	A management report that identifies abnormal computer activity.
Vulnerabilities	Any conditions that exist with the potential for becoming an information security incident, or for making an information security incident possible at a future point in time.
Wide Area Network (WAN)	A network made up of more than one LAN.

Appendix B

Title:	Information Security Program				
Part Number:	XXX	Revision:	A	Effective:	3/1/06

This electronic document supersedes all previous electronic and printed documents or oral statements regarding this policy.
All Company Policies are subject to change at the sole discretion of MYC management.

Overview—Standards for Safeguarding Information

Mission Statement

The Security Director (SD) is responsible for the creation, implementation, and ongoing management of an enterprise-wide information security program (ISP). The ISP will include data security, policy formulation and implementation, user security awareness training, and ongoing system and network monitoring for compliance. The SD will assist with any investigations into unauthorized, illegal, or anomalous activities within the information environment. The SD is the focal point for information security issues and problem resolution and has overall responsibility for ensuring information assets are appropriately protected and maintained within the enterprise.

Vision Statement

The information security organization will be the most trusted and valued source for data security communications and information, and will be the source for ensuring confidentiality, integrity, accountability, and availability of enterprise information assets.

Scope

The scope of the ISP involves MYC customers, partners, customer information, partner information, MYC's information systems, service providers, and MYC employees entrusted with the maintenance of information.

Information Security Program

MYC shall implement and maintain a comprehensive ISP that includes administrative, technical, and physical safeguards appropriate to the size and complexity of MYC information assets and the nature and scope of its activities. All elements of the ISP must be coordinated.

Objectives

MYC's ISP shall be designed to

- Ensure the confidentiality, integrity, accountability, and availability of information assets
- Protect against any anticipated threats or hazards to the security or integrity of such information
- Protect against unauthorized access to or use of such information that could result in substantial harm or inconvenience to any customer or employee

Business Assumptions

The ISP is predicated on the mission statement and values for MYC:

- Create and provide leading-edge solutions that enable the delivery of wireless communications services worldwide
- Deliver clear and lasting value to employees, customers, shareholders, and the community
- Stretch. Lead through innovation. Recognize that change leads to growth. Be accountable for your decisions
- Treat each individual with dignity, consideration, respect, and integrity, whether an employee, colleague, customer, vendor, shareholder or the general public
- Take risks, learn lessons, share in rewards together, and encourage teamwork
- Be the standard by which others are measured for safety, quality, employee and customer care, and overall excellence

Guiding Principles

- Prevent problems through an empowered, educated, and vigilant employee base
- Enhance information security response and monitoring capability through planning, training, and exercising
- Build enterprisewide capabilities and augment resources based on assessed threats and vulnerabilities to our information assets
- Protect our information assets through safe and effective methods using standardization and interoperability
- Support and sustain created capacity into the future

General Objectives

- Minimize risk, impact, and costs to systems, information, and schedules
- Assist in meeting regulatory compliance, contractual requirements, and non-contractual requirements
- Build a comprehensive information security environment
- Maintain flexibility to respond to changing needs of information using good business practices, high-quality management, and innovative ideas
- Support multiple customer information protection needs
- Incorporate new information technologies to meet business needs
- Maximize the use of available resources
- Keep channels of open communication with others, such as the auditors, systems personnel, facilities, users, and management

Definitions

1. The term *information* is defined as any written, recorded, or graphic material generated or received in any form: paper, electronic, drawing, photograph, microfilm, diskette, magnetic tape, optical disk, voice mail, electronic mail, audio tapes, maps, indices, electronic media, video tapes, intellectual property, reference materials, or other data compilation from which information can be obtained or recorded, or any copy of printout that has sufficient information value to warrant its retention.
2. The term *customer* partner is used to define an entity (internal or external to MYC) that has established a continuing relationship within MYC, for which MYC provides products or services used by the entity for business purposes.
3. The terms *customer information* and *partner information* are defined as any records containing nonpublic information. This includes records, data files,

or other information in paper, electronic, or other form that is maintained by any service provider on behalf of an entity.

4. The term *MYC information systems* is used to define electronic and physical methods used to access, collect, store, use, transmit ,or protect customer information or enterprise information assets.

5. The term *service provider* is defined and limited to any person or entity that maintains, processes, or is otherwise permitted access to customer information through its provision of services directly to MYC.

6. The term *MYC employee* is defined as any full-time or part-time staff member, visitor, consultant, contractor, vendor, partner, or service provider performing any service for MYC.

Strategic Goals

The following guidelines will be applied for corporate information security strategy decisions and planning.

Strategic Priorities

1. Assessing and protecting key information assets and critical infrastructure, including interdependent physical and cyberinformation systems.
2. Fusing and sharing information security among all business units.
3. Planning for and providing continuity of business operations before, during, and after large-scale disasters within information technology.
4. Protecting and supporting continuous functioning of interoperable communication systems surrounding our information assets.
5. Executing proactive deterrence, preemption, and prevention initiatives.

Strategic Themes

■ Partnership and Leadership. A collaborative environment for sharing information, resources, assistance, and expertise as we jointly strive to enhance our information security environment.

■ Communication. Interoperable systems that provide critical information in a timely fashion to those who need it and in a form that is easy to use and understand.

■ Prevent Attacks. A wide spectrum of prevention efforts including intelligence and warning capabilities to ensure situational awareness and hardening of critical infrastructure.

- Reduce Vulnerabilities. Protection of our enterprise by improving the protection of the individual pieces and interconnecting systems that make up our critical information infrastructure.
- Compliance. Network environment compliance with corporate policies and regulations.

Strategic Objectives

1. Information security technology solutions will be evaluated in terms of benefits realization, cost, and risk.
2. MYC will not invest in newer "leading-edge" information security technology solutions without proven track records. Proposed new systems should be successfully installed in a significant percentage (e.g., 25% to 33%) of other corporate environments.

Development and Implementation of Information Security Program

Audit

1. Approve MYC's written ISP
2. Oversee the development, implementation, and maintenance of MYC's ISP, including assigning specific responsibility for its implementation and reviewing reports from management

Assess Risk

1. Identify reasonably foreseeable internal and external threats that could result in unauthorized disclosure, misuse, alteration, or destruction of customer information or customer information systems or any information assets
2. Assess the likelihood and potential damage of these threats, taking into consideration the sensitivity of customer information and information assets
3. Assess the sufficiency of policies, procedures, information systems, information assets, and other arrangements in place to control risks

Manage and Control Risk

1. Design the ISP details to control the identified risks, commensurate with the sensitivity of the information assets as well as the complexity and scope of MYC's activities. MYC must consider whether the following security measures are appropriate for the enterprise and, if so, adopt those measures MYC concludes are appropriate:

a. Controls on customer information systems, including ones to authenticate and permit access only to authorized individuals and controls to prevent employees from providing customer information to unauthorized individuals who may seek to obtain this information through fraudulent means.

b. Restrictions at physical locations, such as buildings, computer facilities, and records storage facilities, containing customer information to permit access only to authorized individuals.

c. Encryption of electronic customer information, including while in transit or in storage on networks or systems to which unauthorized individuals may have access.

d. Procedures designed to ensure that information system modifications are consistent with MYC's ISP.

e. Dual control procedures, segregation of duties, and employee background checks for employees with responsibilities for access to information assets.

f. Monitoring systems and procedures to detect actual and attempted attacks on or intrusions into information systems and assets.

g. Response programs that specify actions to be taken when MYC suspects or detects that unauthorized individuals have gained access to information systems and assets, including appropriate reports to regulatory and law enforcement agencies.

h. Measures to protect against destruction, loss, or damage of information assets due to potential environmental hazards, such as fire and water damage or technological failures.

2. Train staff to implement MYC's ISP through user security awareness during the new hire process and at least on an annual basis.

3. Regularly test the key controls, systems, and procedures of the ISP. The frequency and nature of such tests should be determined by MYC's risk assessment. Tests should be conducted or reviewed by independent third parties or staff independent of those who develop or maintain the security programs.

Oversee Service Provider Arrangements

1. Exercise appropriate due diligence in selecting service providers

2. Require its service providers by contract to implement appropriate measures designed to meet the objectives of the Information Security Strategic Plan

3. Where indicated in the MYC's risk assessment issues, monitor the service providers to confirm that they have satisfied their obligations to mitigate the documented risk issues

As part of this monitoring, MYC should review audits, summaries of test results, or other equivalent evaluations of its service providers.

Assisting in Acquisition Information Technology Due Diligence

1. Exercise appropriate due diligence when reviewing the new businesses' information technology environment
2. Require acquisitions by contract to implement appropriate measures designed to meet the objectives of the Information Security Strategic Plan
3. Where indicated in the MYC's risk assessment, monitor the acquisition to confirm the service provider is fulfilling his/her obligations required by the acquisition contract

As part of this monitoring, MYC should review audits, summaries of test results, or other equivalent evaluations of its acquisitions.

Adjust the Program

The SD shall monitor, evaluate, and adjust, as appropriate, the ISP in light of any relevant changes in technology, the sensitivity of information assets, internal or external threats to information, and MYC's own changing business arrangements, such as mergers and acquisitions, alliances and joint ventures, outsourcing arrangements, and changes to customer information systems.

Report to the Board of Directors and Audit Committee

The SD shall report to the MYC's Board of Directors and the Audit Committee at least annually. This report should describe the overall status of the ISP and MYC's compliance with corporate policies and federal regulations. The reports should discuss material matters related to its program, addressing issues such as risk assessment, risk management and control decisions, service provider arrangements, results of testing, security breaches or violations and management's responses, and recommendations for changes in the ISP.

Standard Security Director Tasks

- Coordinate the annual Information Security Risk Assessment
- Promote Internal Information Security Awareness (newsletter articles, brown bags, etc.)
- Provide Information Security Training to new employee classes
- Maintain the Corporate Information Security Policy architecture

- Maintain information security templates, guidelines (e.g., data/information security)
- Maintain the Corporate Information Security Program
- Implement actions to External Audit, Regulatory, Consulting findings
- Maintain, monitor, and test the Business Continuity Planning
- Maintain, monitor, and test disaster recovery planning
- Collect and review disaster recovery test records and report to management
- Maintain and coordinate network incident response
- Evaluate proposed changes to systems and procedures
- Provide Information Security Status Reports to the management
- Serve as the information security liaison for business units within the organization
- Provide consulting services to IT management, IT staff, and the enterprise
- Serves as sponsor as appropriate, or as designated by the Chief Information Officer, for information security related efforts, including implementation or upgrade of hardware or software

Appendix C

Sample Policy Format

Title	Doctitle		Document Number	Docnumber
Department	Dept		Document Owner	Docowner
Effective Date	XX/XX/XX		Last Review Date	XX/XX/XX

Purpose

Scope

References

> **Definitions**
>
> **Acronyms**
>
> **Document References**
>
> **Roles and Responsibilities**

Policy

Consequences

Approvals

Revision History

Note: This document and the information disclosed is proprietary and is not to be reproduced, used, or disclosed to anyone without the written permission of MYC. A hard copy of this document is for reference only and the latest approved version is located in the enterprise document management system.

Sample Guideline Format

Title	Doctitle		Document Number	Docnumber
Department	Dept		Document Owner	Docowner
Effective Date	XX/XX/XX		Last Review Date	XX/XX/XX

Purpose

Scope

References

    Definitions

    Acronyms

    Document References

    Roles and Responsibilities

Guideline Statement

    Acceptable Use Examples

Approvals

Revision History

Note: This document and the information disclosed is proprietary and is not to be reproduced, used, or disclosed to anyone without the written permission of MYC. A hard copy of this document is for reference only and the latest approved version is located in the enterprise document management system.

Sample Standard Format

Title	Doctitle		Document Number	Docnumber
Department	Dept		Document Owner	Docowner
Effective Date	XX/XX/XX		Last Review Date	XX/XX/XX

Purpose

Scope

References

   Definitions

   Acronyms

   Document References

   Separation of Duties with Roles and Responsibilities

Standard Statement/Detailed Specification

   Technology

   Configurations

Approvals

Revision History

Note: This document and the information disclosed is proprietary and is not to be reproduced, used, or disclosed to anyone without the written permission of MYC. A hard copy of this document is for reference only and the latest approved version is located in the enterprise document management system.

Sample Procedure Format

Title	Doctitle		Document Number	Docnumber
Department	Dept		Document Owner	Docowner
Effective Date	XX/XX/XX		Last Review Date	XX/XX/XX

Purpose

Scope

References

> **Definitions**
>
> **Acronyms**
>
> **Document References**
>
> **Separation of Duties with Roles and Responsibilities**

Step-by-Step Instructions

> **Screen Shots**
>
> **Flow Charts**
>
> **Steps to Accomplish Activity**

Approvals

Revision History

Note: This document and the information disclosed is proprietary and is not to be reproduced, used, or disclosed to anyone without the written permission of MYC. A hard copy of this document is for reference only and the latest approved version is located in the enterprise document management system.

Appendix D

Topic	Included in Existing Policy Architecture
INFORMATION SECURITY ORGANIZATION	
Information Security Policy	
■ Information Security Policy (and Review) ■ Senior Management Support ■ Accountability and Responsibility	
Information Security Organization	
■ Independent Review of Information Security Policy ■ Sharing Information with Other Organizations ■ Segregation of Duties	
CLASSIFYING INFORMATION AND DATA	
Setting Classification Standards	
■ Defining, Handling, Storing, Classifying, and Labeling Information ■ Ownership for Classified Information ■ Managing Access Control to Information	
CONTROLLING ACCESS TO INFORMATION AND SYSTEMS	
Controlling Access to Information and Systems	
■ Managing Access Control Standards (device, application, operating system) ■ Managing User Access (direct, remote, wireless)	

Topic	Included in Existing Policy Architecture
■ Securing Unattended Workstations ■ Segregation of Duties ■ Third-Party Service Management ■ Managing Passwords and Authentication ■ Securing Against Unauthorized Physical/Logical Access ■ Monitoring Access and Use ■ Acceptable Usage of Information Assets	
PROCESSING INFORMATION AND DOCUMENTS	
Networks	
■ Configuration Management ■ Network Segregation ■ Controlling Shared Networks ■ Network Access (direct, remote, wireless) ■ Defending Your Network Information from Malicious and Accidental Activities	
System Operations and Administration	
■ System Administration (segregation of duties, review) ■ System Utilities and Use ■ System Use Procedures ■ Managing Electronic Keys ■ Managing System Documentation ■ Synchronizing System Clocks ■ Scheduling Changes and Maintenance to Devices ■ Monitoring Operational Audit and Error Logs ■ Responding to System Faults (incidents, corruption of data, corruption of controls) ■ Managing or Using Transaction/Processing Reports	
Acceptable Use	
■ Downloading Files and Information from Different Sources ■ Electronic Business Communications	

Topic	Included in Existing Policy Architecture
■ Digital Signatures ■ Records Retention ■ Using Enterprise Assets for Work Purposes ■ Exceeding Authority ■ Filtering Inappropriate Material from Different Sources ■ Encryption and Key Management Procedures	
Data Management	
■ Transferring and Exchanging Data ■ Permitting Emergency Data Amendment ■ Setting Up and Maintaining Folder/Directory Structure and AccessSharing Data ■ Archiving Documents ■ Using Version Control Systems ■ Updating Customer Information ■ Using Meaningful File Names	
Backup, Recovery, and Archiving	
■ Restarting or Recovering your System ■ Archiving Information (what, where, how) ■ Recovery and Restoring of Data Files	
Data Handling	
■ Managing Hard Copy Printouts ■ Signing/Countersigning/Electronic Signature for Documents ■ Approving Documents ■ Verifying Signatures ■ Copying Confidential Information ■ Transporting Sensitive Data ■ Using Good Data Management and Destruction Practices	
Securing Data	
■ Encryption Techniques ■ Sending Information to External Parties	

Topic	Included in Existing Policy Architecture
■ Maintaining Customer Information Confidentiality ■ Sharing Information	
Other Information Handling and Processing	
■ Loading Personal Screen Savers ■ Speaking to Outside Parties (media, customers) ■ Need for Dual Control/Segregation of Duties ■ Using Clear Desk Policy ■ Using External Disposal Firms ■ Using Photocopier for Personal Use ■ Verifying Correctness of Information ■ Traveling on Business.	
PURCHASING AND MAINTAINING COMMERCIAL SOFTWARE	
Purchasing and Installing Software	
■ Specifying User Requirements for Software ■ Implementing New/Upgraded Software ■ Selecting Business Software Packages ■ Using Licensed Software (types of software valid on the network) ■ Technical Vulnerability Management	
Software Maintenance and Upgrade	
■ Patch Management ■ Interfacing Applications Software/Systems ■ Recording and Reporting Software Faults ■ Software Disposal	
SECURING HARDWARE, PERIPHERALS, AND OTHER EQUIPMENT	
Purchasing and Installing Hardware	
■ Specifying Information Security Requirements for New Hardware ■ Specifying Detailed Functional Needs for New Hardware	

Topic	*Included in Existing Policy Architecture*
■ Installing New Hardware ■ Testing Systems and Equipment (burn-in) ■ Power and Air Requirements ■ Disposing of Obsolete Equipment ■ Recording and Reporting Hardware Faults ■ Clear Screen Policy ■ Maintaining Hardware (on-site or off-site support) ■ Insuring Laptops/Portables for Use Domestically or Abroad	
Telecommunications	
■ Using Fax Machines/Fax Modems ■ Using Modems/ISDN/DSL/DS3/T1/MPLS Connections ■ Installing and Maintaining Network Telecommunications ■ Maintaining and Ownership of Connections	
Working off Premises or Using Outsourced Processing	
■ Contracting or Using Outsourced Processing ■ Using Mobile Devices ■ Using Removable Storage Media including Diskettes and CDs ■ Laptop/Portable Computers to Personnel (acceptable use) ■ Working from Home or Other Off-Site Location (Tele-working) ■ Moving Hardware from One Location to Another	
Using Secure Storage	
■ Using Lockable Storage Cupboards ■ Using Lockable Filing Cabinets ■ Using Fire-Protected Storage Cabinets ■ Using a Safe	
COMBATING CYBER CRIME	
Combating Cyber Crime	
■ Defending against Premeditated Cyber Crime Attacks ■ Minimizing the Impact of Cyber Attacks	

Topic	Included in Existing Policy Architecture
■ Collecting Evidence for Cyber Crime Prosecution ■ Handling Virus and Worm Warnings ■ Handling SPAM ■ Defending against Virus Attacks ■ Responding to Incidents	
CONTROLLING E-COMMERCE INFORMATION SECURITY	
E-Commerce Issues	
■ Architecting, Securing, and Configuring E-Commerce Networks ■ Using External Service Providers for E-Commerce ■ Accessing E-Commerce Networks	
DEVELOPING AND MAINTAINING IN-HOUSE SOFTWARE	
Controlling Source Code	
■ Controlling Source Code and Objects during Software Development ■ Controlling Old Versions of Programs ■ Managing Program Source Libraries ■ Acquiring Third-Party Developed Software	
Software Development	
■ Software Development (coding, database) Standards ■ Justifying New System Development ■ Managing Change Control Procedures ■ Making Emergency Amendments to Software ■ Separating Systems Development and Operations (segregation of duties) ■ Documentation	
Testing and Training	
■ Controlling Test Environments ■ Using Live Data for Testing	

Topic	*Included in Existing Policy Architecture*
■ Testing Software before Transferring to a Live Environment ■ Capacity Planning and Testing of New Systems ■ Parallel Running ■ Training in New Systems ■ Documentation	
DEALING WITH LOCATION-RELATED CONSIDERATIONS	
Premises Security	
■ Physical Protection ■ Challenging Strangers on the Premises ■ Delivery and Loading Areas ■ Ensuring Suitable Environmental Conditions (power, air, humidity) ■ Physical Access Control to Secure Areas	
ADDRESSING PERSONNEL ISSUES RELATING TO SECURITY	
Contractual Documentation	
■ Preparing Terms and Conditions of Employment ■ Using Nondisclosure Agreements (staff and third party) ■ Misuse of Organization Stationery ■ Lending Keys to Secure Areas to Others ■ Complying with Information Security Policy ■ Establishing Ownership of Intellectual Property Rights ■ Employing/Contracting New Staff (background reviews) ■ Contracting with External Suppliers/Other Service Providers ■ Employees' Responsibility to Protect Confidentiality of Data	

Topic	Included in Existing Policy Architecture
Confidential Personnel Data (privacy)	
■ Respecting Privacy in the Workplace ■ Handling Confidential Employee Information ■ Giving References on Staff ■ Checking Staff Security Clearance ■ Sharing Employee Information with Other Employees ■ Sharing Personal Salary Information	
Staff Leaving Employment	
■ Handling Staff Resignations ■ Completing Procedures for Terminating Staff or Contractors ■ Obligations of Staff Transferring to Competitors	
DELIVERING TRAINING AND STAFF AWARENESS	
Awareness	
■ Delivering Awareness Programs to All Staff ■ Drafting Top Management Security Communications to Staff ■ Third-Party Contractor: Awareness Programs ■ Providing Regular Information Updates to Staff	
COMPLYING WITH LEGAL, REGULATORY AND POLICY REQUIREMENTS	
Complying with Legal/Regulatory Obligations	
■ Legal/Regulatory Obligations ■ Copyright and Software Licensing ■ Complying with the Data Protection Act or Other Equivalent Regulations ■ Copyright Legislation ■ Legal Safeguards against Computer Misuse	

Topic	*Included in Existing Policy Architecture*
DETECTING AND RESPONDING TO INFORMATION INCIDENTS	
Reporting Information Security Incidents	
■ Reporting Information Security Incidents (inside and outside requirements) ■ Notifying Information Security Weaknesses ■ Witnessing an Information Security Breach	
Investigating Information Security Incidents	
■ Responding to and Investigating Information Incidents ■ Collecting Evidence of an Information Security Breach ■ Recording Information Security Breaches	
PLANNING FOR BUSINESS CONTINUITY	
Business Continuity Management	
■ Business Continuity (project, evaluating risk, plan, testing, maintenance) ■ Training and Staff Awareness on Business Continuity	

Appendix E

Assessment	Activity Is Documented (Y = 1, N = 0)	Has Been Implemented (Enterprise-wide) (Y = 1, N = 0)	Staff Knowledge Adequacy (High = 3, Medium = 2, Low/No = 1)
Technology Administration			
Technology is structured in a manner that supports the company business goals and objectives.			
An Information Technology organizational chart exists and reports to a senior executive.			
An Information security organizational chart exists.			
Roles and responsibilities are clearly defined and monitored (segregation of duties). Position descriptions have been reviewed and approved by management.			
Contracts and/or service level agreements are in place for outsourced functions.			

Assessment	Activity Is Documented (Y = 1, N = 0)	Has Been Implemented (Enterprise-wide) (Y = 1, N = 0)	Staff Knowledge Adequacy (High = 3, Medium = 2, Low/No = 1)
Management responds to business requests and is supportive of business goals and objectives.			
Information Security and Technology have a strategic plan in place and it is being followed.			
A matrix has been developed to document the global regulations that apply to the enterprise.			
A matrix has been developed to document the privacy requirements of all enterprise locations and customers.			
Configuration management for computing systems and network environments are documented and in place.			
The systems that support the mission critical functions are clearly defined and documented (in-house and packaged solutions).			
The network, servers, and applications to servers are identified in a matrix or a summary graphic.			
Key external network connections are clearly documented.			

Assessment	*Activity Is Documented (Y = 1, N = 0)*	*Has Been Implemented (Enterprise-wide) (Y = 1, N = 0)*	*Staff Knowledge Adequacy (High = 3, Medium = 2, Low/No = 1)*
A project management methodology is defined.			
Information Security Policies and Procedures exist and ownership and updating responsibilities have been assigned.			
Procurement and distribution of equipment and software is controlled centrally.			
All departments comply with all specific, international, state, and federal regulations.			
Host and Application Logical Security			
Established procedures and practices for information security and for restricting access to operating systems, databases, and application software.			
Security related policies and procedures are complete, appropriate, and in use.			
A security/administration function has been created and performs job functions that impart an adequate.			
User IDs and passwords are not shared. If shared, there are valid and documented reasons for sharing.			

Assessment	Activity Is Documented (Y = 1, N = 0)	Has Been Implemented (Enterprise-wide) (Y = 1, N = 0)	Staff Knowledge Adequacy (High = 3, Medium = 2, Low/No = 1)
Password use, uniqueness, and strong configuration is enforced for all accounts on all systems.			
Disabled accounts require System Administrator or Help Desk personnel to reactivate them after verification of user identification.			
Security tools are run on a regular basis to ensure that staff follow procedures.			
Data owners are aware of their access authorization and data classification responsibilities.			
Procedures exist for granting access for new staff, removing access for terminated staff, and changing access for transferred staff.			
Procedures exist for granting access for new third parties, removing access for terminated third parties, and changing access for transferred third parties.			
Procedures exist for expiring unused IDs after X number of days.			

Assessment	Activity Is Documented (Y = 1, N = 0)	Has Been Implemented (Enterprise-wide) (Y = 1, N = 0)	Staff Knowledge Adequacy (High = 3, Medium = 2, Low/No = 1)
Responsibility has been assigned to the appropriate personnel for creation and deletion of accounts relating to all systems and applications.			
User ID lists and access level reports are generated on a periodic basis and are reviewed by data owners for appropriateness to ensure timely implementation of requested access changes.			
Human Resources (or a central group) reports on staff status to ensure user accounts have been appropriately updated.			
Audit trails/reports for security violations are reviewed on a regular basis and Information Security representatives conduct appropriate follow-ups with users.			
A security awareness program is in place to periodically inform and make users aware of the client's security practices.			
Anti-virus controls are in place to protect network devices from viruses and are updated on a regular basis.			

Assessment	Activity Is Documented (Y = 1, N = 0)	Has Been Implemented (Enterprise-wide) (Y = 1, N = 0)	Staff Knowledge Adequacy (High = 3, Medium = 2, Low/No = 1)
Physical Security			
Physical security considers the environmental aspects that help ensure company computing assets and that resources are physically secure and systems are periodically tested.			
Policies and procedures related to physical security are documented and periodically updated.			
Sensitive documents, such as operations manuals, guides, network control guides, are properly secured from unauthorized access.			
In areas where equipment is located, all entrances from noncontrolled areas are locked/access secured at all times.			
Guests must sign in and/or are escorted at all times if they do not have access badges.			
Access to the facility is restricted and monitored.			
Lists/reports are maintained showing individuals authorized to enter/access computing facilities.			

Assessment	Activity Is Documented (Y = 1, N = 0)	Has Been Implemented (Enterprise-wide) (Y = 1, N = 0)	Staff Knowledge Adequacy (High = 3, Medium = 2, Low/No = 1)
The individuals who can access restricted areas are appropriate, and management periodically reviews and updates the access lists.			
Environmental systems and devices are properly maintained per vendor requirements, including HVAC/humidity control, fire detection/suppression or extinguishers, water/leak detection, and UPS/battery back up and surge/sag controls where key assets are located.			
Periodic tests of environmental systems are performed to ensure proper operation.			
The computing facility and the IT area are maintained in a clean and orderly fashion.			
Business Continuity and Disaster Recovery Planning			
A formal disaster recovery/business continuation plan is documented and tested.			
A business impact analysis (BIA) has been conducted for the enterprise.			

Assessment	Activity Is Documented (Y = 1, N = 0)	Has Been Implemented (Enterprise-wide) (Y = 1, N = 0)	Staff Knowledge Adequacy (High = 3, Medium = 2, Low/No = 1)
A set of disaster recovery plan are documented, implemented, tested, and remediated based on the BIA.			
All critical and key applications and systems are identified with recovery priorities, time the business can do without the services, and support personnel.			
Different disaster scenarios are outlined, with detailed recovery time guidelines, support roles, tasks and responsibilities defined.			
Recovery responsibilities are clearly defined for executives, managers, leaders, and personnel.			
Contact lists are up to date and the calling sequence is prioritized.			
All key vendors and suppliers have been identified, along with their contact numbers, in the plan.			
The disaster recovery plans provide for continuation of appropriate security measures and adequate controls.			

Assessment	Activity Is Documented (Y = 1, N = 0)	Has Been Implemented (Enterprise-wide) (Y = 1, N = 0)	Staff Knowledge Adequacy (High = 3, Medium = 2, Low/No = 1)
The file recovery procedures documented in the disaster recovery plan are adequate and will adequately support an emergency.			
An uninterruptible power supply, electric generators, or similar system is used and is tested regularly. These meet recovery requirements in the case of prolonged power outage.			
Hardware, Software, Data, and Operating System Maintenance and Support			
Processes for change and configuration management are established.			
Change management procedures exist to ensure only authorized personnel can perform production software updates with management authorization.			
Back-up copies of the old versions of programs are available on-site or through the vendor, if back-up is required.			
All changes are documented.			

Assessment	Activity Is Documented (Y = 1, N = 0)	Has Been Implemented (Enterprise-wide) (Y = 1, N = 0)	Staff Knowledge Adequacy (High = 3, Medium = 2, Low/No = 1)
Procedures are current and approved, reflect the current environment, and address requirements for key issues such as: ■ Classifying changes based on priority or severity; ■ Management approval for changes; ■ User testing and documented test plans; ■ Back-out plans; ■ Outage windows and notices; ■ Segregation of duties.			
An audit trail exists in the change management process to determine who is responsible and accountable for the change.			
Software is in use to implement the software change management function (code access, code promotion, check in/out, etc.).			
Regular reviews with business units and management for approving changes are scheduled.			
A separate environment is used to test all changes and data used for tests does not contain confidential or sensitive financial information.			

Assessment	Activity Is Documented (Y = 1, N = 0)	Has Been Implemented (Enterprise-wide) (Y = 1, N = 0)	Staff Knowledge Adequacy (High = 3, Medium = 2, Low/No = 1)
Personnel making application changes are different from the ones who requested the changes (segregation of duties) and developers do not have access to the production library or production program codes AFTER the code has been moved into the production environment.			
Audit trails exist for User IDs that are used to make program changes.			
Management periodically reviews the audit trail reports for mission critical systems or systems that process sensitive information, including financial systems, to ensure changes made were appropriate and authorized.			
Policies and procedures exist related to database administration.			
Production databases are included in back-up and restore schemes, including authorizations.			
The number and individuals devoted to Database Administration are appropriate, their duties are not conflicting, and they have unique IDs.			

Assessment	Activity Is Documented (Y = 1, N = 0)	Has Been Implemented (Enterprise-wide) (Y = 1, N = 0)	Staff Knowledge Adequacy (High = 3, Medium = 2, Low/No = 1)
Logging that details changes and who made them been activated. Transaction histories are maintained.			
Network/LAN/Telecommuni-cations & Network Security			
Network, local area network, and telecommunications monitoring procedures and established access controls, security, intrusion detection, and disaster recovery planning processes are documented and in use.			
Network schematics are in place, are current, and have secured access.			
Alternate or redundant network communication lines are available to minimize downtime.			
Security devices are used to regulate network traffic from the outside? Servers used for internal purposes and those accessed by personnel via the internet are placed behind a firewall.			
Remote access provisions are secured and logged.			
A method is used to monitor network activity for each platform.			

Assessment	Activity Is Documented (Y = 1, N = 0)	Has Been Implemented (Enterprise-wide) (Y = 1, N = 0)	Staff Knowledge Adequacy (High = 3, Medium = 2, Low/No = 1)
Some criteria is used to set alarms as opposed to just logging entries for events.			
Security/Firewall Administrators receive, review, and act upon alerts and advisories for the enterprise.			
Personnel responsible for security use audit and/or security vulnerability software, e.g., Crack, Tripwire, Satan, or ISS security tool has been used to assess vulnerabilities the production environment may be facing for external and internal sources.			
There are network device ingress and egress standards or policies in place.			
User ID and passwords are required for device administration and devices are accessed in a secure manner.			
The network/LAN contains an intrusion detection or prevention system application.			
Incident response policies and procedures have been documented to define response activities that are required to be taken.			

Assessment	Activity Is Documented (Y = 1, N = 0)	Has Been Implemented (Enterprise-wide) (Y = 1, N = 0)	Staff Knowledge Adequacy (High = 3, Medium = 2, Low/No = 1)
Third party access to the network is controlled.			
End-User Computing			
End-user computing platforms (laptops, desktops, Blackberrys, PDAs, faxes, etc.), enforce security, end-use, and asset management controls.			
Policies and procedures exist for the effective management, operation, security, and control of the end-point devices.			
End-point software is updated on a regular basis through bundled or systematic releases.			
Workstation software is monitored and inventoried to ensure compliance with licensing standards and to check for unauthorized software.			
Virus scans and patching are automatically administered through log-on scripts or similar methods to ensure regular checking and patching of workstations			
Lockable screen savers are used to hide sensitive data when end-points are unattended.			

Assessment	Activity Is Documented (Y = 1, N = 0)	Has Been Implemented (Enterprise-wide) (Y = 1, N = 0)	Staff Knowledge Adequacy (High = 3, Medium = 2, Low/No = 1)
Sensitive Data Computing Environment			
Sensitive data is protected and monitored.			
Policies and procedures exist and are in use for data classification, storage, use, and destruction.			
Data access controls are in use, maintained, and monitored.			
Transmission of sensitive data is protected by adequate security.			

Appendix F

Executive Summary

Project type:	Enterprise Infrastructure		
Project Category:	Improved protection quality, information protection, customer requested, legislative mandate, contract required		
PROJECT TITLE:	Information Security Policy Architecture		
Business Unit/Area:	Enterprise	Priority to Business Area:	☐ Crltical ■ High ☐ Medium ☐ Low
Functional Area:	Corporate	Requestor:	CSO
Executive Sponsor:	CEO	Project Sponsor:	CSO
Initial Request Date:		Desired Target Date:	2006/12/31
Project Objectives Statement:	Develop and implement an information security policy architecture that provides information assurance to MYC's information assets.		
Estimated Costs:	Optimistic	Most Likely	Pessimistic
IT:	$0 (–10%)	$a	$ (+25%)
Business:	n/a	n/a	n/a
Estimated 12-mo ROSIb:	>$0	$0	$0

a Estimate based on actual quote from Dimension Data, plus a 20% additional contingency added for potential revisions during procurement.
b ROSI—Return on Security Investment

Steering Committee

Initial Date Reviewed:		Initial Disposition:		
		☐ Prioritize ☐ Need More Detail ☐ Reject		
Final Date Reviewed:		Final Disposition:		
		☐ Prioritize ☐ Need More Detail ☐ Reject		
Approval Log:				
Priority to Company:	☐ Critical ☐ High ☐ Medium ☐ Low	Target Project Initiation Date:		
Approved Budget:		Target Solution In-Use Date:		

Project Request

Overview
Project Description:
An information security architecture provides a framework within which an organization can plan, implement, and enforce a security policy. Broad organizational guidance and direction for security technologies and structure are in the process of being developed as part of the architecture. Recommendations regarding network security, organizational structure, data value, and Internet services should be a part of MYC's security architecture. A well-developed information security policy architecture will provide the framework for security and technology implementation and can serve as a reference measure for successful implementation and operation.
At this time, MYC does not have a formal written set of security policies. Policies need to be formalized to include assets, network security, remote access, confidentiality agreements, physical security, Internet usage, auditing, handling of information, and disaster recovery. Security policies need to be included within the Employee Handbook or in another highly visible and well-known place and supported by upper management. Also, MYC does not have a complete set of security procedures. Security procedures are operational steps that employees take to achieve a certain goal. There are no

documented information security procedures in place at MYC. Information security procedure use and effectiveness need to consider dependencies on information flow among departments or personnel. In order to implement information security procedures effectively and consistently, MYC needs to ensure that security related procedures are able to provide the controls to meet security policy requirements. Security procedures must be expandable to include new technologies, to improve security actions that require effective communications, and to implement auditing mechanisms.

Business Justification:

Information assurance depends not only on the soundness of the design strategy but also on the assurance of correctness of the implementation of security controls. Information assurance is about defining standards, controls, and guidelines for maintaining information privacy, protecting information soundness, and ensuring information accessibility by staff.

MYC's information requirements continue to expand on a daily basis. As MYC sells and supports customer products, MYC is required by customers and international laws to protect information. An information security policy architecture will give the enterprise guidance on assuring those assets are protected.

Benefits/Consequences:

Project benefits will be obtained in the following areas:

■ Support for Customer Service: Provide standardize responses to customer inquiries about MYC's information assurance program and improve customer confidence in MYC security standards.

■ Application Support: MYC-purchased and internally developed applications will have standard business requirements and security requirements to ensure the protection and integrity of information.

■ Business Continuity and Disaster Recovery: Standardized and complete documentation prepares a business for emergency recovery situations.

Major Risks:

■ Significant initial investment could take longer to recoup if benefit estimates are not immediately realized.

■ There could be civil and criminal customer lawsuits, because MYC did not effectively and efficiently protect customer related information.

Alternatives Considered: None

Key Stakeholders:	CSO, CIO, COO, CFO, CEO
Other Business Units/Areas Affected:	None

Project Scope

In Scope:

- High level enterprise information assurance policies, guidelines, standards, and work instructions
- Developing an information security document manual of style
- Developing a basic information awareness program for staff
- Implementing the high level information assurance policy
- Implementing an initial information awareness program

Out of Scope:

- Implementing any additional manual or automated controls for compliance to the high level information assurance policies

Deliverables:

Phase 1

Two critical aspects of MYC's security policies will be to clearly define the corporate assets and appropriate uses of MYC's information systems to the entire organization. The corporate assets must include tangible and intangible assets. In order to hold employees accountable for their actions and to have effective enforcement mechanisms, employees must clearly understand what behaviors and uses are acceptable or unacceptable. Without a clear definition of what inappropriate behavior is, employees cannot realistically be held accountable. Base security architecture policies should be written and published for the following:

- Corporate Assets and Resources and Expected Level of Privacy
- Corporate Authority and Responsibility Policy
- Acceptable Use of Corporate Assets and Resources
- Business Ethics and Code of Conduct
- Information Assurance Policy

These first three policies are the base architecture for the remaining policies because they will provide a definition of all assets and resources belonging to MYC, who is responsible for what actions, and what the appropriate uses are of those assets. Before the intial set of policies is developed, an information security manual of style will be developed to ensure the information security policy architecture set of documents is standardized and easily followed. This manual of style will also include a glossary of basic information security definitions and an acronym reference.

Phase 2

From the three base policies, the following can be added on for a complete set of MYC security architecture policies:

- Record Retention and Control Policy
- Equipment and Transmission Monitoring Policy
- Disaster Recovery and Business Resumption Policy
- Public Information and Media Policy
- Third Party/Partner Access Policy

Phase 3

Once the corporate level security policies are in place, then Information Technology and Communications and Network Services can take over to create a more detailed set of security architecture policies. These policies have to be supported by management and highly visible, but they are the responsibility of Information Technology and Communications and Network Services. Some of the following policies have been instituted, but may not be formally published.

- Account and Password Policies
- Access Control and Authorization Policy
- Remote Access Policy
- Anti-Virus Policy
- Change Management
- Media and Material Disposal Policy
- Incident Handling Policy
- TCP/IP and Other Protocols Policy

Phase 4

Once the base set of security policies is in place, then the security procedures supporting these policies can be written, published, and implemented. The procedures should be owned by individual departments responsible for the various activities. These documents will expand as new technologies and software are implemented within the MYC environment. This phase will take the longest to develop and implement, due to the individual department responsibilities. The following is an initial list of security procedures and best and standard practices:

- IT standards for the production supported hardware and software
- Password management, protection, reset, and change on all devices
- Account addition, change, deletion, and reset procedures
- Group addition, change, and delete procedures
- Administrative account security and access control procedures for all devices
- Windows server security
- Solaris server security
- Linux server security

- Business continuity
- Incident handling
- Information and media disposal
- Desktop/laptop security
- Remote access security
- Gateway administration and security for each of our supported installations, for example:
    Individual application installation, administration, and security, for example, anti-virus
    System and audit log procedures
    Internet access category reporting
    System monitoring procedures
    Access control procedures.

	Projections	Year 1	Year 2	Year 3
	Savings/Cost Reductions/Benefits*			
A.	Prevent/Reclaim Income/Asset Loss			
B.	Reduced Operating Costs			
C.	Prevent/Reclaim Increased Operating Costs			
TOTAL Benefits:				
	Project and Support Costs			
A.	Capitalized Software & Equipment			
B.	Capitalized External Labor			
C.	Capitalized Internal Labor			
D.	Support/Maintenance Expense			
TOTAL Costs:				
NET 3-Year Financial Projections:				

* The benefits are estimates on industry survey results and the estimates costs within the enterprise for the recovery or investigation of an incident.

HISTORY:

Revision Date:		Revised by:	
Revision Description:			
Review Date:		Revision Disposition:	
		☐ Prioritize ☐ Need More Detail ☐ Reject	

Appendix G

Title:	INFORMATION ASSURANCE				
Part Number:	PL00550	Revision:	1.0	Effective:	20050930
Owner:	CEO			Last Review:	20070501

This electronic document supersedes all previous electronic and printed documents or oral statements regarding this policy.
All Company Policies are subject to change at the sole discretion of MYC management.

Scope

This policy applies to all MyCompany (MYC) enterprise information and any MYC staff member who accesses information within MYC locations.

Definitions

See the Information Assurance glossary.

Policy

Information and information systems are critical and vital to MYC's mission and objectives. MYC has a fiduciary duty to protect, limit risk, preserve, improve, and account for MYC information at all times. MYC must take appropriate steps to assure information protection from risks and threats. MYC's information must be protected in a manner commensurate with its sensitivity, value, and criticality. Security measures must be employed regardless of the media on which information is stored, the systems which process it, or the methods by which it is moved. Such protection includes restricting access to information based on the need to know. MYC staff must devote sufficient time and resources to ensure that information is properly protected and to properly protect and manage this property. Management reserves the right to audit, monitor, and log all data stored in or transmitted by these systems.

Responsibility

Information Security	Will perform regular risk and compliance reviews against MYC information and will coordinate any information incidents.
Information Technology	Will maintain the technology required for information assurance.
Management	Must make sure that information is protected in a manner that is at least as secure as other organizations in the same industry handling the same type of information and as required by law.
Staff	Must be provided with sufficient training and supporting reference materials to allow them to properly protect and otherwise manage MYC information.

Violations

Unauthorized access, disclosure, duplication, modification, diversion, destruction, loss, misuse, or theft of MYC information by staff, willingly and deliberately, may result in the loss of computer and/or network resources up to and including termination and legal prosecution. Disciplinary measures are on a case-by-case basis.

/Name/, Chief Executive Officer

Appendix H

Title:	Computing Resources				
Part Number:	GD00300	Revision:	1.0	Effective:	20050930
Owner:	CIO			Last Review:	20070501

This electronic document supersedes all previous electronic and printed documents or oral statements regarding this policy.
All Company Guidelines are subject to change at the sole discretion of MYC management.

Scope

This guideline applies to MYC staff and all MYC computing resources. Staff are required to be familiar with and comply with this guideline. Questions about the guideline should be directed to the Information Security Manager (ISM).

Definitions

See the Information Assurance glossary.

References

PL00550, Information Assurance Policy

Guideline

MYC has a variety of computing resources that store, transmit, and manipulate information. Staff and computing resources introduce a level of risk to the information. Staff access to MYC computing resources in based on business need/justification and limiting the risk to the information asset.

Responsibility

Management	■ At any time and without prior notice, MYC management reserves the right to examine and authorize examinations of electronic mail messages, portable storage devices, files on desktops and laptops, Web browser cache files, Web browser bookmarks, and other information stored on or passing through MYC computing resources. Such management access assures compliance with internal policies, assists with internal investigations, and assists with the management of MYC information systems. ■ Management ensures staff are performing functions within their assigned rights and permissions.
Staff	■ Staff should ensure compliance with this guideline. ■ Staff are responsible for their own activities. ■ Staff are responsible for reporting violations to all policies and guidelines.
IT Operations	■ MYC logs e-mail, Web sites visited, files downloaded, time spent on the network and Internet/Intranet, and related information. IT Operations ensures that logging and monitoring is constantly enabled. ■ IT ensures supporting documentation for logging and monitoring devices exists and is implemented.

Computing Resource Areas

Internet Information Reliability

All information taken from the Internet should be considered suspect until confirmed by a separate information source. There is no quality control process on the Internet, and a considerable amount of its information is outdated and inaccurate and, in some instances, even deliberately misleading.

Personal Use

MYC computing resources are for business use only. Use of MYC computing resources for certain personal purposes is permissible as long as the incremental cost of the usage is negligible and no MYC business activity is interrupted or preempted by the personal use.

No Default Protection

Staff using MYC computing resources and the Internet should realize that their communications are not automatically protected from viewing by third parties. Unless the enterprise standard encryption is used, staff should not send information over the Internet if they consider it to be confidential or private.

Notification Process

If sensitive MYC information is lost, disclosed to unauthorized parties, or suspected of being lost or disclosed to unauthorized parties, the ISM must be notified immediately. Similarly, whenever passwords or other system access control mechanisms are lost, stolen, or disclosed, or are suspected of being lost, stolen, or disclosed, the ISM must be notified immediately. The specifics of security problems should not be discussed widely.

Virus Checking

Downloaded information from non-MYC computing resources must be screened with anti-virus software prior to being used. If an external provider of the software is not trusted, downloaded software should be tested on a stand-alone non-production machine that has been recently backed up. Downloaded files must be decrypted and decompressed before screening for viruses. Separately, the use of digital signatures to verify that a file has not been altered by unauthorized parties is recommended, but this does not assure freedom from viruses.

Spoofing Users

Unless tools such as digital signatures and digital certificates are employed, it is relatively easy to spoof the identity of another user on the Internet. Before staff release any MYC information, enter into any contracts, or order any products via public networks, the identity of the individuals and organizations contacted must be confirmed. Identity confirmation is ideally performed via digital signatures or digital certificates, but in cases where these are not available, other means such as letters of credit, third-party references, and telephone conversations may be used.

User Anonymity

Misrepresenting, obscuring, suppressing, or replacing a staff's identity on the Internet or any MYC electronic communications system is forbidden. The staff name, electronic mail address, organizational affiliation, and related information included with messages or postings must reflect the actual originator of the messages or postings. If staff have a need to employ remailers or other anonymous facilities, they must do so on their own time, with their own computing resources, and with their own Internet accounts. Use of anonymous FTP log-ins, anonymous UUCP log-ins, HTTP (Web) browsing, and other access methods established with the expectation that staff would be anonymous is not permissible.

Web Page Changes

Staff may not establish new Internet Web pages dealing with MYC business, or make modifications to existing Web pages dealing with MYC business, unless they have first obtained the approval of the Web page owner, the Director of Marketing or the Chief Executive Officer. Modifications include the addition of hot-links to other sites, updating the information displayed, and altering the graphic layout of a page.

Information Exchange

Agreements signed by staff, MYC software, documentation, and all other types of internal information must not be sold or otherwise transferred to any non-MYC party for any purposes other than business purposes expressly authorized by management.

Message Interception

Wiretapping and other types of message interception are straightforward and frequently encountered on the Internet. MYC proprietary or private information must not be sent over the Internet unless it has first been encrypted by approved methods. Unless specifically known to be in the public domain, source code must always be encrypted before being sent over the Internet.

Security Parameters

Credit card numbers, telephone calling card numbers, fixed log-in passwords, and other security parameters that can be used to gain access to goods or services must not be sent over the Internet in readable form. The SSL and SET encryption processes are both acceptable Internet encryption standards for the protection of security parameters. Other encryption processes, such as PGP, are permissible if they are approved by the Director of Engineering.

External Representations

Staff may not indicate their affiliation with MYC in mailing lists (listservs), chat sessions, and other offerings on the Internet. This may be done by explicitly adding certain words or it may be implied, for instance via an electronic mail address. Whenever staff provide an affiliation, they must also clearly indicate that opinions expressed are their own and not necessarily those of MYC. Likewise, if an affiliation with MYC is provided, political advocacy statements and product/service endorsements are also prohibited unless they have been previously cleared by the Chief Executive Officer. With the exception of ordinary operations and customer service activities, all representations on behalf of MYC must first be cleared by the Chief Executive Officer.

Appropriate Behavior

To avoid libel, defamation of character, and other legal problems, whenever any affiliation with MYC is included with an Internet message or posting, "flaming" or similarly written attacks are strictly prohibited. Staff must not make threats against another user or organization over the Internet or over any internal mechanisms. All Internet messages intended to harass, annoy, or alarm another person are similarly prohibited.

Removal of Postings

Those messages sent to Internet discussion groups, electronic bulletin boards, or other public forums, which include an implied or explicit affiliation with MYC, may be removed if management deems them to be inconsistent with MYC's business interests or existing company policy. Messages in this category include: (a) political statements, (b) religious statements, (c) cursing or other foul language, and (d) statements viewed as harassing others based on race, creed, color, age, sex, physical handicap, or sexual orientation. The decision to remove electronic mail must be made by the Director of Engineering, Chief Technology Officer, Corporate Counsel, Chief Executive Officer, or Human Resource Officer. When practical and feasible, individuals responsible for the message will be informed of the decision and given the opportunity to remove the message(s) themselves.

Disclosing Internal Information

Staff must not publicly disclose via the Internet internal MYC information that may adversely affect MYC's security, customer relations, or public image unless the approval of the Chief Executive Officer or Executive Team has first been obtained. Such information includes business prospects, service performance analyses, and the like. Responses to specific customer electronic mail messages are exempted from this guideline.

Inadvertent Disclosure

Care must be taken to properly structure comments and questions posted to mailing lists (listservs), public news groups, and related public postings on the Internet. Before posting any material, staff must consider whether the posting could put MYC at a significant disadvantage or whether the material could cause public relations problems. Staff should keep in mind that several separate pieces of information can be pieced together to form a picture revealing confidential information which could then be used against MYC or the agencies and individuals it serves. Although it may seem to be different from the prevailing Internet culture of openness, to avoid this mosaic picture problem, staff should be reserved rather than forthcoming with internal MYC information.

User Authentication, Inbound

Staff wishing to establish a real-time connection with MYC internal computing resources via the Internet must use two-factor authentication through a secure portal before gaining access to MYC's internal network.

Establishing Network Connections

Unless the prior approval of the Director of Engineering has been obtained, staff may not establish Internet or other external network connections that could allow non-MYC users to gain access to MYC computing resources and information. These connections include the establishment of multicomputer file systems (such as Sun's NIS), Internet Web pages, ftp servers, and the like.

Copyrights

MYC strongly supports strict adherence to software vendors' license agreements. When at work, or when MYC computing resources are employed, copying of software in a manner that is not consistent with the vendor's license is strictly forbidden. Off-hours participation in pirate software bulletin boards and similar activities represent a conflict of interest with MYC work and are, therefore, prohibited. Reproducing, forwarding, or in any other way republishing or redistributing words, graphics, or other materials must be done only with the permission of the author/ owner. Staff should assume that all materials on the Internet are copyrighted unless specific notice states otherwise.

Publicly Writable Directories

All publicly writable directories on MYC computing resources and Internet-connected computers will be reviewed and cleared on a regular basis. This process is necessary to prevent the anonymous exchange of information inconsistent with MYC's business. Staff using MYC computers must not be involved in any way with the exchange of the material described in the paragraph above.

Blocking Sites

MYC prevents staff from connecting with certain nonbusiness Web sites. Staff using MYC computing resources who discover they have connected with a Web site that contains sexually explicit, racist, violent, or other potentially offensive material must immediately disconnect from that site. The ability to connect with a specific Web site does not in itself imply that users of MYC systems are permitted to visit that site.

False Security Reports

The Internet has been plagued with hoaxes alleging various security problems. Many of these hoaxes take the form of chain letters which request that the receiving party send the message to other people. Staff in receipt of information about system vulnerabilities should forward it to the ISM, who will then determine what if any action is appropriate. Staff must not personally redistribute system vulnerability information.

Testing Controls

Staff must not "test the doors" of (probe) MYC computing resource security mechanisms or other Internet sites unless they have first obtained permission from the

ISM. If staff probe security mechanisms, alarms will be triggered and resources will needlessly be spent tracking the activity. Likewise, the possession of tools for cracking information security (such as SATAN) is prohibited without the advance permission of the ISM.

Appendix I

Title:	Electronic Communications Standard				
Part Number:	ST00150	Revision:	1.1	Effective:	20050930
Owner:	Corporate Counsel			Last Review:	20070501

This electronic document supersedes all previous electronic and printed documents or oral statements regarding this policy.
All Company Standards are subject to change at the sole discretion of MYC management.

Scope

This standard is required for and by MYC staff and all MYC computing resources. Questions about the guideline should be directed to the Corporate Security Officer (CSO) or Chief Counsel.

Definitions

See the Information Assurance glossary.

References

PL00550, Information Assurance Policy
GD00300, Computing Resources Guideline
Employee Handbook
Manager's Guide to Human Resource Policies and Procedures

Revision History

Date	Revision Number	Modification
08/16/04	0.0	S. Bacik. Initial release of standard.
08/30/04	0.1	S. Bacik. Added network storage of the I:, F:, N:, and public FTP site storage requirements.

Overview

This Electronic Communications Standard ("Standard") serves to provide guidance to staff regarding the use of any MYC telecommunication system. This Standard applies to any MYC telecommunication system including but not limited to the following: e-mail, voicemail, BlackBerrys, cell phones, and pagers. This Standard sets forth requirements applicable to all employees and third parties that are subject to MYC policies and procedures. Not included in this Standard is information on how to operate any of MYC's telecommunication systems. The Help Desk can assist with "how-to" questions regarding any of MYC's telecommunication systems.

Persons Subject to Electronic Communications Standard

This Standard applies to MYC staff. This Standard also applies to any temporary workers, contractors, consultants, and vendors who provide services to MYC and who are given permission to use its electronic communications systems or services on behalf of MYC.

Any failure to adhere to this Standard and the related business standards, practices, and procedures set forth in MYC's Employee Handbook and Manager's Guide to Human Resource Policies and Procedures can compromise the information and intellectual property of MYC and its business interests, and may result in disciplinary and legal action, including, without limitation, termination of employment or services on behalf of MYC.

Microsoft Exchange is MYC's standard e-mail system using Microsoft Outlook as the standard e-mail client.

Audit and Review

Staff using MYC's electronic communications systems should have no expectation of privacy. MYC reserves the unrestricted right to access, audit, review, delete, disclose, or use all communications and other information stored or transferred on

MYC's electronic communications systems at any time, without notice and without recourse, regardless of the content of the information.

On request, any authorized electronic communications system staff shall furnish to MYC all passwords and codes necessary to access that user's information. Use of any of MYC's electronic communications systems automatically constitutes each staff's consent to any audit, review, and management by MYC's representatives.

Standard Exceptions

The following is the process for requesting exceptions:

1. An e-mail or letter must be written documenting the business reason for the exception with a compensating control for validation with the approval of the requester's manager.
2. The security team will review the exception and document the risk for non-compliance and rate the compensating control for risk.
3. The exception will be forwarded on to the division Vice President, Chief Information Officer (CIO) and the Director of Operations (ITDO) for approval.
4. If the exception is granted by the division Vice President, CIO and ITDO, the exception will be in place for one year (to be reviewed annually) and the documentation for the exception will be held by the CSO.
5. The group requesting the exception will have one year to correct the non-compliant state. If the correction is not made within 12 months, then a new exception will need to be granted.

On an annual basis, the CSO will review the exceptions and ask the requester to renew the exception by going through the above process.

Standard

Network Storage

Excessive network storage has a number of repercussions for MYC. First, there is a cost associated with storing and maintaining e-mail files. As the use and storage on the network drives grow, the cost of storage, backup, and retention increase as well. Second, there are legal implications to consider. Old file versions or abandoned projects would be subject to discovery if MYC were to be involved in litigation.

It is recommended that you review the files you have placed on the network at least once a month, so the electronic clutter does not increase. To assist with the monthly clean up, the following network drive standards will be adhered to.

- **\\MYC_files\users\<username>** The maximum size that each user will be permitted on the network to store files is 400 MBs. This is the approximate size of data that can be stored on a CDRom drive, should the data have to be written to another media.
- **\\MYC_files\groups\<businessunit>** Each business unit will be permitted to use 1 GB of storage on the network.
- **\\MYC_files\shared** The N: drive was created for temporary storage among departments to exchange documents and remove them from the share. This drive will have all files removed once a month. On the 15th of each month, all files will be automatically removed from the N: drive.

Public FTP (ftp.MYC.com)

The public ftp (file transfer protocol) site setup for transferring files to and from the Internet is monitored for content on a regular basis. This public ftp area will have all files automatically removed on the fifth of every month to ensure data is not obsolete.

E-mail Footer

The following e-mail footer shall be attached to every e-mail going outside of *MYC:*

"Confidentiality Notice: The information contained in this e-mail message and its attachments, if any, may be privileged, confidential, and otherwise legally protected from disclosure. This information is solely the property of MYC. If you are not the intended recipient, any disclosure, copying, distribution, reading, or taking of any action in reliance on or in response to this information (except as specifically permitted in this notice) is strictly prohibited. If you have received this communication in error, please erase all copies of the message and its attachments and notify the sender immediately."

E-mail Retention and Storage

Excessive e-mail storage has a number of repercussions for MYC. First, there is a cost associated with storing and maintaining e-mail files. As MYC and its use of e-mail grows, costs increase as well. Second, there are legal implications to consider. If MYC were to be involved in litigation, it is likely that MYC would be subject to a broad request for review of all pertinent MYC records, including electronic records, such as e-mail communications. The more e-mail messages that are retained on individual computers, the more costly it is to search through them to identify relevant information. It becomes more likely that internal communications not intended for publication could be discovered, misconstrued, and potentially used against MYC. For all of these reasons, it is extremely important that all persons subject to this Electronic Communications Standard understand the implications of creating and storing e-mails.

It is recommended that you clean up mail at least once monthly, so you don't trade office clutter for electronic clutter. Your e-mail is a virtual mailbox, and its messages and enclosures are stored in a database on MYC's mail server.

- **120 days of e-mail.** To assist in being compliant with our departmental records retention policy, only 120 days of e-mail will be stored on the mail server per mailbox. There will be an automatic delete process that will remove all items stored on the mail server that are over 120 days old.
- **Mailbox size of 100 MBs.** The inbox size on the mail server has a size limit of 100 MBs per user and, as with your mailbox at home, can get too full. If you exceed the limit, the system will notify you and you will not be able to send or receive any mail until some is deleted. The more messages in your mailbox, the slower your mail will be, especially when connecting from a non-MYC location. You should erase obsolete e-mail from all your e-mail folders, including "sent mail" and "deleted mail," or store the material in a folder in your private directory.
- **Automatic archive once every 15 days.** When you archive, the original items are copied to the archive file, and then removed from the current folder. When you archive, your existing folder structure is maintained in your new archive file. If there is a parent folder above the folder you choose to archive, the parent folder is created in the archive file, but other items within the parent folder are not archived. In this way, an identical folder structure exists between the archived file and your mailbox. Folders are left in place after being archived, even if they are empty. Several Outlook folders are set up with AutoArchive turned on. These folders and their default aging periods are Calendar (3 months), Tasks (3 months), Journal (3 months), Sent Items (2 months), and Deleted Items (2 months). Inbox, Notes, Contacts and Drafts do not have AutoArchive activated automatically.

Voicemail Retention

The repercussions of voicemail storage are the same as the e-mail repercussions. For these reasons, it is extremely important that all persons subject to this Standard understand the implications of creating and storing voicemails. Once a voicemail is deleted from the system, there is no way to recover the message or information about the message.

It is recommended that you clean up voicemail at least once weekly. Your voicemail is a virtual message box and you are limited to 1200 seconds of storage. The voicemail system is configured so that the maximum length of any message is 300 seconds.

A message can be stored within the voicemail system for a maximum of 10 days. This 10 day period includes the new inbox messages, old inbox messages, unopened inbox messages, and saved messages. There is an automatic delete process that removes all messages after 10 days.

BlackBerry Message Retention and Synching

It is recommended that you clean up the messages stored on your BlackBerry at least weekly. Your BlackBerry is another virtual storage device for e-mails and other documents that can run out of memory or become cluttered.

It is recommended that you synchronize your BlackBerry with your desktop at least once weekly to ensure you have the most current contact and appointment information from your Outlook client.

Cell Phone Retention

The repercussions of MYC-issued cell phone use and message storage are the same as the e-mail repercussions. For these reasons, it is extremely important that all persons subject to this Standard understand the implications of using a MYC-issued cell phone.

It is recommended that you clean up MYC-issued cell phone voice-mail at least once weekly.

Pager Retention

The repercussions of MYC-issued pager use and message storage, again, are the same as the e-mail repercussions. For these reasons, it is extremely important that all persons subject to this Standard understand the implications of using an MYC-issued pager.

It is recommended that you clean up MYC issued pager messages and numbers at least once weekly.

Fax Retention

Leaving fax pages on a machine in an open area could disclose confidential information to anyone within the area of the fax machine. For these reasons, it is extremely important that all persons subject to this Standard understand the implications of using an MYC fax machine.

It is recommended that someone within your area clean up MYC fax machine messages that are left on the fax machine at least once weekly. If no owner can be determined for the fax, the fax should be placed in the shred bin.

If you have a fax number that forwards received faxes into your e-mail account, the received faxes are subject to the above rules defined for e-mails.

Fax Footer and Header

The following fax footer shall be attached to every fax going outside of MYC:

"Confidentiality Notice: The information contained in this fax may be privileged, confidential, and otherwise legally protected from disclosure. This information is the property solely of MYC, Inc. If you are not the intended recipient, any disclosure, copying, distribution, reading, or taking of any action in reliance on or in response to this information (except as specifically permitted in this notice) is strictly prohibited. If you have received this communication in error, please erase all copies of the fax and notify the sender immediately."

A sample fax cover sheet can be found below.

My Address
My City, State Zip
Date: _____

To: _____

Fax Number: _____

Pages (including cover): _____

From: _____

Phone Number: _____

Fax Number: _____

RE: _____

Comments:

Confidentiality Notice: The information contained in this fax may be privileged, confidential, and otherwise legally protected from disclosure. This information is solely the property of MYC. If you are not the intended recipient, any disclosure, copying, distribution, reading, or taking of any action in reliance on or in response to this information (except as specifically permitted in this notice) is strictly prohibited. If you have received this communication in error, please erase all copies of the fax and notify the sender immediately.

Appendix J

Title:	Solaris Server Build Security Standard				
Part Number:	ST00185	Revision:	5.0	Effective:	20001101
Owner:	Dir IT Operations			Last Review:	20070301

This electronic document supersedes all previous electronic and printed documents or oral statements regarding this policy.
All Company Standards are subject to change at the sole discretion of MYC management.

Specification

This Solaris Security Standard Practice defines the security practice which should be implemented on all Solaris servers within the development, test, and production enterprise environments.

The basic goal of computer security is to protect MYC computing and information assets from *unauthorized* activities. Security is the responsibility of *everyone*. Information and computer security involves at least three concepts—confidentiality, integrity, and availability. With an expanding network environment and the ability to access and transfer data both into and out of the network environment, it becomes increasingly important that we implement effective security practices to help us perform due diligence. An open and diverse network environment requires strong host-based security. An out-of-the box Solaris installation is not secure and extra precautions need to be taken after installing the operating system.

Intended Use and Exceptions

All exceptions must be documented and approved by Information Technology and Information Security.

Solaris servers (development, test, and production) must follow this standard and any Solaris server not in compliance will be removed from the enterprise network and shut down until compliance can be achieved.

Rationale

This standard practice is required to secure the company's critical business, financial data, and assets, and to ensure reliable operation of critical applications which are stored and maintained on a Solaris server. Compliance with this standard practice is necessary to adhere to MYC's security policies.

The purpose of this Solaris Security Standard Practice is twofold. First, it is to provide consistency on critical aspects of UNIX server security. Secondly, this practice is to provide consistency with the UNIX server installations.

Overview

This standard practice addresses

- securely configuring a UNIX server
- administrative duties for the UNIX server
- network service controls

Additionally, requirements for specific business applications are outside the scope of this standard. Refer to application-specific documentation for installation details and additional configuration information.

Intended Audience

Knowledge of corporate security policies is required.

The intended audience for this document includes Solaris server administrators and business Information Technology (IT) support staff who install, configure, and administer Solaris servers throughout the MYC network environment. To effectively perform the security administration functions outlined in this document, it is assumed that the staff member has the following:

- Formal training and/or experience with
  UNIX shell scripting
  UNIX servers
  TCP/IP
- Familiarity with network terms such as *TCP/IP, protocols.*

Separation of Function

Individual accountability clearly establish for duties that are performed for the ongoing, day-to-day support of a Solaris server. The separation of duties can be achieved by unique, individual accounts for each user/function.

Computer Operations Personnel

- Authorizes and schedules all operating system software changes
- Authorizes and schedules all hardware changes
- Authorizes and schedules all application software changes
- Maintains a log of all software/hardware change activity

System Administration

- Performs all operating system software changes
- Reviews all hardware changes

Account Administration

- Performs user ID additions, changes, and deletions

Security Administration

- Monitors operating system security controls
- Reviews operating system logs for unauthorized access or use
- Aids business units in determining risks to the MYC network environment
- Reviews access control changes for risks to the MYC environment
- Reviews operating system for compliance with corporate and all security policies

Application Support

- Reviews all application software changes
- Implements access control changes

There should be both a *primary* administrator and a *backup* administrator. Both must be trained and proficient in Solaris and application software and security administration duties.

References

The recommended configurations listed below are based on the following documents:

- PL00550, Information Assurance Policy
- GD00300, Computing Resources Guideline
- Employee Handbook
- Manager's Guide to Human Resource Policies and Procedures
- Sun Solaris Security by Sun (www.sun.com/software/white-papers/wp-security)
- NIS+ PSD/FAQ (http://www.ebsinc.com/solaris/network/nis+.html)
- Security in Open Systems, NIST Special Publication 800-7, July 1994, www-08.nist.gov/nistpubs/800-7

System Monitoring

The following files and processes need to be monitored or ensured on the server:

- Monitor the /etc/passwd on a monthly basis to ensure all accounts have a purpose to locally logon and that all unused accounts are removed
- Monitor the /etc/group on a monthly basis to ensure all groups and group members have a business reason for their presence and ensure that all accounts listed can be found in the /etc/passwd file
- Ensure that ROOT logon is restricted to CONSOLE only
- Ensure the /etc/services file contains only the services required to execute on and through the machine
- Ensure the /etc/inetd.conf file contains only services which are listed in the /etc/services file and only required services are initialized upon system reboot
- Monitor that ports on and through the box are contained in the /etc/services file (netstat)
- Monitor for failed logins
- Monitor for users that use the su program
- Monitor for successful logins

- Monitor all successful and failures of login and init
- Monitor /var/log/syslog for other miscellaneous messages

Solaris Operating System

It is recommended that the server be migrated to a secure (trusted) system. Implementation of this option may be incompatible with other features or third-party software.

Network Access

The following items require monitoring or configuring to maintain secure access via the network:

- For Network File System, the uniformity of user ID values (UID) and group ID values (GID) must be maintained for the server and client systems
- Ensure that the Windows manager cannot be started, except on the console
- Use the control features available for inetd. See inetd(1M) in the man pages
- Review /etc/inetd.conf and comment out any unneeded services
- Define /etc/exports to specifically list file systems and hosts that can mount files via Network File System
- Eliminate or restrict use of finger to superuser only. Change file permissions with "chmod 500 /usr/bin/finger" on the client
- RPC should be limited to local access only
- Ensure root can login only through the console. This will require non-console users to su to root, providing an audit trail via the sulog. It also would force would-be hackers to know two passwords instead of one
- If a modem is connected to your system, the accountable manager is obligated to document its existence and use

ROOT

ROOT is required to conform to the following items:

- Only one individual knows the password for the ROOT account. If two or more individuals need ROOT or SUPERUSER access, define unique accounts with UID=0.
- Ensure the root account has a login directory of /root instead of / and ensure the /etc/passwd file is updated to reflect the change.
- Ensure that the "." is removed from the PATH statement.
- ROOT should be restricted to console login only.

User IDs

User IDs are required to conform to the following items:

- Only one person may use a USERID. A person may have more than one USERID.
- The /etc/passwd file will be shadowed.
- All USERIDs will have passwords and password aging will be turned on.
- All USERIDs will have a unique UID value. Any UID of 0 will always log as root, not the UID.
- The COMMENT field of /etc/passwd will contain the name, mail sort, and telephone number (in that order) of the individual responsible for the activity of a USERID. See COMMENT Field Layout for detailed description.
- All passwords will be a minimum of six characters, including a least two alpha characters and at least one numeric or special character.

UID and GID Uniformity

Maintain uniformity of user ID and group ID for server and client systems. Owner and group specification for a file is based on UID/GID value, not login/group name.

Login Banner Text

A login banner will be defined for all services and any login banner will not contain the system name or operating system and version. /etc/issue should be used for the warning banner file, because the warning banner will be displayed prior to the login prompt. /etc/motd will display a message after a user has logged into the system.

There are two forms for the Login Banner Text. The long form is the preferred text and should be used if technically possible. The short form is reserved for situations where the long form cannot be technically implemented.

Long form	**WARNING:** This is a private network. All usage is subject to audit. Unauthorized access or use may lead to prosecution.
	This system is for the exclusive use of authorized MYC employees and associates. Anyone using this system is subject to having all of his or her activities on this system monitored and recorded by system administration staff. Anyone using this system expressly consents to such monitoring and is advised that if such monitoring reveals possible evidence of criminal activity, system administration staff may provide the evidence from such monitoring to law enforcement officials.
Short form	**NOTICE:** This is a private network.

Passwords & /etc/passwd

For nonemployee accounts, an account expiration date should be set to no more than one year from the account creation date.

Password shadowing should be enabled.

Password aging should be turned on using the /etc/default/passwd file with the following values:

- MAXWEEKS=16
- MINWEEKS=0
- TIMEOUT=300
- PASSLENGTH=6

Passwords must be constructed to meet the following requirements:

- Each password must have at least PASSLENGTH characters, where PASS-LENGTH is defined in /etc/default/passwd and is set to 6. Only the first eight characters are significant.
- Each password must contain at least two alphabetic characters and at least one numeric or special character. In this case, *alphabetic* refers to all upper or lower case letters.
- Each password must differ from the user's login name and any reverse or circular shift of that login name. For comparison purposes, an upper case letter and its corresponding lower case letter are equivalent.
- New passwords must differ from the old by at least three characters. For comparison purposes, an upper case letter and its corresponding lower case letter are equivalent.

COMMENT Field Layout

The COMMENT field of /etc/passwd will be the home of the record of the individual responsible for the activity of that specific login ID on that specific operating system. This field is subdivided into four fields: name, mail sort, office telephone number, and comment.

This field and its contents will be used for various cross references and contact lists. In no case should generic or descriptive names be placed in lieu of an individual name and contact information.

The format of the COMMENT field follows the specifications given below.

Subfield	Content Specifications
Name	First name, either full or common, and last name. Use upper and lower case letters, use a single space between the first and last names. Example: Jane Smith

Subfield	Content Specifications
Mail sort	Use the company mail sort or local interoffice mail identifier. Examples: WTC G123 Scale #4
Office telephone	Use the full number. Examples: 667–4998 (no area code specified) 206–667–4998 (area code specified)
Comment	This can be used for a general comment.

File/Directory Permissions

File and directory permissions are required to have the following features:

- All files that have the suid or sgid bits set must be protected from tampering; that is, they cannot be written by others. All files that have the suid or sgid bits set must have known and approved purposes.
- All files must have a known owner and group associated with them.
- Ensure that no files are world writeable, unless there is a documented business reason.
- Default UMASK for user accounts (uid>0) will be 077. If an application requires a different UMASK value, have the UMASK value set by the application or a logon script.
- Default UMASK root accounts (uid=0) will be 022.
- Eliminate the use of .netrc files. It is a security risk to have plain text passwords in a file. See netrc(4) in the man pages.
- Know and justify the use of $HOME/.rhosts files. Use of $HOME/.rhosts files implies a trust relationship between the local system and the systems named in the file. All hosts listed in .rhost must comply with or exceed the security classification (critical/non-critical) of local host. Protect your .rhost files and home directory to prevent unauthorized users from gaining rcp access to your remote account and host.
- Know and justify the use of /etc/hosts.equiv. The risk of using hosts.equiv is similar to $HOME/.rhosts. There are somewhat better controls available. See hosts.equiv(4) in the man pages and review the material discussed in Using APRA Services.
- Files referenced by *cron, at,* or *batch,* should not have group or other write permission.
- No application or user files should be located in the ROOT (/) directory.
- System shutdown files will not have group or other write permission.

- System startup files will not have group or other write permission and verify that sys group only can use.
- User profile files will not have group or other write permission.
- Use Access Control Lists (ACLs) to provide discretionary access control to files. NOTE: Not all file backup methods (e.g., TAR & CPIO) copy ACLs.

Permission definitions:

r	read
w	write
x	execute (file), read (directory)
s	set uid at execution
c	character device

The following files should always have the listed owners, groups, and permissions:

File Name	File Owner	File Group	Permissions
$home/.profile. for all root and superuser accounts remove the "." from the path statement.	the user	the user's initial group	-rw-------
$home/.rhost. If .rhosts file is to be used the following rules must be used: permissions on the .rhost file should be set to 0600(-rw-------). protect your remote home directory with at least 0711(-rwx--x--x)	the user	the user's initial group	-rw-------
/bin/login	root	bin	-r-sr-xr-x
/dev/console	root	tty	crw--w--w-
/dev/kmem	bin	sys	crw-r-----
/dev/mem	bin	sys	crw-r-----
/etc/cron	root	bin	-r-xr-xr-x
/etc/cron.d/at.allow	root	sys	-rw-r--r--
/etc/cron.d/at.deny	root	sys	-rw-r--r--

File Name	File Owner	File Group	Permissions
/etc/cron.d/cron.allow	root	sys	-rw-r--r--
/etc/cron.d/cron.deny	root	sys	-rw-r--r--
/etc/getty	root	sys	-r-xr--r--
/etc/group	root	sys	-rw-r--r--
/etc/hosts	root	sys	-rw-r--r--
/etc/inet/*	root	sys	-rw-r--r--
/etc/inetd.conf	root	sys	-rw-r--r--
/etc/inittab	root	sys	-rw-r--r--
/etc/mount	bin	bin	-r-xr-xr-x
/etc/oshadow	root	sys	-r--------
/etc/passwd	root	sys	-r--r--r--
/etc/profile	bin	bin	-rw-r--r--
/etc/services	root	sys	-r--r--r--
/etc/shadow	root	sys	-r--------
/etc/skel/.profile	root	sys	-rw-r--r--
/etc/skel/local.cshrc	root	sys	-rw-r--r--
/etc/skel/local.login	bin	bin	-rw-r--r--
/etc/skel/local.profile	root	sys	-rw-r--r--
/etc/vfstab	root	sys	-rw-r--r--
/opt/local/config/files/netgroup	bin	bin	-rx-r--r--
/sbin/mount	root	bin	-r-xr-xr-x
/usr/adm/sulog	root	root	-rw-------
/usr/bin/login	root	bin	-r-sr-xr-x
/usr/bin/savecore	root	bin	-r-xr-xr-x
/usr/sbin/cron	root	bin	-r-xr-xr-x
/usr/sbin/in.*	root	bin	-r-xr--r--
/usr/spool/cron/atjobs	root	sys	dr-xr-xr-x

File Name	File Owner	File Group	Permissions
/usr/spool/cron/crontabs	root	sys	dr-xr-xr-x
/var/adm/utmp	adm	adm	-rw-r--r--
/var/adm/utmpx	adm	adm	-rw-r--r--
/var/adm/wtmp	adm	adm	-rw-r--r--
/var/adm/wtmpx	adm	adm	-rw-r--r--
/var/cron/log	root	root	-rw-------
/var/log/syslog	root	other	-rw-r--r--

Services/Utilities

General

Services/utilities, in general, are required to conform to the following items:

- Know and review any program that allows memory to be examined or changed.
- Use the most current version of FTP. Apply any FTP patches as they become available from the vendor.
- Use the most current version of sendmail. Apply any sendmail patches as they become available from the vendor.
- Use cron.allow/cron.deny and at.allow/at.deny to specifically control use of the cron and at/batch utilities.

Allowable Services

FTP

Whenever possible, the /etc/ftpusers file should be used. The /etc/ftpusers file contains a list of users who are not allowed to use FTP to access files. At a minimum /etc/ftpusers should be used to deny users and systems from accessing FTP. /etc/ftpusers should contain the following accounts and any other account that does not belong to a human user:

- root
- uucp
- news

- bin
- nobody
- daemon

If anonymous FTP is required, then the following items can be used to minimize threats using anonymous FTP (Endnote 1):

- Disable the FTP account by placing an asterisk in the password field of the password file. This will prevent users from logging onto the system using a user name of FTP.
- Verify that the anonymous FTP root directory and its subdirectories are not owned by the FTP account and are not in the same group as the FTP account. Anonymous FTP subdirectories generally include FTP/bin, FTP/etc, and FTP/pub. These directories should be write protected.
- In order to print user names and group names when files are listed, a passwd and group file are needed in the FTP/etc directory. To prevent crackers from obtaining copies of the system's /etc/passwd and /etc/group files, a dummy copy of each file should be used. All password fields should be changed to asterisks.
- An administrator should not provide writeable anonymous FTP directories unless the threats of providing writeable directories are known and precautions are taken to minimize these threats.
- Limit large file transfers by putting a file quota on an FTP user or locate the FTP account's home directory on an isolated partition.
- The contents of the pub directories should be monitored and any suspicious files should be deleted.

NIS+

The following should be reviewed to ensure a secure NIS+ operation (Endnote 2):

- The /etc/hosts.equiv file should not consist a single line containing a "+" because trusted access should never be granted to all hosts on the network. If the /etc/hosts.equiv file is used, it should contain entries for specific host names. Specific user names may also be specified.
- Netgroups, which group various users and hosts together, can be defined in the file /etc/netgroup and maintained as an NIS map. Using netgroups can simplify the task of granting or denying access to users. Netgroups can also be used in the password file.
- When NIS password or group file information is to be accessed, a line of the format "+:" should be used to indicate NIS server access. The format

"+::0:0:::" should not be used because if the leading "+" is accidentally deleted, unintended access can be granted.

■ NIS map files should be writeable only to the superuser.

■ The program ypbind should not be started with options that allow ypbind to listen to locally issued ypset commands. This prevents a cracker from using ypset to obtain information from an unauthorized NIS server. It also prevents a cracker from obtaining unauthorized copies of databases by guessing the name of a NIS domain, binding to the NIS server using the ypset command, and requesting a database.

■ Password aging can be used to force users to change their passwords periodically. Although password aging cannot be centralized using NIS, password aging can be individually implemented on each system a user can log in to.

■ Do not run NIS on a secure gateway.

■ To prevent unintended disclosure of information contained in the NIS databases, the ypserv program can be modified to respond to requests only from authorized NIS clients. This modification requires access to NIS source code.

■ Patches for bugs in ypserv, ypxfrd, and portmap utilities should be attained from Sun Microsystems.

■ Security is an integral part of NIS+. When properly configured, NIS+ prevents unauthorized sources from reading, changing, or destroying naming service information.

rcp, rsh, & rlogin

The "r" commands imply that the hosts listed in .rhosts are trusted. The administrator and owner of the server and data must decide if it is more secure to trust hosts so that passwords do not go across the network in plain text versus having passwords go across the network in plain text. The use of the "r" commands should be documented. The system administrator should monitor the contents of /etc/hosts.equiv and all copies of .rhosts.

sendmail

The following should be reviewed to ensure a secure sendmail operation (Endnote 3):

■ Verify that the version of sendmail used is recent. Older versions of sendmail have several bugs that allow security violations.

■ Remove the "uudecode" and "decode" alias from the aliases file. This file is usually /etc/aliases or /usr/lib/aliases.

- For aliases that allow messages to be sent to programs, make sure that there is no way to obtain a shell or send commands to a shell from these programs.
- Verify that the "wizard" password is disabled in the configuration file sendmail.cf.
- Verify that sendmail does not support the "debug" command. This can be done with the following commands:

```
% telnet localhost 25
Connected to localhost
Escape character is "^]".
220 hostname sendmail 5.61 ready at Fri, 18 Sep 92 15:10:48 EDT
debug
500 Command unrecognized
quit
%
```

If sendmail responds to the "debug" command with the message "'200 Debug set'," then sendmail is vulnerable to attack and should be replaced with a newer version.

telnet

The main security issue with telnet is that passwords are transmitted in plain text across the network. Whenever possible, use /bin/false as the initial program/shell to deny specific users TELNET access to a system. The file /etc/shells should be defined. See shells(4) in the man pages. At a minimum /bin/false should contain the following accounts and any other account that does not belong to a human user:

- root
- uucp
- news
- bin
- nobody
- daemon

NFS

If possible use Secure NFS over NFS. Know and justify all NFS mounted file systems and directories. Know and justify all NFS export directories. Use available access options in all exported file systems to control NFS mounts, preferably read-only. If possible, have the same system administrator for both client and server systems. The system administrator should monitor the contents of /etc/exports, which contains directories that can be exported. The following are the requirements when using NFS:

- Do not export the /usr directory
- Files should be read-only and owned by root
- Export the minimal subdirectory
- Use the nosuid option on the mount command

Disallowed Services

chargen	chargen should be disabled.
echo	echo should be disabled.
finger	finger should be disabled.
TFTP	TFTP should be disabled. TFTP is based on UDP which provides no security.
uucp	uucp should be disabled.

Endnotes

1. Security in Open Systems, NIST Special Publication 800–7, July 1994, section "Improving the Security of FTP."
2. Security in Open Systems, NIST Special Publication 800–7, July 1994, section "Improving the Security of NIS."
3. Security in Open Systems, NIST Special Publication 800–7, July 1994, section "Improving the Security of Mail Services."

Definitions

Cron	Clock daemon. Used for scheduling processes.
finger	Takes an account as input and returns information about the user who owns the account and other miscellaneous information.
ftp	File Transfer Protocol.
Nfs	Network File System.
nis+	Network Information Service Plus.
Pam	Pluggable authentication module

rcmd	Routines for returning stream to a remote command.
rexec	Return stream to a remote command.
rlogin	Establishes a remote login session from your terminal to a remote machine named hostname.
sendmail	Mail service.
telnet	User interface to a remote system.
tftp	Trivial file transfer protocol.
udp	Unreliable datagram protocol.
uucp	Unix-to-Unix Copy, a Unix utility and protocol that enables one computer to send files to another computer over a direct serial connection or modems.

Appendix K

Title:	Disk/Data Wipe Work Instruction				
Part Number:	PD00150	Revision:	1.0	Effective:	20060801
Owner:	Dir IT Operations			Last Review:	20070801

This electronic document supersedes all previous electronic and printed documents or oral statements regarding this policy.
All Company Work Instructions are subject to change at the sole discretion of MYC management.

Change History

Date	Revision #	Author	Revision Description	Approved?
08/01/06	1.0	S. Bacik	Initial Version	Yes

Introduction

This procedure defines Disk Wipe and Data Wipe processes for ensuring all data is wiped from personal computers, servers, and any other device with a bootable Windows or UNIX/LINUX Operating System upon disposal/release from MYC.

Purpose and Scope

All systems that store MYC specific data on a hard drive will utilize a program to delete the data and then overwrite with randomized data to ensure old data cannot be recovered. Currently MYC utilizes Darik's Boot and Nuke, free to use under GNU public license.

This process is to be used on all devices with MYC specific data being removed from the environment, including any temporary facilities used for testing or developing offsite.

References

The instructions below are based on the following documents:

- PL00550, Information Assurance Policy
- GD00300, Computing Resources Guideline
- ST01505, IT Windows Standard Configuration

Acronyms

Acronym	Description
IT	Information Technology
CSO	Corporate Security Officer
ISO	International Standards Organization

Roles and Responsibilities

IT Management Team	Designate personnel authorized to facilitate or oversee data wipe processes.
IT Operations Team	Utilize data wipe procedure and document its use either in a Service Desk ticket or as a completed item on a project plan on equipment approved for disposal or temporary equipment before its return.
Information Security Team	Monitor operation and conduct periodic review of the effectiveness of implemented disk wipe procedure and associated application(s).

Process Description

This section contains a description of the process for destroying data on a hard drive.

Process Flow

1. Obtain the Disk Wipe Utility ISO image or create a bootable CD diskette from the software found in the IT Operations software cabinet on \\MYCGHOST.
2. The Disk Wipe Bootable CD can be created from the ISO image found at \\MYCGHOST\apps\diskwipe\dban-1.0.6_i386.ISO.
3. Alternatively, for machines that cannot boot from CD, you can create a bootable floppy image by running the dban-1.0.6_i386.EXE file contained within the \\MYCGHOST\apps\diskwipe\dban-1.0.6_i386.zip file.
4. Ensure that the machine you are working with is set to autoboot from either the CD-ROM drive or floppy drive (depending on which option you are using).
5. Insert the bootable CD or floppy with Darik's Boot and Nuke. Power cycle the machine to ensure a clean boot to this bootable disk. If the devices will not autoboot to either the CD or Floppy, then you will need to physically remove the drive and mount the drive as a secondary drive in a device that supports this option.
6. You will see a blue screen with the following text:

```
Darik's Boot and Nuke

- - - - - - - - - - - - - - - -

Warning: This software irrecoverable destroys data.

        This sof Tables 3,4,5tware is provided without any warranty; without

        even the implied

        warranty of merchantability or fitness for a particular purpose. In no event

        shall the software authors or contributors be liable for any damages

        arising

        from the use of this software. This software is provided "as is".

http://dban.sourceforge.net/

Press the F2 key to learn about DBAN.

Press the F3 key for a list of quick commands.

Press the ENTER key to start DBAN in interactive mode.

Enter autonuke at this prompt to start DBAN in automatic mode.

boot:
```

7. Type **autonuke** and hit enter.
8. A secondary processing screen will appear:

```
               Darik's Boot and Nuke beta.2003052000
 ┌──────────── Options ──────────┐┌──────────── Statistics ──────────┐
 │Entropy: Linux Kernel (urandom)││Runtime:    00:00:21               │
 │PRNG:    Mersenne Twister (mt19937ar-cok)││CPU Load:   96%          │
 │Method:  DoD 5220 22.M         ││Throughput: 5973 KB/s              │
 │Verify:  Last Pass             ││Limiter:    Disk I/O               │
 │Rounds:  1                     ││Errors:     0                      │
 └───────────────────────────────┘└───────────────────────────────────┘

  (IDE  0,0,0,-,-) VMware Virtual IDE Hard Drive
    [04.33%, round 1 of 1, pass 1 of 7] [writing] [5973 KB/s]
```

9. Once you are at this screen, you can remove the disk and continue on to another machine as you wait for the wipe procedure to complete.
10. This runs at a rate of a little over 10 gigabytes per hour for a 7 pass run (default); return to the machine after the appropriate time has passed.
11. Validate the results by looking to see that 7 of 7 passes completed successfully.
12. The process is complete for the primary drive. If other drives are mounted in the system, the procedure will need to be repeated for those drives using the ENTER option to go to interactive mode.

Anomalies

If the drive cannot be wiped due to errors or a physical limitation, log a service desk ticket noting the failure to complete successfully and escalate to Data Center Operations management with notification to the CSO.

If the disk was part of a RAID volume (excluding mirrors), any single disk does not contain enough data to reconstruct any files and therefore does not need to be wiped prior to being disposed of or returned to the vendor. However, if multiple disks from the same RAID volume are being sent outside MYC, they must first be wiped.

Any exceptions to this procedure must be approved in writing by the CSO and Manager of Data Center Operations.

Quality Records

Quality records are documentation that provides evidence of conformance to the process. The erasing of data is upon request and there may not be any records of this request.

Appendix L

Title:	Internet Access Reports				
Part Number:	PD00175	Revision:	1.0	Effective:	20060801
Owner:	Dir IT Operations			Last Review:	20070801

This electronic document supersedes all previous electronic and printed documents or oral statements regarding this policy.
All Company Work Instructions are subject to change at the sole discretion of MYC management.

Change History

Date	Revision #	Author	Revision Description	Approved?
08/01/06	1.0	S. Bacik	Initial Version	Yes

References

The recommended instructions documented below are based on the following documents:

- PL00550, Information Assurance Policy
- GD00300, Computing Resources Guideline
- ST01505, IT Windows Standard Configuration

Procedure

This procedure defines the weekly reporting for Human Resources (HR) and the Chief Information Officer (CIO) on the MYC Internet access from the MYC enterprise network. The report is processed on Monday morning based on the previous week's data from the Pix firewall ported into the Websense SQL database.

The current data acquisition and reporting functions are performed using Websense, MSAccess, and perl. The software, command script, and perl script master copies can be found on the HQSECURITY01 file server. The permissions on this server are limited; please see the Director of Information Security (DIS) for access.

Weekly Processing

As of October 15, 2002, this process can only be executed from the HDQ-SECURITY server, due to the Websense application setup and the perl scripts.

Websense/MSAccess

The Websense application is subscription based to update the Web sites that fall into specific categories. See Table 15—Monitored Categories for a listing of the possible categories and the categories reported to HR.

1. Log into the workstation initially as the security administrator.
2. Start the Websense application (Start -> Programs -> Websense Reporter -> Reporter 6.2).
3. Open the Favorites container.
4. Double click on the Favorites HR1 -> Summary -> User -> Destinations by date.
5. Update the Dates tab section to use the dates for the previous week (Sunday through Saturday).
6. Select the Generate button.
7. The report will be processing for a while; when the data is displayed in the right window, then the data can be exported.
8. On the tool bar there will be a white envelope with a red arrow, this is the export tool. Select Export.
9. In the Export window from the Format drop down, select ODBC -> MS Access Database and click OK.
10. Change the directory to the websense.mdb file in c:\data\monitoring\data\hr
11. Create the table name to be CREXPORT and click OK. If you receive the error "Table already exists. Please use another table name, or you can retry after removing the table," then open the websense.mdb file, delete the

CREXPORT table, close the websense.mdb file, and attempt the export again.

12. The exporting screen will display and this processing will take a few minutes.
13. When the export is complete, open the websense.mdb file and rename the CREXPORT table to CREXPORT-<date>-HR1.
14. Double click on the Favorites HR2 -> Summary -> User -> Destinations by date.
15. Update the Dates tab section to use the dates for the previous week (Sunday through Saturday).
16. Select the Generate button.
17. The report will be processing for a while; when the data is displayed in the right window, then the data can be exported.
18. On the tool bar there will be a white envelope with a red arrow, this is the export tool. Select Export.
19. In the Export window from the Format drop down, select ODBC—MS Access Database and click OK.
20. Change the directory to the websense.mdb file in c:\data\monitoring\data\hr
21. Create the table name to be CREXPORT and click OK. If you receive the error "Table already exists. Please use another table name, or you can retry after removing the table," then open the websense.mdb file, delete the CREXPORT table, close the websense.mdb file, and attempt the export again.
22. The exporting screen will display and this will take a few minutes processing.
23. When the export is complete, open the websense.mdb file and rename the CREXPORT table to CREXPORT-<date>-HR2.
24. Open the websense.mdb file and export the CREXPORT-<date>-HR1 and CREXPORT-<date>-HR2 tables to a tab delimited text file (Text Files for the Save as type) in c:\temp\ using the same names. When exporting the HR1 table, export the column names in the first row and do not export the column names in the first row for HR2.
25. Close the websense.mdb file.

Command Line/MS Access

1. Open the command line prompt
2. Change to the c:\temp directory
3. Combine the CREXPORT-<date>-HR1.txt and CREXPORT-<date>-HR2.txt files into one file using the command

   type CREXPORT-<date>-HR2.txt >> CREXPORT-<date>-HR1.txt

4. Open the websense.mdb file, open the tables section, select New from the menu bar

5. Select Import Table from the New Table window and click OK
6. Change directories to c:\temp and select the CREXPORT-<date>-HR1.txt file.
7. In the Import Text Wizard window, select Delimited and Next
8. Select Tab delimited file, First Row Contains Field Names, and Text Qualifier {none}, and Next
9. Select In a New Table and click Next
10. When selecting the field options, do not change anything and select Next
11. Select No primary key and click Next
12. Change the import table name to CREXPORT and click Finish
13. Change to the Queries objects and double-click CREXPORT Query
14. When the query displays, select File -> Export, then select the Save as type to be text file and the filename to be c:\data\monitoring\data\hr\badsite-<date>
15. Click Export All
16. Select delimited file and Next
17. Select the tab delimiter and the text qualifier as {none} and click Next
18. Validate the file name and click Finish
19. Click OK upon the good export and close the websense.mdb file

Perl

1. Open the command line prompt.
2. Change to the c:\data\monitoring\scripts directory.
3. Run the following perl script command to document the workstation and account accessing the Web site: Websense-hr.pl c:\data\monitoring\data\hr\badsite-<date> <startdate-mm/dd/yyyy> 7
4. The perl script will run gathering the log in information from the remote dial-up logs (\\hqsec01\logs\TACACS+ Accounting\TACACS+ Accounting YYY-MM-DD.csv) and the network log in information from the network logs (\\hqfile03\logging$\AssetMgmt\Queue\Julianday.done).
5. The perl script will then parse the bad sites input file and try to find the IP address in the array built from the dial-up and network login access files. If the IP address cannot be found, then a "ping -a" is tried against the IP address to see if the address is still on the network and attempts the gather the machine name.
6. The perl script will display a tab delimited file containing the following information:
   - Date of access
   - Time of first network/dial-in login for the day
   - Account name
   - Machine name
   - IP address of machine
   - Number of hits to the Web site

- Web site name
- Websense category
- Additional login times for the IP address

Excel

1. Open the tab delimited output file from the perl script using Excel
2. Sort the sheet by Account Name, Date, and Time
3. Delete all records with the account of INFOSEC-RESEARCH
4. Start reviewing all of the account names starting with UNKNOWN
5. Using the machine name, attempt to determine the possible account name that used the machine and update the Account Name field to have it appended onto the information (Possibly <name>)
6. Repeat until all UNKNOWN account names have been accounted for, as best as possible
7. Open a Notepad session for Web sites to review
8. Search the Web sites for the following words or numbers and place the Web site name in the Notepad session:
   - All numbers or garbled letters
   - teen
   - lolita
   - 18
   - kid
   - youth
   - little
   - young
9. Save the Notepad file to c:\temp\checksites.txt
10. Save and close the Excel spreadsheet in Excel format

Internet Explorer/Excel

1. Log off the workstation and log into the HDQ-SECURITY workstation as INFOSEC-RESEARCH.
2. Open the Notepad file of c:\temp\checksites.txt.
3. Open Internet Explorer and validate whether the list of sites contains children or youth approximately 18–25 years of age. Note which sites qualify.
4. Log off the workstation and log into the HDQ-SECURITY workstation as Sandra Bacik.
5. Open the tab delimited output file from the perl script using Excel.
6. For each site that was found to include children or youth from approximately 18–25 years of age, bold and italicize the Web site name in the Excel spreadsheet.

Sending the Report

1. Using PGP, encrypt the Excel spreadsheet
2. E-mail the encrypted file to HR and CIO using a subject line of "Weekly report <date> thru <date>"

Ad Hoc

As of October 15, 2002, this process can be executed only from the HDQ-SECURITY laptop, due to the Websense application setup and the perl scripts. This would be requests from HR or a manager to report on all of the Internet activity for a specific person. The request must contain the person's name and a specific date range for the report to display.

Perl/Excel

1. Open the command line prompt.
2. Change to the c:\data\monitoring\scripts directory.
3. Create a DOS batch file containing the following command for each Julian day to be reviewed, then saved as <username>.bat:

   readfile-loginlogs.pl 0 2 "Sandra Bacik" <JulianDay> <sandrabacik>

5. Run the newly created batch file from the c:\data\monitoring\scripts directory.
6. The perl script (readfile-loginlogs.pl) will run gathering the login information from the network logs (\\hqfile03\logging$\AssetMgmt\Queue\Julianday. done).
7. The perl script will output a tab delimited file containing the IP address, machine name, date, and time the person logged into the network for the specified date range.
8. Open Excel and open the output file from the c:\data\monitoring\data\ review directory.
9. Copy a line containing "Login Date   Login Time   Logout Date" to the first line in the file—this will be your column heading line.
10. Sort the file by Logout Date (actually user name), Login Date, and Login Time.
11. After the last valid date line, delete the rest of the lines in the file.
12. Autofit the columns in the file.
13. Hopefully, the user will have logged into the network obtaining the same IP address for all dates. If not, note each day and each IP address on the day.

Websense/MSAccess

1. Start the Websense application (Start -> Programs -> Websense Reporter -> Reporter 6.2)
2. Open the Favorites container
3. Double click on the Favorites HR1 -> Summary -> User -> Destinations by date
4. Update the Dates tab section to use the dates for the previous week (Sunday through Saturday)
5. Select the Generate button
6. The report will be processing for a while; when the data is displayed in the right window, then the data can be exported
7. Double click on the Favorites HR2 -> Summary -> User -> Destinations by date
8. Update the Dates tab section to use the dates for the previous week (Sunday through Saturday)
9. Select the Generate button
10. The report will be processing for a while; when the data is displayed in the right window, then the data can be exported

Perl

The Websense application is subscription based to update the Web sites that fall into specific categories. See Table 15—Monitored Categories for a listing of the categories.

Sending the Report

The Websense application is subscription based to update the websites that fall into specific categories. See Table 15—Monitored Categories for a listing of the categories.

Table 15

Monitored Categories

Monitored Category	Category Title	Category Description
	Abortion Advocacy	All Abortion Advocacy sites are contained within the subcategories. See their descriptions below.
	Abortion Advocacy: Pro-Choice	Sites with neutral or balanced discussion of the issues.
	Abortion Advocacy: Pro-Life	Sites with neutral or balanced discussion of the issues.
	Advocacy Groups	Sites sponsored by or devoted to organizations that promote change or reform in public policy, public opinion, social practice, economic activities, and relationships. Excludes commercially sponsored sites, sites dedicated to electoral politics or legislation or to the abortion issue, sites advocating hate or violence.
Yes	Adult Material	All Adult Material sites are contained within the subcategories. See their descriptions below.
Yes	Adult Material: Adult Content	Sites featuring full or partial nudity reflecting or establishing a sexually oriented context, but not sexual activity; sexual paraphernalia; erotica and other literature featuring, or discussions of, sexual matters falling short of pornography; sex-oriented businesses such as clubs, nightclubs, escort services, password/ verification sites. Includes sites supporting online purchase of such goods and services.
Yes	Adult Material: Lingerie and Swimsuit	Sites offering views of models in suggestive but not lewd costumes; suggestive female breast nudity. Also classic "cheesecake" art and photography.

Monitored Category	Category Title	Category Description
Yes	Adult Material: Nudity	Sites offering depictions of nude or seminude human forms, singly or in groups, not overtly sexual in intent or effect.
Yes	Adult Material: Sex	Sites depicting or graphically describing sexual acts or activity, including exhibitionism.
	Adult Material: Sex Education	Sites offering information on sex and sexuality, with no pornographic intent.
	Business and Economy	Sites sponsored by or devoted to individual business firms, but not supporting e-commerce and not firms engaged in computer or Internet businesses or the sale of alcohol or tobacco, travel services, vehicles, or weaponry. Includes commercial real estate, but not residential real estate.
	Business and Economy: Financial Data and Services	Sites offering news and quotations on stocks, bonds, and other investment vehicles and investment advice, but not online trading. Includes banks, credit unions, credit cards, and life insurance.
	Drugs	All Drugs sites are contained within the subcategories. See their descriptions below.
Yes	Drugs: Abused Drugs	Sites that discuss, promote, or provide information about prohibited, scheduled, or otherwise controlled or regulated drugs and their abuse; also, paraphernalia associated with such use and abuse. *Note:* As legality of drugs varies by country, the drug laws of the United States are used.
Yes	Drugs: Marijuana	Sites whose primary function is to provide information specifically about or promoting the use of marijuana.
	Drugs: Prescribed Medications	Sites providing information about approved drugs and their medical use.

Monitored Category	*Category Title*	*Category Description*
Yes	Drugs: Supplements/ Unregulated Compounds	Sites providing information about or promoting the use of chemicals not regulated by the FDA (as naturally occurring compounds, for example).
	Education	All Education sites are contained within the subcategories. See their descriptions below.
	Education: Cultural Institutions	Sites sponsored by museums, galleries, theaters (but not movie theaters), and other cultural institutions.
	Education: Educational Institutions	Sites sponsored by schools and other educational facilities or by faculty or alumni groups, or that relate to educational events and activities.
	Education: Educational Materials	Sites that discuss or provide information about educational materials.
	Entertainment: Popular Entertainment	Sites that provide information about or promote motion pictures, non-news radio and television, books, humor, music, and magazines (other than those devoted primarily to sex, business, electronic games, computers and related technology, alcohol and tobacco, health, hobbies, sports, travel, vehicles, or weaponry). *Note:* Computer magazines containing technical information are not included in this category.
Yes	Entertainment: MP3	Sites that support downloading of MP3 files or that serve as directories of such sites.
Yes	Gambling	Sites that provide information about or promote gambling or that support online gambling. Risk of losing money possible.

Monitored Category	Category Title	Category Description
Yes	Games	Sites that provide information about or promote electronic games, video games, computer games, role-playing games, or online games, but not board or card games; also sites that support or host online games. Includes sweepstakes and giveaways.
	Government: Civil Government	Sites sponsored by government branches or agencies; all levels of government (i.e., *.gov).
	Government: Military	Sites sponsored by military branches or agencies (i.e., *.mil).
	Government: Political Groups	Sites sponsored by or providing information about political parties and interest groups focused on elections or legislation. Excludes all official government sites.
	Health	Sites that provide information or advice on personal health or medical services, health insurance, procedures, or devices, but not drugs. Includes self-help groups.
Yes	Illegal/ Questionable	Sites that provide instruction in or promote nonviolent crime (except computer crime) or unethical or dishonest behavior, or evasion of prosecution thereof. *Note:* United States laws are used as a guide.
	Information Technology	Sites sponsored by or providing information on computer and Internet industry firms.
Yes	Information Technology: Hacking	Sites providing information on or promoting illegal or questionable access to or use of communications equipment and/or software.
Yes	Information Technology: Proxy Avoidance Systems	Sites that provide information on how to bypass proxy server features or to gain access to URLs in any way that bypasses the proxy server.

Monitored Category	Category Title	Category Description
	Information Technology: Search Engines & Portals	Sites that support searching the Web, news groups, or indices or directories thereof.
	Information Technology: URL Translation Sites	Sites that offer online translation of URLs.
	Information Technology: Web Hosting	Sites of organizations that provide hosting services, or top level domain pages of Web communities.
	Internet Communication	All Internet Mediated Communication sites are contained within the subcategories. See their descriptions below.
Yes	Internet Communication: Web Chat	Sites that host Web Chat services, Chat sites via HTTP, on-IRC chat rooms. Home pages devoted to IRC. Sites that offer forums or discussion groups.
	Internet Communication: Web-Based E-Mail	Sites that host Web-based e-mail. Any Web-based e-mail service, either browser or software-based.
	Job Search	Sites that offer information on or support of seeking employment.
Yes	Militancy/Extremist	Sites that offer information on or promote or are sponsored by groups advocating antigovernment beliefs or actions.
	News and Media	Sites that offer current or real-time news, including those sponsored by newspapers, magazines, trade and academic journals, radio and television stations and networks, and wire services. Does not include current financial quotes or sports.
	News and Media: Alternative Journals	Online equivalents to supermarket tabloids or nonmainstream periodicals. *Note:* This category may contain material that is sexual in nature.

Monitored Category	*Category Title*	*Category Description*
	Premium Group I	Categories that enhance Websense customers' ability to manage and report on Internet use. Premium Group I categories are purchased separately as a bundle.
	Premium Group I: Advertisements	Sites that provide advertising servers. Individual banner ads from the most frequently visited Internet sites.
	Premium Group I: Freeware/Software Download	Sites whose primary function is to provide freeware/software downloads.
Yes	Premium Group I: Instant Messaging	Sites that enable instant messaging.
	Premium Group I: Message Boards and Clubs	Sites that allow people to post messages and give information about specific clubs.
	Premium Group I: Online Brokerage and Trading	Sites that support active trading of securities and management of investments.
	Premium Group I: Pay-to-Surf	Sites that pay for people to surf or pay to e-mail.
	Premium Group II	Categories that enhance Websense customers' ability to manage and report on Internet use. Premium Group II categories are purchased separately as a bundle and primarily focus on saving bandwidth.
	Premium Group II: Internet Radio and TV	Sites whose primary purpose is to provide radio or TV programming on the Internet.
Yes	Premium Group II: Internet Telephony	Sites that enable users to make telephone calls via the Internet or obtain information on or acquire software for this purpose.
Yes	Premium Group II: Peer-to-Peer File Sharing	Sites that provide client software to enable peer-to-peer file sharing and file transfer.

Monitored Category	Category Title	Category Description
	Premium Group II: Personal Network Storage/Backup	Sites that store personal files on Internet servers for backup or exchange; e.g., digital photo storage and album services.
	Premium Group II: Streaming Media	Sites that primarily provide streaming media content such as movie trailers.
	Premium Group II: Message Boards and Clubs	Sites for personal and business clubs, personal and business discussion groups, and list servers that are not blocked elsewhere.
	Premium Group II: Sport Hunting/Gun Clubs	Gun club sites or directories of gun club sites. Includes war game and pinball sites.
	Premium Group II: Educational Materials	Sites whose primary function is to provide historical information, scientific/research pages, or educational curriculum materials.
	Premium Group II: Personal Web Sites	Web sites published by an individual for personal use and interchange; not published by an organization.
Yes	Racism/Hate	Sites that promote the identification of racial groups, the denigration or subjugation of groups (racially identified or otherwise), or the superiority of any group.
	Religion	All religion sites are contained within the subcategories. See their descriptions below.
	Religion: Non-Traditional Religions	Sites that provide information on or promote religions not listed under Traditional Religions, and on other unconventional religious or quasi-religious subjects, including cults.
	Religion: Traditional Religions	Sites that provide information on or promote Buddhism, Baha'i, Christianity, Christian Science, Hinduism, Islam, Judaism, Mormonism, Shinto, and Sikhism; also atheism.

Monitored Category	Category Title	Category Description
	Shopping	Sites that support online purchasing of consumer goods, but not including sexual paraphernalia, investments, computer software or hardware, supplements, alcohol and tobacco, travel services, vehicles and parts, or weaponry. Included are sites exclusively devoted to selling sports or religious goods. *Note:* The entire site is blocked if the intent of the site is to sell.
	Shopping: Internet Auctions	Sites that support the offering and purchasing of goods between individuals.
	Shopping: Real Estate	Sites that provide information on renting, buying, and selling residential real estate.
	Society and Lifestyles	Sites that provide information on matters of daily life, excluding sex, entertainment, jobs, sports, and those topics covered in the subcategories below.
	Society and Lifestyles: Alcohol and Tobacco	Sites that provide information on, promote, or support the sale of alcoholic beverages, tobacco products, and any associated paraphernalia. Excludes self-help groups such as AA, which are in Health.
	Society and Lifestyles: Gay and Lesbian Issues	Sites that provide information on or cater to gay and lesbian lifestyles, including those supporting online shopping, but not sexually oriented or issue-oriented.
	Society and Lifestyles: Hobbies	Sites that provide information on or promote private and largely sedentary pastimes, but not electronic, video, or online games.
	Society and Lifestyles: Personals/Dating	Sites that promote interpersonal relationships, excluding those of exclusively gay or lesbian appeal.
	Society and Lifestyles: Personal Web Sites	Sites that contain material specific to an individual.

Monitored Category	*Category Title*	*Category Description*
	Society & Lifestyles: Restaurants & Dining	Sites that list, review, advertise, or promote food, catering, or dining services.
	Special Events	Sites devoted to a current event that requires separate categorization owing to objectionable content, bandwidth demand, or potential effect on productivity. Some such sites will disappear; others will be reviewed after 90 days for possible reclassification.
	Sports	Sites that provide information on or promote sports, active games, and recreation.
	Sports: Sport Hunting/Gun Clubs	Sites that provide information on or promote sport hunting, including gun clubs.
Yes	Tasteless	Sites that cannot be categorized elsewhere but offer offensive, grotesque, frightening, or lurid material with no redeeming value.
	Travel	Sites that provide information on or promote various travel-related services and destinations, including those that support online purchase or reservations.
	User-Defined	Category used to contain user-defined URLs.
	Vehicles	Sites that provide information on or promote vehicles, including those that support online purchase of vehicles or parts.
Yes	Violence	Sites that provide information on or promote violent activity. Sites containing excessive profanity may be classified here if not in Society and Lifestyles.
Yes	Weapons	Sites that provide information on, promote, or support the sale of weapons and related items.

Appendix M

RE	Standards of Conduct Consequences
Date	August 1, 2006
To	All Staff
From	Office of the CEO

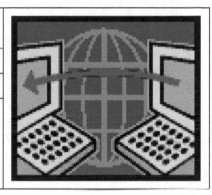

MYC functions in an environment in which overall program quality and reliability are extremely important. Staff are expected to contribute to the quality and reliability of MYC services within the scope of their job responsibilities.

MYC may follow an approach of progressive consequences with staff in circumstances where management believes staff behavior should be changed or that the process would be useful. The intent of this process is to attempt to change staff performance or behavior through instruction.

Any action taken will be based on the seriousness of the situation and the specific circumstances. Actions up to discharge may take the form of a verbal warning, a written warning, a Performance Enhancement Review indicating below-standard performance in one or more areas, probation, or suspension. Which of these options is chosen, or whether any of them is used before discharge, will depend on MYC's assessment as to the seriousness of the problem.

The following is a partial list of examples of conduct that may result in specific consequences, up to and including discharge:

- Failure or refusal to carry out job assignments and management requests
- Unauthorized release of confidential information

- Falsification of any work, personnel, or other organizational records
- Unauthorized taking, mishandling, or removal of employer or coworker funds or property, or unauthorized charges to a MYC account
- Engaging in dishonest or misleading practices or communications
- Misuse of MYC assets, electronic files, system access, signatures, or passwords
- Discrimination against or harassment of coworkers
- Possession, consumption, sale, or being under the influence of alcohol or a controlled substance at work or on work premises (except for medications as prescribed by a physician)
- Possession of a firearm or other weapons, legal or illegal
- Deliberate damage to MYC property, vehicles, or assets, or the property of other employees
- Fighting with or threatening another employee
- Inefficient, negligent, or below-standard performance
- Excessive absenteeism, tardiness, or failure to report in when absent or late for work
- Violation of any MYC policy

In addition to these examples, any other conduct that adversely affects job performance or the reputation of The MYC, including its relationship with other staff, customers, vendors, or partners, also may be grounds for action, up to and including discharge.

Appendix N

RE	**Preventing Laptop Theft**
Date	July 15, 2007
To	All Staff
From	Sandy Bacik, CSO

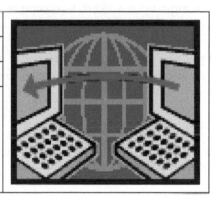

Each day, almost 3,000 laptops are stolen globally. Many of these thefts could have been prevented. Below is a reminder of practical steps you can take to prevent MYC's laptop from being a police and MYC statistic.

- Lock your notebook in your office during off-hours, shutting it down before removing it from the docking station.
- Whenever possible, take your laptop home with you so you always know where it is.
- Keep only the most necessary proprietary information on the laptop.
- Do not load passwords on the laptop, particularly those allowing remote and e-mail communication with clients and the officer.
- Never leave your laptop unattended in a public space.
- Back up your files and store them on the network because laptop devices are not backed up automatically.
- Ensure that the laptop contains an MYC asset tag or MYC markings on the external side.

- Do not install any additional software without the consent of IT, so the software source and licensing can be validated before installation.
- Pay attention to where you use the laptop. Be aware that someone behind or next to you can see your computer screen.

When traveling with the MYC laptop, also remember

- Carry your laptop in a strong, padded, nondescript bag. Do not use a carrying case that advertises there is a computer inside.
- Never leave a laptop in full view in your car, and never check the laptop as luggage at the airport. Do not leave the MYC laptop unattended.
- At airport checkpoints, be observant. Do not place the laptop on a conveyor belt until you are ready to walk through the checkpoint.

If you have any additional questions or would like other standard tools to assist in physical protection the MYC laptop, please contact me or open a Help Desk Request.

Sincerely,

Sandy Bacik
Chief Security Officer

Appendix O

Effective E-Mail Usage

Electronic Mail (e-mail) continues to grow as a communications method. We have had thousands of years to hone our oral and written communications skills and about 100 years with the telephone. But many of us have been using e-mail for less than 15 years. We are all still learning how to use the communication method better.

E-mail has opened our communications ability but with this openness, there is great responsibility and higher risk.

Communication Considerations

- *Speed:* With the click of a mouse, you can send, or reply to, a message almost instantaneously. But faster is not always better.
- *Permanence:* Just because you delete a message does not mean that it is gone. People who received your message have copies. Remember when you send e-mail, it is not sent from computer to computer, but copied from computer to computer, will likely exist forever as a written electronic record, and will be stored on system backups long after the message has been sent and long after it has been deleted from both the sender's and recipients' mailboxes. Your message may actually have unintended readers as it can always be forwarded. Don't say anything in e-mail that you wouldn't want to be published in the newspaper or wouldn't say to someone face-to-face. Once you press Send, what happens to that information is out of your control.
- *Accessibility:* E-mail is accessible to every person regardless of position or title—that means that no matter who you are, you can access everyone from the CEO on down. This, itself, is consequential.

Considerations in Sending and Replying to Messages

■ *Use the Subject Line Effectively:* An understandable subject line header will help your message to be read and understood, but it will also help the recipients effectively manage their mail. Experienced e-mailers tend to start their messages with a one- or two-word subject category, followed by a subheading. The MYC Management has identified the following as helpful e-mail headers:

Urgent: Need reply by date—SUBJECT
(Urgent messages: Read and reply by specified date)

Urgent: Read by date—SUBJECT
(Urgent messages: Read as soon as possible, no reply required)

DIVISION: subject
(Divisional information)

FYI: subject
(For Your Information: informative messages that require no response)

FYI: Employees Only—subject
(For Your Information: informative messages that require no response)

FYI: Organizational Announcement—subject
(For Your Information: informative messages that require no response)

FYI: News Article—subject
(For Your Information: informative messages that require no response)

FYI: Press Release—subject
(For Your Information: informative messages that require no response)

Outage Notification—subject
(IT outage notices)

If you are sending to distribution lists, please use the above recommendations or standardize them for your business unit. For example, Meeting—Requirements for network monitoring.

■ *Is this the best way to communicate?* When developing your communication, ask yourself—"Is this the best way to communicate?" In some cases, it may not be. It may be more effective to call, schedule a face-to-face meeting, or simply get up and walk to the person's office to talk.

- *Keep it short:* Try to keep to one topic per message. Your message will be clearer and easier to respond to. Long e-mail messages are difficult for some people to read on the screen; you may want to explore other avenues of communicating.
- *Keep your audience in mind in constructing your To and CC list:* Ask yourself, "Does everyone need this information?" when sending or replying to a message.
- *BCC—consider the audience:* BCC stands for "Blind Carbon Copy." When sending an e-mail anyone in the BCC field will receive a copy of the message, but not be known as having received that message by the other recipients. When using this feature, you should be mindful that some people will take offense to being deliberately left in the dark as to who else has received a copy of the message. Often, disclosure of who has been blind-copied is out of the original sender's control. For example, if a blind-copied recipient performs a Reply to all then all of the recipients on the To and CC lines of the original e-mail will be made aware of the blind copy. A good time to use BCC is when sending an e-mail to a large distribution list. By blind-copying all recipients, you eliminate the possibility that any number of the recipients will Reply to all and create unnecessary spam for the wider audience.
- *Reply to all:* A common faux pas is to use Reply to all to respond to a message when replying to the original sender was the intent. Always review the addressing of any message you compose prior to hitting Send.
- *Be specific about what you are asking someone to do:* If you want someone to do something for you, say what it is and when you need it to ensure understanding.
- *Avoid large attachments:* Large e-mail attachments, such as PowerPoint presentations, are troublesome to a mobile workforce such as MYC. Files with graphics can be huge and take ages to open over a remote dial-up connection. Use secured shared network drives to post sensitive documents for review, then use e-mail to notify the appropriate group and include a link to the document.
- *Expectations:* Just because e-mail is instantaneous does not mean that you should expect an immediate reply.
- *Manners and courtesy:* In keeping your messages short, don't forgo manners and courtesy in your messages and replies.
- *Check your emotional space:* When sending or replying, don't hit the Send button when you are upset or angry. It may be better to call the person to check for understanding before sending something that you may regret. E-mail is not a recommended method to resolve a disagreement.
- *Use broadcast distribution lists sparingly:* Messages sent to whole departments, offices, or organizations should be reserved for special occasions or important notifications.

Considerations When Receiving

- *Manage your e-mail interruptions:* E-mail is a tool to help you in your work. Do not let it interrupt what you are doing. Practice good time management techniques and set aside some specific times in your day to deal with it.
- *Deal with it and delete it or save it:* When reviewing your messages, scan subject headers and determine if you need to do something or not. If you do, respond and delete it. If you need to keep it, save it to your personal directory on the server or in one of your personal folders.
- *Take advantage of the Outlook Inbox Assistants:* Outlook has Inbox Assistants to "pre-sort" and file your e-mail based on sender, recipient, or subject. Setting up Assistants will save you time and effort.

If you have any problems using Microsoft Outlook software:
Contact MYC's IT Help Desk

If you have any questions on IT security policy and processes:
Contact MYC's Corporate Security Officer

Appendix P

Title:	MYC LAN to Lan VPN Request Form				
Part Number:	FM00055	Revision:	5.1	Effective:	20001101
Owner:	Dir IT Operations			Last Review:	20070301

Purpose

Any entity that requires connectivity to the MYC enterprise network must abide by MYC Information Assurance Policy. Connectivity to MYC must be through a dedicated encrypted tunnel using a minimum of 128-bit authentication encryption and must be to a specific set of no more than 255 hosts. Access will be immediately terminated if there is an increase of risk to MYC by the activities being performed through the requested connection.

Requester Information

Requesting Organization: [   ]   Requestor: [   ]

Approved By: [   ]   Data: [   ]

Classification: ☐ Customer   ☐ Partner   ☐ Reseller/Vendor   ☐ Lab

Project Information:

Project Description or Purpose of Request:

```
```

Required Date: [   ]   Ending: [   ]

Non-Disclosure Agreement Signed: [   ]   Original Located at: [   ]

Contacts

Project/Contact Point of Contact:

Contact		MYC	Staff/Customer/Partner/Reseller
Primary	Name		
	E-mail		
	Telephone		
	Cellular		

Network Contact:

Contact		MYC	Staff/Customer/Partner/Reseller
Primary	Name		
	E-mail		
	Telephone		
	Cellular		
Secondary	Name		
	E-mail		
	Telephone		
	Cellular		

Security Contact:

Contact		MYC	Customer/Partner/Reseller
Primary	Name		
	E-mail		
	Telephone		
	Cellular		

Equipment:

Host Information	MYC VPN Device	Customer/Partner/ Reseller VPN Device
IP Address		
VPN Device Version		
VPN Device Module		

Method of Encryption:

Phase 1 Properties	MYC Parameters	Customer/Partner/ Reseller Parameters
Authentication Mode		
Authentication Algorithm		
Encryption Algorithm		
Diffie–Hellman Group		
Main or Aggressive Mode		
Lifetime Measure		
Time Lifetime (seconds)		
Phase 2 Properties	MYC Parameters	Customer/Partner/ Reseller Parameters
PreShare Key		
Encryption Algorithm—IPSEC		
Authentication Algorithm		

Perfect Fwd Secrecy—IPSEC		
Lifetime Measure		
Time Lifetime (seconds)		

Domain of Encryption:

Network Information	MYC	Customer/Partner/Reseller
Encrypted network/hosts		

Access Rules:

Policy Rules	Source IP Address	Destination IP Address	Service (TCP, UDP port #)	Action (Allow/Deny)
Rule 1				
Rule 2				
Rule 3				
Rule 4				
Rule 5				
Rule 6				

Note: Every attempt will be made to accommodate private internal IP addresses with the restriction that they do not conflict with existing VPN tunnels or internal MYC IP addresses.

Appendix Q

Title:	Third-Party Service Provider Standard				
Part Number:	ST00225	Revision:	1.0	Effective:	20060429
Owner:	CSO			Last Review:	20070301

This electronic document supersedes all previous electronic and printed documents or oral statements regarding this policy.
All Company Standards are subject to change at the sole discretion of MYC management.

Revision History

Date	Revision Number	Modification
2005/08/15	0.0	Sandy. Initial Release.
2006/04/29	1.0	Jim. Additions Sect. 4 and 7 Orig. to IT Admin.

Specification

A contract is a binding agreement between two or more parties for the performance of an agreed-upon action by each party. For example, one party might agree to provide a product or service within an agreed-upon time and the other party will agree to pay for the product or service within an agreed-upon time. Failure by either party to perform its duty under the contract causes a breach of the contract and can result in adverse consequences to the party who failed to perform. A contract can be called different things, such as an agreement, a memorandum of understanding, or a letter of intent.

Good business practices and regulatory requirements mandate that Information Technology (IT) oversee its third-party service provider (TPSP) arrangements. Specifically IT shall, as specified later per Sarbanes-Oxley (SOX) compliance:

- Exercise appropriate due diligence in selecting IT TPSPs
- Require IT TPSPs by contract to implement appropriate measures designed to meet the objectives of this standard
- Require that IT TPSP controls
  1. Provide reasonable assurance that third-party service connections and data transfers are secure, accurate, available, and support processing integrity
  2. Are defined approximately as performance requirements

It is important to remember to review all contract provisions with great care and try to negotiate any changes that will reduce risk and costs for MYC.

IT Separation of Functions/Duties

The purpose of the IT separation of functions and duties is to clearly establish individual accountability within IT for the activities that occur in connection with the ongoing and day-to-day support of IT TPSP. This section of separation of functions and duties identifies the personnel responsible for establishing and maintaining IT TPSP communications and overseeing the contracts with IT TPSPs.

IT Management Team

- All IT work unit managers shall be required to review TPSP contracts applicable to their work units to ensure they understand and follow the IT TPSP standards that apply their work units
- CIO shall approve all exceptions to the above-stated requirement of this standard
- CSO is to review the annual report of each TPSP contract for compliance with this standard
- Operations will monitor TPSP for misconfigured access, unauthorized access, and changes to access authority and report anomalous events to the CSO
- CSO is to maintain the documentation for any exceptions to this standard

IT Teams

The following teams are required to ensure that specific IT TPSP contracts comply with this standard when executed and during the term of the contract, and to report annually to the CSO with respect to such compliance:

- Systems Development Team
- Financial Systems Development Team
- Applications Development Team
- IT Projects Team
- Knowledge and Database Team
- Server/Network Services Team
- Customer Support Team

Standard

Work units that have an IT TPSP relationship are responsible for the following:

- Creating procedures and monitoring TPSP system controls and measurements
- Recording management and support documentation
- Reporting these activities to the CSO at least annually
- Reporting to the IT work unit manager and the CSO immediately if control concerns (e.g., anomalous activity, breaches of security, significant internal control weaknesses) are identified

Before execution, all IT TPSP contracts shall be submitted to MYC's Legal Department or outside counsel approved by MYC's Legal Department for review in order to assure compliance with various regulations and to protect against unacceptable risk to MYC. Contracts to be submitted include, but are not limited to

- Contracts involving mission critical systems, critical systems, or systems that, should they fail, would cause significant business disruption to MYC
- Contracts for tax and flood certification
- Contracts that involve the release of MYC or customer information to third parties for marketing of a third party's products or services
- Nondisclosure agreements

Contracts that are purchase orders or invoices based on master contracts do not need legal review. The information set forth below can help negotiate and execute the most favorable contract terms possible given the circumstances of the transactions contemplated in such contract.

Please involve counsel early in the TPSP selection process. Do not forget that the counsel can also help after the contract has been signed to assist in answering questions about MYC's rights and duties during the term of a contract and to help with negotiations for contract renewals. Any amendment, waiver, or modification to any IT TPSP contract shall also require the prior review and written approval of MYC's Legal Department prior to its execution.

Approval of all IT TPSP contracts must comply with applicable sections of MYC's "Signature Approval Level Policy" issued by the Internal Audit Department as Financial Policy and the sections on "Recurring Contracts (Excluding Ground Leases)" and "Operating and Selling, General and Administrative (SG&A) Expenses." All IT Approvers of TPSP contracts are required to immediately provide the IT Executive Assistant with the original signed contract. Refer to section "Who Manages after Contract Signing" of this document.

Service Level Agreements

The business arrangement defines the key terms of any contract and should spell out in great detail what each party agrees to do. These terms are extremely important and should be carefully reviewed and understood. No assumptions should be made when interpreting the contract's provisions, and all duties and responsibilities should be spelled out clearly. At a minimum, under this standard the items set forth in "Business Items to Be Addressed" below are required to be reviewed prior to executing any IT TPSP contract.

Specific Legal Terms

The legal terms are equally important terms of any contract that should be carefully reviewed and understood. "Legal Terms" provides a list of specific legal issues that shall be reviewed prior to execution of each contract with an IT TPSP. To help in contract review and negotiations, review each of the issues in this section before beginning the negotiation of a proposed contract. Many of these issues will also have relevance once the contract has been signed, so use this section as a guide as the contract is managed during its term.

Who Manages after Contract Signing

Attention to the contract is as important after the contract has been signed as it is before signing. The signed contract sets out the operating rules between the parties. It is, in effect, the plan of actions that the parties have agreed to follow during the term of the contract. The IT Executive Assistant is designated as the "keeper" of the signed contract, "IT Approvers of TPSP contracts are required to immediately provide the IT Executive Assistant with the original signed contract."

The IT Executive Assistant shall be responsible for tracking critical contract dates and for knowing what MYC's responsibilities are under the contract. This is a lot of responsibility, but is manageable if the "keeper" of the contract is familiar with the content of the contract (and even reads it periodically as a refresher to make sure all is going according to the contract). With respect to MYC's efforts to manage the costs and risks associated with contracts, nothing could be worse for MYC than a contract that, once signed, is tucked away in a drawer and forgotten.

Tracking Critical Contract Dates

An essential aspect of managing a contract, once signed, is the tracking of critical performance dates under the contract. Observing critical dates will prevent losing important rights, such as the right to terminate the contract at the end of its initial term. The IT Executive Assistant managing the contract for MYC shall maintain a calendar system set up to identify critical dates under the contract, including dates by which decision making must begin and end. One of the purposes of this calendar is to ensure that all decisions relevant to a critical date—and necessary communications to the other party—are made in a timely and proper manner. The final decision to renew or not to renew should be made, and all negotiations completed within, a minimum of three days prior to the date that the contract requires notice of renewal to be delivered.

All critical dates should be marked on the face of the contract (or on a sheet that is attached to the front of the contract) and on the calendar. Mark the following critical dates:

1. Date on which contract term commences
2. Date on which contract term ends
3. Last date on which notice of termination in initial or renewal terms will be treated as valid
4. Five business days before the date that the contract requires notice of renewal to be delivered (e.g., mark as "Deadline for Delivery of Notice of Termination of Initial Term to Avoid Automatic Renewal")
5. Date on which decision making must begin regarding renewal or nonrenewal of contract (e.g., 60 days prior to termination date)

SOX Compliance

SOX regulations require that controls (1) provide reasonable assurance that TPSP services affecting financial reporting are secure, accurate, and available and support processing integrity and (2) are defined appropriately in performance contracts. SOX requires that businesses safeguard customer and financial reporting information; therefore, MYC has established appropriate standards relating to administrative, technical, and physical safeguards to

- Ensure the security and confidentiality of customer information
- Protect against any anticipated threats or hazards to the security or integrity of such information

- Protect against unauthorized access to or use of such information that could result in substantial harm or inconvenience to any customer

SOX requires that each functional area should

- Exercise appropriate due diligence in selecting its TPSPs
- Regularly monitor its TPSPs to confirm that they have satisfied their obligations under any applicable contracts. As part of this monitoring, a department should review audits, summaries of test results, and other equivalent evaluations of its TPSPs.

Managing TPSP services may include the use of outsourced TPSPs to support financial applications and related systems. Deficiencies in this area could significantly impact financial reporting and disclosure of a reporting entity. For instance, insufficient controls over processing accuracy by a TPSP may result in inaccurate financial results. The following identifies the key SOX TPSP requirements that are applicable to all TPSP contract (*even if there is no potential impact on MYC's SOX compliance or financial statements*):

- IT management determines that, before selection, potential third parties are properly qualified through an assessment of their capabilities to deliver the required service and conducts a review of their financial viability.
- Work unit procedures exist and are followed to ensure that a formal contract is defined and agreed for all TPSP services before work is initiated, including definition of internal control requirements and acceptance of the organization's policies and procedures.
- A regular review of security, availability, and processing integrity is performed for service level agreements and related contracts with IT TPSPs by the CSO.
- Each TPSP contract addresses the risks, security controls, and procedures for information systems and networks in the contract; accordingly, each of the following shall be undertaken by the CSO:
  1. Obtain and review the TPSP's Third Party/Independent Information Technology Audit, such as an SAS 70 Type II audit, to determine
     a. The possibility of significant or material control weaknesses applicable to MYC (Note: The audit report should identify the controls reviewed and the level of compliance with those controls, especially where a control is applicable to MYC's compliance with SOX requirements).
     b. The adequacy of the TPSP management's corrective actions to significant exceptions identified in the report.

  c. If a status report from the TPSP management that describes corrective actions planned and/or taken in response to reported issues should be requested.

  d. That a copy of the examination report, the TPSP's status report, and the summary assessment of these items is provided to the CSO on an annual basis.

2. Ensure the TPSP will maintain a disaster recovery plan that is sufficient to support the continuance of its services in the event of a disruption of normal business operations. The TPSP will provide a description of its disaster recovery test results annually to MYC. Upon request, the TPSP will also provide sufficient information to MYC to allow MYC to develop a disaster recovery plan that will work with the TPSP's disaster recovery plan.

3. Prepare and provide a completed and signed copy of the TPSP Management Report (see p. 313) to the CSO on an annual basis. This report should also identify whether any of these items cannot be achieved and what mitigating controls have been completed for such issues. This report is required to be provided to the CSO by the end of the third quarter of each fiscal year.

4. Report immediately any significant concerns (e.g., control deficiencies) that are noted during the year to the CSO and CSI as soon as they become known.

Business Items to Be Addressed

The following identifies certain business issues, among others, that shall be reviewed and carefully considered prior to signing any contract with a TPSP. This list is not intended to identify all issues to be considered in connection with the negotiation of a TPSP contract but is merely representative of some of the more common issues. The facts and circumstances are specific and unique to the transactions contemplated in any TPSP contract and may result in other issues not identified below. Such issues shall be carefully considered as well.

- A detailed description of the work to be performed by the vendor, and the frequency and general content of the related reports. A description of "support services" is too broad and could result in unsatisfactory performance from the vendor. Some items to request and document include
  1. The obligations of each party (i.e., identify any responsibilities and important response times of each party to the contract)
  2. The times and days on which the services being provided will be available (if necessary, take fallback facilities into account or require other backup coverage or support)

3. The right to supervise the activities of users (and the right to revoke this right)
4. A requirement that the vendor keep the software current by incorporating all telecommunication and public company regulatory changes and updates
5. Responsibilities for installing and maintaining equipment and software
6. Permitted methods of access and the management and use of user identifications (IDs) and passwords
7. TPSP's obligation to a keep a list of authorized persons and a corresponding authorization procedure for user access rights

■ An outline of the training to be provided for our personnel, including the type and number of personnel to be trained and the related costs, if training is needed or requested.

■ Established time schedules for receipt and delivery of work products or services.

■ The availability of on-line communications, security related to access controls, transmissions, and alternate data entry considerations.

■ A detailed description of liability responsibilities for source documents while in transit to and from the service center.

■ Maintenance of adequate insurance by the vendor for fidelity and fire liability, reconstruction of physical properties, data reconstruction, and resumption of normal operations, as well as for data losses resulting from errors and omissions.

■ Confidentiality of information. Measures to ensure that all information learned about MYC, including names and addresses and any internal data, is treated as confidential. The TPSP and its agents shall be prohibited from using or disclosing this information except as necessary to provide the contracted services. The TPSP is responsible for maintaining appropriate security measures (e.g., policies, procedures, and practices) to ensure confidentiality of all MYC information. The TPSP will fully disclose breaches in security resulting in unauthorized intrusions into the TPSP that may materially affect MYC information. Measures to ensure that confidential information is returned to MYC after the TPSP contract's expiration.

■ Ownership of software, intellectual property, and related documents, if the vendor is writing or selling software and documentation for MYC. If a vendor is providing source code, access to vendor's source code and maintenance documentation via escrow agreement for turnkey operations.

■ Ownership of master and transmission data files and their return in machine-readable format upon the termination of the contract.

■ Processing priorities for normal and emergency situations.

■ Mandatory notification of MYC by the vendor of all systems changes that affect MYC.

■ A guarantee that the vendor will provide necessary levels of transition assistance if MYC decides to convert to other automation alternatives.

- The management process for information security at the TPSP, such as a recent SAS 70 Type II audit report to ensure at least the following for operations and financial information:
  1. Controls for authentication and authorization
  2. Access controls for data access
  3. Controls for backup and recovery
  4. Business continuity and disaster recovery plans
- Covenants regarding the reporting and investigation of any security incidents, including contact persons for urgent security incidents.

Legal Terms

The following identifies certain business issues, among others, that shall be reviewed and carefully considered prior to signing any contract with a TPSP. This list is not intended to identify all issues to be considered in connection with the negotiation of a TPSP contract but is merely representative of some of the more common issues. The facts and circumstances are specific and unique to the transactions contemplated in any TPSP contract and may result in other issues not identified below. Such issues shall be carefully considered as well.

Costing and Hidden Costs

Please review contracts for any provisions that obligate MYC to pay costs that are not readily and specifically identifiable (e.g., provisions that require payment of "standard" or "reasonable" costs without capping or scheduling the amounts).

Assignments/Subcontracting

Prohibit assignments or subcontracting of the obligations under the contract by the vendor or TPSP without the prior written consent of MYC.

Licensing Terms

See CSO for specific items to look for or ask for assistance from legal.

Length of Contract

Most contracts will run for a fixed period of time that is specified in the contract—one year, two years, three years, and so on. The length of the contract is called the "term of the contract" or "contract term." When negotiating a contract, consider carefully the length of the contract. If the proposed length is longer than two years, consider carefully what changes could come about (advances in technology, for example) that might render the service, technology, equipment, or something else obsolete.

When considering the length of a contract, always think about time and resources needed to get up and running with the product or services, the cost of switching again in a couple of years, the trends in technology (if technology is involved), and whether business direction is consistent with the product or services in the future. Generally, for larger contracts and for systems contracts, three years is probably an average length of the contract term. If a contract is less than three years, it could be too expensive, and if it is more than three years, it could inappropriately obligate the MYC in the future.

Commencement Date

Most contracts will specify a commencement date, also sometimes called the "effective date." The commencement date is typically the date on which the term of the contract begins (that is, the beginning of the fixed time period for which the contract runs). The commencement date is extremely important because the commencement date typically determines the anniversary date on which the term of the contract ends (the "termination date"). The termination date may determine the final date by which MYC must give notice of termination of the initial term to avoid automatic renewal of the contract for another fixed term (see "Contract Termination and Automatic Renewal", below).

The commencement date may be stated as a month, day and year (for example, "The initial term of this contract commences on May 1, 2001"), or the commencement date may be triggered by an event specified in the contract, such as commencement of service or delivery of a product. If the commencement date is triggered by an event, then very carefully read the contract to determine the event that triggers commencement. When the triggering event occurs, note on the face of the contract the date and note it as the commencement date.

Contract Termination and Automatic Renewal

A key provision of any contract is how and when the contract terminates. Most contracts will run for a fixed period of time (two years, for example) and will contain an "automatic renewal" clause stating that the contract will automatically renew at the end of the contract term unless written notice of termination is given within the time frame specified in the contract.

Finally, when giving notice of termination, the person handling the contract for MYC must look at not only the termination provisions of the contract, but must also the "notice" provisions of the contract to determine exactly how proper notice must be given to the other party. Failure to give notice according to the requirements of the contract can make the notice of termination invalid. Most contracts will have a section entitled "Notice," the provisions of which must be followed in order to have a legally binding termination. See "Giving and Receiving Notices under a Contract" below.

Giving and Receiving Notices under a Contract

An easily overlooked but extremely important provision of a contract is the "Notices" provision. This clause tells the parties how to notify each other regarding information related to the contract. Most contracts will contain requirements that certain information be communicated in a particular way to the other party and, typically, those requirements will be set out in the "Notices" provision. If information is not communicated as required by the contract, the communication can be treated by the other party as invalid.

It is a good idea to review the contract to be aware of what type of information must be communicated in a particular way. The contract may not always be completely clear on this, so in general when communicating with the other party, other than on routine matters, look carefully at the contract to find out whether the contract dictates how that information must be communicated (e.g., via e-mail, facsimile, or overnight courier).

Representations and Warranties by Other Party

The "Representations and Warranties" section of a contract tells you the limits of performance of the product or service that is the subject of the contract. Most often the product or service will be limited to standard specifications identified by the TPSP in its standard documentation supporting the product or service. It can easily happen that the "Representations and Warranties" section states that performance of the product or service is less than what MYC thinks it will be. Even worse, it will be very difficult to decipher from the "Representations and Warranties" section what level of performance is actually assured or how the performance level translates into reality. The contract protects MYC only to the extent of the performance warranted in the "Representations and Warranties" section of the contract—even have a different expectation is based on conversations with the TPSP. Often, many vendors require a "Disclaimer" of expressed or implied warranties. Disclaimers severely limit our rights to recover in the event that a product or service is inadequate and should be carefully considered.

One final note: If the TPSP states during the sales process or contract negotiations that the product or service will do something especially important to MYC, but that thing does not seem explicit in the contract, make sure that the information is included in the contract in the "Representations and Warranties" section.

Limitation of Liability

The limitation of liability provision is extremely important and is typically found in many technology contracts. This provision caps the amount of monetary damages the TPSP will pay to MYC in the event the TPSP breaches the contract or otherwise causes the company to suffer monetary loss or damages as a result of the product or service. Plan to work with MYC's counsel on the limitation of liability section of each contract that is intended to be executed.

Most "Limitation of Liability" provisions in contracts limit damages to a dollar amount that, realistically, will be too low to cover the possible losses under the contract. It is, therefore, essential to carefully review the "Limitation of Liability" section, determine the adequacy of the damages that can be recovered in light of the risks associated with the contract, and attempt to negotiate changes to the "Limitation of Liability" provision to expand MYC's right to recover in the event of vendor's liability.

At a minimum, you should seek to have the "Limitation of Liability" provision be reciprocal—that is, it should apply to both parties. If the amount of damages that can be recovered from the other party is limited by the contract, then the amount of damages that the other party can recover from MYC should also be limited by the same amount.

Indemnification

Many contracts contain an indemnification provision. An indemnification provision, in essence, states that Party A will compensate Party B for losses or liabilities owing to third parties caused by Party A, and vice versa. An indemnification provision must always be read in conjunction with the "Limitation of Liability" section of the contract. This is because the agreement to compensate set out in the indemnification section (even though it may read like a total compensation for all losses) may be limited to the cap on monetary recovery set out in the "Limitation of Liability" section of the contract.

The "Indemnification" section of a contract typically includes reciprocal obligations; that is, each party to the contract should agree to indemnify the other party for losses caused by the party breaching the contract. In such cases, the indemnification language should be the same for both parties. However, with respect to many contracts, the indemnification provisions may be heavily negotiated. Accordingly, the assistance of MYC's counsel should be sought with respect to negotiating indemnification issues.

Confidentiality

Every contract that MYC enters into should have a "Confidentiality" section that requires the other party to keep confidential all information learned about MYC that is not in the public domain and states that all information received about MYC, including names and addresses, must be treated as strictly confidential and may only be used for the purposes identified in the contract.

A confidentiality provision is extremely important because it protects the proprietary information of MYC and ensures the privacy of our information. If a contract lacks a confidentiality provision, or contains one that does not include the above requirements, work with MYC's counsel to put together a confidentiality provision that will protect MYC, or ensure that the MYC Nondisclosure Agreement has been signed.

Governing Law

The "Governing Law" section of a contract identifies the State whose laws will govern the interpretation of the contract. This section will also typically identify in which state any litigation or dispute resolution will take place. Typically, the state whose laws govern the contract and the state in which litigation will take place will be the same.

TPSP Management Report

Instructions

- Identify whether the required activity has been completed by placing an "X" in the appropriate column.
- Provide a brief narrative comment to support your response to each section in this Report. Identify the name and date of the source document, describe your review assessment findings, identify planned corrective actions to exceptions, and list references of supporting documentation (e.g., contracts, reports) and their filing location, for review by management and audit.
- Answer NA in the "No" column if the review requirement does not apply to your TPSP relationship. Provide a brief comment to explain your response.

TPSP Name:				
		Completed		
#	*Review Requirements*	*Yes*	*No*	*Comments*
1	**Contract** Review the TPSP contract to ensure it meets the IT TPSP standard.			

#	Review Requirements	Completed Yes	No	Comments
2	**Audit Reports** Obtain and review the TPSP's Third Party Information Technology Audit Report, such as an SAS 70 Type II or Risk Assessment report.			
2.a	Review the Report for significant or material control weaknesses (e.g., issues that would impact MYC or the TPSP's performance). Note: The report should identify the controls reviewed and the level of compliance with those controls.			
2.b	Determine the adequacy of the TPSP management's corrective actions to significant exceptions identified in the report.			
2.c	Request a status report from the TPSP management that describes corrective actions planned or taken to reported issues, and monitor those actions.			
2.d	Provide a copy of the report, the TPSP's status report, and your summary assessment of these items to the CSO.			
3.	**Disaster Recovery** Obtain and review the most recent TPSP Disaster Recovery Plan (DRP) and Test Report (or summary plans and test results). Determine if adequate provisions and tests of those plans have been documented for the following areas.			
3.a	The plan provides reasonable assurance of the TPSP's ability to continue operations in the event of a disaster at their data processing facility.			
3.b	Test results demonstrate that the TPSP's plan has been adequately tested and validates the plan.			

#	Review Requirements	Completed		Comments
		Yes	*No*	
3.c	Any changes that should be made to MYC's DRPs to ensure compatibility with the TPSP's plan.			
4.	**Performance and Measurement Evaluation** Identify the type and adequacy of TPSP reports to help determine whether they are meeting expected contract terms and measurements.			
4.a	System performance levels (uptime, response time, customer service support, etc.) to monitor the service levels against contracted requirements. Note: Penalties may need to be imposed if contracted performance levels have not been met by the TPSP.			
4.b	Security administration review of user activity, exceptions, or system errors.			
4.c	Breaches of its network, customer data, etc. when (if) they occur. Note: Breaches of customer data files, no matter where they are held, need to be investigated and reported to department management and the CSO to ensure appropriate incident response procedures have been completed.			
4.d	Required audit and security related reports (as listed above in items 2a–d) for clients to review.			
5.	**TPSP Management Report** Maintain this report throughout the year.			
5.a	Provide a copy of the TPSP Management Report to the CSO by the end of the third quarter of each fiscal year.			
5.b	Report immediately to the CSO any significant concerns noted during the year as soon as they are known.			

Appendix R

Title:	Information Security Policy Acknowledgment Form				
Part Number:	FM00085	Revision:	5.1	Effective:	20001101
Owner:	CSO			Last Review:	20070301

Introduction

Information security is for the protection of company information assets from accidental or deliberate misuse. Information resources include, but are not limited to, the following:

- Data
- Client Information
- Personnel records
- Communications
- Software
- Hardware
- Supplies

Personnel Responsibilities

In general, each staff member is responsible for

- Taking precautions to protect company assets
- Their own actions within our environment
- Reporting inappropriate activity to management that they may become aware of in the course of executing their duties

When granted access to MYC computing systems, each person is responsible for

- Keeping sensitive and confidential information secured and properly disposed of when information is no longer needed
- Not sharing or documenting IDs and passwords
- Selecting strong passwords
- Logging out or locking the personal workstation when leaving the work area
- Reporting suspicious or compromising activity to the Information Security department
- Using company resources for company business, as stated in the Acceptable Use Policy, anything else is considered misuse
- Protecting resources from destructive, nonlicensed, and nonauthorized software

Acknowledgment

Signing this form acknowledges that you have read and understand the existing security policies for MYC. Signing this form also acknowledges that you will comply with all MYC security policies. MYC, as stated in the security policies, reserves the right to log, audit, and monitor information flow across company assets. Information flow could be defined as e-mail, voicemail, file copying, production processing, or Web surfing.

I have read and understand MYC security policies and the information presented above.

_____   _____
Signature   Date

_____   _____
Printed Name   Personnel Number

Appendix S

TO: All MYC Employees (Regular & Contract) and the Board of Trustees

FROM: The Office of the CSO

RE: Information Security Policy Annual Acknowledgment

The purpose of this e-mail is to remind everyone about complying with MYC's guidelines and policies related to the use of MYC assets as stated in the Electronic Communications Policies republished on January 31, 2000. MYC assets are both tangible and intangible and we have the privilege of using the MYC assets. MYC provides you with electronic communications systems ("systems") to improve productivity and communications between individuals. The systems include, but are not limited to e-mail, voicemail, cell phones, facsimiles, laptops, palm pilots, workstations, servers, and Intranet and Internet access. The systems, messages, information, and conversations or data ("data") created, transmitted, or stored on them are MYC property. There is no right to expect privacy in the data. MYC reserves, and will exercise as it deems necessary, the right to review, audit, intercept, access, and disclose the data, including information and messages received, sent, or forwarded by the Internet.

As a system is assigned to you, an account is also assigned to you. You are responsible for the activity on that system and of that account, no matter if you are directly connected to the network, dialing into the network, or connecting via a virtual private network. The use of the systems and accounts needs to correspond with MYC's Standards of Conduct and Standards of Ethical Conduct. The following are some examples of activities for which you would be responsible:

- Should you log into the network from your workstation or laptop, then permit a non-MYC person or a youth to use your system to access the Internet, print to a printer, or access the MYC network, you will be held responsible for that activity.

■ Should you take your laptop from the office and dial into the MYC network, and then someone else in the house uses your machine or account to access the MYC network or the Internet to view inappropriate content, you will be held responsible for that activity.

■ Should you give your account password to someone else in or out of the office, then that person logs into the MYC network using your account to access the MYC network or the Internet to view inappropriate content, you will be held responsible for that activity.

When you receive access to a MYC asset, there are specific access controls, scripts, and auditing and monitoring configurations in place to ensure the MYC asset is protected to the level of its importance. Modifying your assigned account or system or having your assigned account or system modified to bypass any login scripts, access controls, or other security measures for monitoring and auditing the use of an MYC asset can be constituted as deliberately evading processes and procedures and could imply dishonest behavior. This type of activity may result in disciplinary actions, up to and including termination. The following are some examples of this type of activity:

■ All network accounts should have their passwords changed at least every 90 days. Configuring an account to have a non-expiring password would constitute a violation.

■ All network accounts have a network login script that alerts the network that you are requesting services. Configuring an account to by-pass or avoid the network login script would constitute a violation.

■ Deliberately deleting or erasing system logs to hide your network activity would constitute a violation.

The Electronic Communications Policy (http://mycweb.myc.com/policy_manual/general/organizationn.htm), the Standards of Conduct (http:// mycweb.myc.com/guidelines/personnel/responsibilities09.htm), and the Standards of Ethical Conduct (http:// mycweb.myc.com/policy_manual/general/organizationc.htm) are available on MYCWeb. Please review that information and reply to this e-mail *by no later than October 30, 2007*, by choosing one of the buttons located at the top of this e-mail:

■ **Yes** = I have read the Electronic Communications Policy, Standards of Conduct, and Standards of Ethical Conduct and I ***DO AGREE*** to abide by them.

■ **No** = I have read the Electronic Communications Policy, Standards of Conduct, and Standards of Ethical Conduct and I ***DO NOT AGREE*** to abide by them. (If so, please explain in detail.)

Your response to this e-mail will go directly to a confidential e-mail box ("Communications and Conduct") that will be accessed by Human Resources. The e-mail return address will serve as your electronic signature. Questions should be directed to XXXXX.

Thank you for your attention to this matter.

Appendix T

Title:	Non-MYC Staff Policy Acknowledgment Form				
Part Number:	FM00105	Revision:	5.1	Effective:	20060101
Owner:	CSO			Last Review:	20070301

Introduction

In the interest of securing its Intellectual Property and ensuring the integrity of its workplace and its assets, MYC has adopted several policies with which non-MYC staff must comply. It is in the best of interest of MYC and its non-MYC staff that non-MYC staff accessing MYC locations and assets must read, understand, and acknowledge these policies. These policies are

- MYC Policy 100, Acceptable Use of Communication and Information Systems
- MYC Policy 205, Non-MYC Network Connection
- MYC Policy 60, Prevention of Workplace Violence and Harassment
- MYC Policy 65, Alcohol and Drugs in the Workplace
- MYC Policy 205, Information Assurance

Personnel Responsibilities

In general, each non-MYC staff member is responsible for:

- Protecting MYC tangible and intangible assets from a breach of confidentiality, integrity, availability, and authorization
- Reporting to MYC management inappropriate, suspicious, or compromising activity of which they may become aware in the course of performing their duties

When granted access to MYC computing systems, each person is responsible for

- Keeping sensitive and confidential information secured
- Properly disposing of sensitive and confidential information when it is no longer needed
- Not sharing or documenting IDs and passwords
- Logging out or locking the personal workstation when leaving the work area
- Using MYC resources for MYC business only, as stated in Policy 205 and Policy 100, Information Assurance and Use of Communication and Information Systems, respectively
- Protecting MYC resources from destructive, nonlicensed, and nonauthorized software

Acknowledgment

Signing this form acknowledges that you have read and understood the accompanying MYC policies and Rules of Use, and acknowledges that you will comply with these policies. MYC, as stated in these policies, reserves the right to log, audit, and monitor information flow across company assets. Information flow includes e-mail, voicemail, file copying, production processing, or Web surfing. I have read and understood this statement and the MYC policies listed above. Violations can result in contract termination.

_____   _____
Signature   Date

_____
Printed Name

Appendix U

Title:	Information Security Policy Architecture Exception Work Instruction				
Part Number:	PD005750	Revision:	1.0	Effective:	20060801
Owner:	CSO			Last Review:	20070801

This electronic document supersedes all previous electronic and printed documents or oral statements regarding this policy.
All Company Work Instructions are subject to change at the sole discretion of MYC management.

Change History

Date	Revision #	Author	Revision Description	Approved?
08/01/06	1.0	S. Bacik	Initial Version	Yes

Purpose and Scope

This procedure defines the process for an exception to any document within the information security policy architecture. The scope of this document will apply to all publishing information security policy architecture documents that are owned and maintained by the information security group.

References

The documented instructions below are based on the following documents:

- PL00550, Information Assurance Policy
- GD00300, Computing Resources Guideline
- ST01505, IT Windows Standard Configuration
- ST1510, UNIX Standard Configuration

Acronyms

Acronym	Description
IT	Information Technology
CSO	Corporate Security Officer

Roles and Responsibilities

Management Team	Management personnel who are requesting an exception.
Information Security Team	Monitor operation and conduct periodic review of the effectiveness of the approved policy exceptions.

Process Description

This section contains the steps required when applying for an exception to any document in the information security policy architecture.

Process Flow

The only acceptable circumstances for requesting an information security exception are as follows:

- Accidental noncompliance. The business unit was unaware of the published information security policy architecture. A new hire was unaware of the location of the information security policy architecture.
- Another acceptable solution is available. The business unit is recommending a solution with better information assurance controls and the exception can be granted until the published documented has been updated.

- A legacy system is being allowed to go to its end-of-life. This would be a managed risk with a definitive end date.
- Lack of resources. There is a new piece of software being implemented, there are not enough available resources for the segregation of duties, and this risk needs to be managed.

Exception Request

If the noncompliance is caused by anything other than a better solution, the requesting manager must complete the form at the end of this work instruction and include the following information:

- Description of the noncompliance
- Anticipated length of noncompliance, no more than 12 months
- Risk assessment associated with noncompliance
- Plan for alternate means of risk management or compensating controls
- Method for monitoring and evaluating the risk
- Review date to evaluate progress toward compliance

If the noncompliance is a result of a superior solution, an exception will automatically be granted until the information security policy architecture document is updated with the new information.

Process Flow

1. A member of the management team will complete the policy exception form.
2. The policy exception form must be submitted to the CSO.
3. The information security team will review the request, the enterprise asset risk, and the compensating risk control.
4. Within 5 business days, the information security team will respond to the CSO with comments about the acceptable level of risk.
5. If the exception is granted, the CSO will meet with the requesting manager and explain that the information security team will perform monitoring throughout the exception period until the date when the exception needs to be corrected.
6. If the exception is not granted, the CSO will meet with the requesting management, explain the situation, and offer an alternative solution to the request manager.
7. The information security team will log the request, set up a routine for monitoring, and setup the review schedule.

Quality Records

Quality records are documentation that provides evidence of conformance to the process. The e-mail trail and the details about acceptance or denial of the request will be kept for two years after the request is initially approved or denied.

EXCEPTION REQUEST FORM

Requestor's Name: Date:

Requestor's Phone Number:

Requestor's E-mail Address:

Requestor's Business Unit:

Information security policy document name and number for which this exception is being requested:

Brief description justifying (business requirements) the request and why compliance cannot be achieved, including organizations that would benefit from the exception:

Risk analysis, including organizations and assets that would be at risk with this exception:

Risk weighting:

Compensating procedure(s) or control(s) to mitigate (manage) risk:

The business unit responsible for implementing the exception:

Technical description of the situation that is to exist after grant of exception:

Estimated duration (length of time) for the exception, no more than 12 months:

Information Security risk review:

Information Security recommendation:

Date of next review:

Information Security Officer approval (The exception is not approved until signed by the Information Security Officer.):

Date for review of exception

Appendix V

Title:	Security Monitoring Work Instruction				
Part Number:	PD005785	Revision:	1.0	Effective:	20060801
Owner:	CSO			Last Review:	20070801

This electronic document supersedes all previous electronic and printed documents or oral statements regarding this policy.
All Company Work Instructions are subject to change at the sole discretion of MYC management.

Change History

Date	Revision #	Author	Revision Description	Approved?
08/01/06	1.0	S. Bacik	Initial Version	Yes

Purpose and Scope

This procedure defines what network access in monitored on a regular basis by IT and Security Teams on the MYC corporate network. The current data acquisition and reporting functions are performed using freeware software, command scripts, and perl. The software, command script, and perl script master copies can be found on the HQSECURITY01 file server. The permissions on this server are limited; please see the CSO for access approval.

References

The documented instructions below are based on the following documents:

- PL00550, Information Assurance Policy
- GD00300, Computing Resources Guideline

Acronyms

Acronym	Description
IT	Information Technology
CIO	Chief Information Officer
CSO	Corporate Security Officer

Roles and Responsibilities

Management Team	Management personnel who will review and present the output to the executive team.
Information Security Team	Perform the monitoring, auditing, and gathering of information to present to the CSO and CIO.

Process Description

This work instruction provides information relative to the monitoring of activity on various network devices throughout MYC's network. Included in this document is information relative to:

- Netmon
    - Intrusion detection monitoring
    - Anomalous network activity monitoring
    - Firewall traffic monitoring
- SiteScope
    - Network and server availability monitoring
    - Domain monitor
    - Monitoring network resource access
- Alert/log review
    - RSA token authentication
    - Domain accounts and privileges

Server access
Application access

The current software utilized for monitoring includes Netmon tools (including SnortSnarf, ntop, and HTML interfaces into network device statistics and alerts), and proprietary in-house applications for Domain and Authentication (Domain Monitors).

In addition to the out-of-band software that is utilized to monitor the systems, regular review of logged information relative to usage, authorization, and activity is performed. Notifications and alerts sent via e-mail from organizations and application vendors (such as CERT, Symantec, and various third parties) are delivered to and reviewed by the Infrastructure team daily. Any needed actions are passed on to management for review, and if any changes are required, these are put through appropriate change control.

Process Flow

All IT operations and security staff are involved within the various monitoring processes for accounts and application access, with IT Infrastructure/Network Support personnel having primary responsibility for network and server devices. Any event or logged information that is suspect is analyzed and reported to the Help Desk Supervisor, Infrastructure Manager, and as needed, other IT management staff. Any event or logged information that represents a potential risk of data loss, integrity, or confidentiality is reported to the CIO and CSO.

Anomalies

An inability to gather or retain the information necessary to evaluate an activity that is normally available is an anomaly to be addressed immediately. Activity that does not conform to observed patterns, but does not represent an identified or known risk, should be reported as an anomaly for further evaluation. Coordination and cooperation with subject matter experts will be required to allow evaluation of observed patterns as normal or anomalous.

Tools

NetMon

NetMon is a collection of tools to analyze activity that might indicate

- ▪ Intrusion attempted or successful intrusion—SnortSnarf
- ▪ Performance issues relative to anomalous activity:
  - – ntop
  - – HTML interfaces to read statistics from routers, firewalls, switches
  - – HTML interfaces to VM session activity
  - – Alert log retrieval from network core switch

SiteScope

SiteScope is a monitoring, alerting, and reporting tool that analyzes systems availability, alerts on preset thresholds for systems performance and availability, and alerts on possible predefined security events.

Domain Monitor

Domain Monitor is a collection of various programs that are running to report on specific activity, including

- ▪ Any change to privileged domain accounts is monitored and immediately alerted via e-mail to all infrastructure staff (DomainSecurityMonitor)
- ▪ Password expiration is reported to alert on user accounts not within password policy compliance (PEAS Audit)

Log Review

Administrative access and security event logs are reviewed at various intervals for detecting improper security levels granted or indicators of undesired or unauthorized activity. Log file size is reviewed quarterly to ensure at least seven days of logs are stored for review. Additionally, these log files are included in daily incremental and weekly full backups, and can be restored and reviewed as needed.

Activities

24/7 Monitoring

Sitescope sends e-mail alerts concerning system performance and availability, infrastructure related outages, and limited security related events, such as bad password attempts, as well as indicators of problems via query result analysis against established thresholds. Specific platforms and devices monitored include

- All routers, firewalls, and backbone switches
- All production servers (Windows NT/2000 and Sun/Solaris) for
    CPU utilization
    Disk space usage
    I/O utilization
    All data circuits for IP traffic flow
    All applications for availability (simple up/down state of services)

Domain monitors send e-mail to Infrastructure staff on any change in membership of privileged accounts.

The appropriate on-call personnel within Help Desk and Infrastructure take appropriate action to continue to monitor, notify appropriate parties, and take action to rectify any problems associated with the alert.

Extended Business Day Monitoring

The Netmon systems and log review processes are performed daily for

- Firewall traffic
- Network/device administrative access
- Virus activity
- RSA token authentication access

Vulnerability assessments utilizing Nessus are run once monthly, and the results are reviewed by Infrastructure staff. Any concerns are reported to the Infrastructure Manager and CSO. This is done in parallel with review of advisories and patch releases from OS and application vendors. Proposals for implementation of needed patches are discussed and presented as change control requests.

The log review processes are performed regularly (minimum once per month) for

- Password policy compliance
- Domain group membership (privileged accounts—can modify domain security)
- Password policy compliance
- Dial-In/VPN account access
- Application access
- Restricted IT area access (badge assignment review) for data center, inventory area, and wiring closets

The log review processes are performed regularly (minimum once quarterly) for

■ Domain group membership (nonprivileged accounts)
■ E-mail accounts and domain user accounts only for active employees/contractors
■ Network devices for validation of configuration

On review of the information found in these logs, the activity and security settings that are considered to be anomalous are reported to Infrastructure Manager, and appropriate actions are taken.

Scheduled Monitoring

Daily

WebMail

Processing: The WebMail access using Outlook Web Access will be monitored on a daily basis to ensure that:

■ Unauthorized access is not being attempted;
■ The accounts of personnel on sabbatical or who are no longer with MYC are not attempting access.

The perl script, Read_webmail_Eventlog.pl, reviews HQEXCH04 security eventlog for the following activities

Event Id	Description
528	Successful logon
529	Unknown user name or bad password
530	Logon failure due to time restrictions
531	Logon failure due to disabled account
532	Logon failure due to expired account
533	Logon failure due to account cannot access computer
534	Attempting to log onto system with an invalid method
535	Logon failure due to expired password

Event Id	Description
536	Netlogon component not active
537	Unexpected logon failure
538	Successful logout
539	Account locked out
675	Pre-authentication failed
681	Login failed from domain

The output is a tab delimited file containing the read information. If anomalies are discovered, the report reviewer will contact the account owner and document the responses to close the incident.

Dial-up

Processing: The remote dial-up access (RAS) will be monitoring on a daily basis for the following:

- Invalid attempts to log into the domain through RAS
- Valid attempts of logging into the domain through RAS

The perl script, Read_failed_TACACS.pl, reviews HQCA01\logs share and the specific filename for the previous day's date in the subdirectories of Passed Authentications and Failed Attempts.

The output is a tab delimited file containing the read information. If anomalies are discovered, the report reviewer will contact the owner of the account and document the responses to close the incident.

Security Eventlogs

Processing: Each of the Windows-based production servers will be monitored on a daily basis to ensure that:

- The server reboots were authorized and shut down rather than powered off
- The personnel with the right authority are maintaining accounts, groups, and user rights
- The personnel with the right authority are maintaining the server configurations

- The account owner locked out receives training
- Service accounts are not being logged into by individuals accessing data and the Internet inappropriately

The perl script, Read_Security_Eventlog.pl, reviews each Windows-based production server's security eventlog for the following activities

Event ID	Description
512	System starting up
513	System shutting down
516	Some audit messages lost
517	Security eventlog cleared
528	Successful logon
529	Unknown user name or bad password
530	Logon failure due to time restrictions
531	Logon failure due to disabled account
532	Logon failure due to expired account
533	Logon failure due to account cannot access computer
534	Attempting to log onto system with an invalid method
535	Logon failure due to expired password
536	Netlogon component not active
537	Unexpected logon failure
538	Successful logout
539	Account locked out
540	Successful network login
608	Assignment of a user right
609	Removal of a user right
610	Added a trusted domain
611	Removed a trusted domain
612	System audit policy modification

Event ID	Description
615	Service is shutting down
620	Trusted domain information modified
624	New account created
625	User account type changed
626	User account enabled
627	Account password changed
628	Account password set
629	User account disabled
630	Account deleted
631	Global group created
632	Account added to global group
633	Account removed from global group
634	Global group removed
635	Local group created
636	Local group member added
637	Local group member removed
638	Local group removed
639	Local group changed
641	Global group changed
643	System account policy modification
644	Account locked out
668	Group type changed
669	Add SID history
670	Add SID history
682	Session reconnected to winstation
683	Session disconnected from winstation

The output is a tab delimited file containing the read information. If anomalies are discovered, the report reviewer will contact the account owner or the server lead and document the responses to close the incident.

Server Configurations

Processing: From the security$ share on each server that is monitored, the following instructions are run on a daily basis:

- Using SECEDIT, verify that the user configuration settings have not been changed
- Using SECEDIT, verify that the policy configuration settings have not been changed
- Using DumpSec, verify that the system account policy settings have not been changed
- Using DumpSec, verify that the share settings on the server have not been changed
- Using DumpSec, verify that the service settings on the server have not been changed
- Using DumpSec, verify that the security settings on the security$ share have not been changed
- Using the AT command, verify that the settings for executing dailysecurity.bat have not changed
- Verify the last modify date on the dailysecurity.bat file

The output is a tab delimited file containing the read information. If anomalies are discovered, the report reviewer will contact the account owner and document the responses to close the incident.

Weekly

Account Policies

Processing: Reviewing the account policies on all Windows-based production servers will ensure that many of the accounts will follow MYC's standard practice of account policies. The standard practice of account policies is as follows:

- Maximum password age is 90 days
- Minimum password age is five days
- Password length is at least seven characters
- Password history is seven passwords
- Accounts will be locked out after five invalid password attempts within 30 minutes and the invalid password counter will be reset after 30 minutes

The perl script, CheckAccountPolicies.pl, uses Somarsoft's DUMPACL to pull the account policies from each server.

The output is a tab delimited file containing the read information. If anomalies are discovered, the report reviewer will contact the account owner and document the responses to close the incident.

Anomalies: If access is denied to the server for more than 2 weeks in a row, then open a Help Desk ticket to review permissions on the server. If the account policy standard deviates from the standard, then open a Help Desk ticket to have the account policy standard reapplied.

Eventlog Sizes

Processing: Reviewing the size of the eventlogs on all Windows-based production servers will ensure that there is a minimum number of online records for reviewing incidents. Seven days of log entries should reside online for the application, security, and system eventlogs.

The perl script, Eventlog_Date_Range.pl, reviews entries from the server's registry to determine the size of the eventlog, then also reads the eventlog to determine how many day's worth of data is stored online.

The output is a tab delimited file containing the read information. If anomalies are discovered, the report reviewer will contact the server owner and document the responses to close the incident.

Anomalies: If the security eventlogs have stopped logging, then notify the server administration team to enlarge the security eventlog size. If the security eventlogs do not contain at least 7 days worth of data, then notify the server administration team to enlarge the security eventlog size.

Security$ Directory Permissions

Processing: Reviewing the permissions on all of the files and directories within the security$ share on monitored servers. Ensure that only the server administrators, MYC\domain admin, and MYC\security admin level 2 groups have permissions to view and access the data. The server administrators should be the owner of the files and directories.

The perl script, CheckSecurityShareConfigs.pl using DumpSec, documents the owner and permissions on all the files and subdirectories within the security$ share.

The output is a tab delimited file containing the read information. If anomalies are discovered, the report reviewer will contact the server owner and document the responses to close the incident.

Anomalies: If the permissions have changed, then investigate as to who may have changed the permissions and why. Open a request to replace with the correct permissions and ownership.

Internet Activity

Processing: Reviewing the Internet activity will ensure that MYC's acceptable use guidelines for MYC assets are being followed. WebSense is the software product used to produce reports on a weekly basis for Internet activity. The two reports executed on a regular basis list the following:

- Number of hits per WebSense category (http://www.websense.com/products/categories/cat_4.cfm)
- Top 50 Web sites that were requested

The report uses the data stored in an MS SQL database that has the data exported from the Cisco Pix logs.

The output is a tab delimited file containing the read information. If anomalies are discovered, the report reviewer will contact the CIO for further instructions. The IT Directors can request copies of these two reports on a regular basis.

Monthly

Internet Activity

Processing: Reviewing the Internet activity will ensure that MYC's acceptable use guidelines for MYC assets are being followed. WebSense is the software product used to produce reports on a monthly basis for Internet activity. The two reports executed on a regular basis list the following:

- Number of hits per WebSense category (http://www.websense.com/products/categories/cat_4.cfm)
- Top 50 Web sites that were requested

The report uses the data stored in an MS SQL database that has the data exported from the Cisco Pix logs.

The output is a tab delimited file containing the read information. If anomalies are discovered, the report reviewer will contact the CIO for further instructions. The IT Directors can request copies of these two reports on a regular basis.

Abandoned Accounts

Processing: Reviewing the abandoned accounts on all Windows-based production servers will ensure that we will help close one of the back doors into the MYC network. The process for reviewing accounts is as follows:

- If the account has not been logged into for 6 months, there is an attempt made to contact the account owner
- If there is no account owner or the account owner does not respond within 5 days, the account will be disabled
- If the account has not been logged into for 12 months and is disabled, then the account will be deleted

This automated quarterly process will be done using a customized perl script, Somarsoft's DUMPACL, or Hyena reviewing all of the accounts in the MYC domain. The output is a tab delimited file containing the read information.

Anomalies: A Help Desk ticket is opened to disable the account that has not been logged into for at least 6 months. A Help Desk ticket is opened to delete the account that have been disabled for 6 months and have not been logged into for at least 12 months.

Quarterly

Invalid Password Duration

Processing: Reviewing all accounts in the MYC domain for the password duration to ensure compliance with MYC's 90-day account password policy change on all Windows-based production servers will help close one of the back doors into the MYC network. The process for reviewing accounts is as follows:

- Verify the list of accounts that have an exemption from the account password policy
- If the account has not had a password change in the last 90 days, then notify the account owner to change the account password
- If the account has not had a password change in the last 180 days, update the account to force a password change on the next logon

This automated quarterly process will be done using a customized perl script, Somarsoft's DUMPACL, or Hyena reviewing all of the accounts in the MYC domain. The output is a tab delimited file containing the read information.

Ad Hoc

Internet Activity

Reviewing the Internet activity will ensure that MYC's acceptable use guidelines for MYC assets is being followed. WebSense is the software product used to product reports. Any manager has the authority to request a confidential report for the activities of an employee. The request must contain the following information:

- Employee name
- Date range to be review

The report will display the various IP addresses the employee has used and what Web sites or categories the employee accessed during the date range. The report uses the data stored in an MS SQL database that has the data exported from the Cisco Pix logs.

The output is a tab delimited file containing the read information. If possible, the report is printed and sent to the requesting manager or converted to a pdf file and sent encrypted to the requesting manager.

Server Review

A division or region officer can request that their production server be reviewed in detail for secure configuration. The review will entail the following information:

- Account policies
- Audit policies
- User rights
- Services
- Share, file, and directory permissions
- Group member
- Key registry settings and permissions

The report will display the findings and recommendations to better secure the server. If possible, the report is printed and sent to the requesting manager or converted to a pdf file and sent encrypted to the requesting division or region officer.

Quality Records

Quality records are documentation that provides evidence of conformance to the process. The e-mail trails, reports, and presentations will be kept for two years on HQSECURITY01.

Index

Milton Keynes UK
Ingram Content Group UK Ltd.
UKHW021631071024
449327UK00020BA/1278